FIGHT TIME

S0-ASV-234

FIGHT TIME

THE NORMATIVE RULES AND ROUTINES OF INTERPERSONAL VIOLENCE

TERANCE D. MIETHE
UNIVERSITY OF NEVADA, LAS VEGAS

GINI R. DEIBERT
TEXAS STATE UNIVERSITY, SAN MARCOS

WAVELAND

PRESS, INC.
Long Grove, Illinois

For information about this book, contact:
    Waveland Press, Inc.
    4180 IL Route 83, Suite 101
    Long Grove, IL 60047-9580
    (847) 634-0081
    info@waveland.com
    www.waveland.com

Copyright © 2007 by Waveland Press, Inc.

ISBN 1-57766-456-6

All rights reserved. No part of this book may be reproduced, stored in a retrieval system, or transmitted in any form or by any means without permission in writing from the publisher.

Printed in the United States of America

7   6   5   4   3   2   1

Contents

Preface

Common public misconceptions about interpersonal violence involve its presumed random and idiosyncratic character. These perceptions are in sharp contrast to a large and growing body of empirical research that reveals strong and consistent patterns in the offender, victim, and situational factors that underlie violence in a variety of different contexts.

Regardless of its expression in criminal behavior, sporting events, street-level encounters or in the privacy of domestic relations, interpersonal violence is incredibly structured and patterned in terms of the characteristics of its combatants, its predisposing and precipitating conditions, and the action sequences that underlie the escalation and de-escalation of these violent encounters. While some aggressive situations lead to physical assaults and have lethal consequences, the structured nature of interpersonal violence is also indicated by the fact that the vast majority of these encounters are terminated without physical injury to the participants.

The primary goal of this book is to describe the normative rules and routines that pattern the nature and consequences of acts of interpersonal violence. After describing the rules of engagement surrounding aggressive situations, we explore some of the interpersonal and situational factors that facilitate and inhibit the escalation of violence in these situations.

This book was inspired by years of unsystematic observation of violent encounters among humans and other animals. We have long been intrigued by the highly structured action patterns and routines often associated with the onset and termination of violent and potentially violent situations. It is from these basic observations, available scientific evidence, and our personal experiences that we develop our perspective about the normative rules and interaction rituals surrounding interpersonal violence.

Several of our colleagues, friends, and family members have contributed to this book in direct and indirect ways. We would especially like to thank Joel Lieberman, Dick McCorkle, Clay Mosher, Mark Stafford, Randy Shelden, and Bill Sousa for the numerous conversations about violence and its patterns. As a mutual participant in various types of agonistic behavior, Lance Miethe provided his younger brother with direct first-hand experiences with sibling violence, its thresholds, and appropriate points of its de-escalation. Jared Shoemaker also contributed to this book by providing valuable library assistance. Finally, the authors greatly appreciate the decision by Carol and Neil Rowe of Waveland Press to publish this book manuscript. In particular, we admire their support of academic work by publishing this type of hybrid trade book that is neither a conventional textbook nor research monograph.

Introduction

Humans share with other animals the propensity to develop and follow patterned behavioral responses to various external threats. These reactions in human nature originate from a complex interplay of biological, environmental, social, and cultural forces. Some of the rules of nature are content-specific (e.g., the fight-or-flight response of animals), but many of these stereotyped or "programmed" action patterns are largely invariant across contexts (e.g., the physiological response to pain).

As shared evaluations of how one should behave in a particular cultural setting, norms are socially constructed rules of human nature that provide order and predictability in a society. Given a particular external stimulus and prior socialization and conditioning, humans rely on well-entrenched normative scripts to guide their course of action. Unfortunately, violation of these normative rules of conduct is almost inevitable in many situations, due to operation of alternative normative rules, inadequate socialization to these rules, or a wide variety of other factors (e.g., effort, opportunity, motivation).

The basic idea that normative rules of conduct are ubiquitous in human society is clearly revealed in the "rules of engagement" that are associated with different types of violent acts. Consider the formal and informal rules that underlie the following situations of violence:

- Rules of the Geneva Convention dictate that prisoners of war be treated with dignity and respect. However, numerous atrocities against prisoners have been committed in direct violation of these rules. In fact, visual images and narrative accounts of war prisoners being physically tortured and brutalized are often used to vilify the enemy and to justify retaliatory actions of equal or greater brutality.

1

- Dueling was a socially acceptable means of resolving threats to honor and other disputes among gentlemen in American history. Normative rules regulated the choice of weapons, the protocol and procedures for dueling, and the consequences of various rule violations (i.e., cheating).

- Fights in professional hockey are often highly ritualized and patterned events that follow normative scripts. In particular, as long as the players remain standing and use only their fists, referees often allow hockey players to fight until someone gets a clear advantage. A "face washing" (raking one's sweaty glove across an opponent's face) rarely elicits any official intervention. However, officials quickly terminate the fight when the players hit the ice or a stick is used as a weapon. A trip to the penalty box is the sanction for the typical hockey fight, but game expulsions and longer suspensions are given for "cheap shots" and attacks involving excessive brutality.

- The "brushback" pitch in major league baseball is shrouded in various normative reactions depending on the situation. After yielding a home run pitch to the previous batter, a pitcher who then hits or brushes back the next batter with an inside pitch will often provoke immediate verbal "jawing" between the parties and a few demonstrative steps toward each other. Pitches aimed at the head ("beanballs") elicit more severe retaliation by the batter and teammates, including the bench-clearing brawl. Even in these collective battles, however, few punches are thrown and bats are rarely used as weapons. When a pitch simply gets away from the pitcher and strikes a batter unintentionally, the pitcher typically hangs his head and avoids eye contact with the batter. This nonverbal cue signals to the batter, the umpire, and both benches that the hit batter was a mistake and not intentional, immediately de-escalating the situation and preempting further retaliation.

- Street fights or rumbles among rival groups and gangs of male youths are rarely lethal. They typically consist of verbal banter, posturing, and "trash talking" rather than acts of physical violence. The risks of physical violence in these group encounters, however, may change dramatically depending on the particular aspects of their situational context (e.g., whether lethal weapons are available, the use of drugs and alcohol, bystander encouragement).

- Various types of physical and/or psychological abuse are widely observed within the context of domestic violence. Prior histories of abuse and an escalation in its frequency, duration, and seriousness are typical response patterns associated with violence within this context. Most physical violence among intimate partners and family members is directed at less vulnerable body parts (e.g., parents spank children on their buttock, siblings punch each other in the stomach rather than the face) and typically use less lethal weapons (e.g., hands/feet rather than knives/guns). However, physical attacks by intimate partners and family members also represent about one-fourth of lethal acts of interpersonal violence in the United States.[1]

Within each of these settings for violence, there are implicit normative rules of engagement that may facilitate or constrain violent behavior. These rules often dictate who should be the combatants (e.g., professional hockey teams will often have an "enforcer" on their roster; the next batter after a home run is the likely recipient of the "high and inside" pitch) and when, where, and how to resolve the conflict. By endorsing and following the expected rules of engagement, violence-prone situations develop a level of consistency and predictability in the social profile of their combatants and the specific behavioral scripts that lead to their escalation or de-escalation.

The goal of this book is to explore the normative rules associated with violent situations and the factors associated with the escalation of aggression in particular settings. We will examine previous research from various disciplines to identify the facilitators and constraints on aggression that contribute to the "rules of engagement" in the expression of violence and its underlying structure. What we currently know about interpersonal aggression, theories of its nature and distribution, and our approach to study the normative rules and rituals of interpersonal violence are summarized below.

GENERAL PATTERNS OF AGGRESSION AND VIOLENCE

Aggression involves physical or verbal behavior that is intended to dominate someone, whereas violence is usually more restricted to the threat or commission of physical injury. Human aggression is either instrumental (a means to some other ends) or hostile (rage-driven anger for its own ends).[2] Violence may be expressed in collective (e.g., wars, mob attacks), interpersonal (e.g., disputes among individuals), or intrapersonal forms (e.g., self-inflicted injuries, suicide). The term "agonistic" behavior is used to describe any activity related to fighting, including acts of aggression, threat, conciliation, and retreat.[3] By exploring its normative context, acts of physical violence may be classified as legitimate or illegitimate. The normative boundaries of legitimate violence are established by law (e.g., states may legitimately impose the death penalty for particular offenses; killings in self-defense are legally justified) and by well-entrenched customs, traditions, and principles (e.g., corporal punishment of children by parents, standing up for your convictions, the "golden rule" norm of reciprocity). In contrast, illegitimate forms of aggression are those that exceed normative boundaries or thresholds in terms of the nature and magnitude of their application. By going "over the line" of acceptable behavior, illegitimate forms of violence may also be called "deviant" violence to further emphasize the departure from normative standards. There is a massive body of research on the extent and causes of aggression and violence, regardless of its normative or deviant forms.

Prevalence of Human Aggression and Violence

Although cultural variation in aggression questions its classification as instinctive behavior, the prevalence of violence throughout world history nonetheless provides strong evidence of its widespread use as a culturally transmitted, adaptive, and learned response to social and environmental conditions. The research literature establishes a strong biological link as well by detailing neural, genetic, and biochemical influences on aggression.[4]

It is difficult to ascertain the precise levels of violence at any historical point. However, history is filled with numerous accounts of massive and prolonged periods of collective and state-sponsored violence. These included, but are not limited to, the annihilations of the indigenous Persian populations by the Mongol leader Genghis Khan; the Crusades and the expansion of the Holy Roman Empire; the "reign of terror" during the French Revolution; the Jewish Holocaust; and Joseph Stalin's purges of political rivals in twentieth-century Russia. These collective acts of violence are not just historical novelties. In fact, at least 110 million people have been killed in the 250 wars that have taken place worldwide in the twentieth century.[5] The penchant for collective violence is also reflected in the defense expenditures for armies and weapons, involving an estimated $2 billion per day worldwide.[6]

The amount of interpersonal violence varies widely across countries of the world. For example, homicide rates are higher in the United States than in other industrialized nations; the same generally applies to serious physical assaults, robberies, and sexual assaults.[7] Risks of violent offending and victimization also vary dramatically across different social groups within countries. Risks of self-inflicted aggression like suicide follow a similar pattern of variation by social group (e.g., males, younger persons, urban residents have higher risks).

There are culture and context-specific rules of engagement for the commission of violence—whether instrumental, collective, or individual acts of rage. For example, modern soldiers are taught proper protocol in handling enemy forces that surrender during combat; siblings who fight learn to stop their actions before inflicting serious injury; and different cultural standards exist concerning when suicide is appropriate, who should do it, and how it is done. However, within each of these contexts, there is both conformity to and defiance of the normative rules of aggression. The basic research issues in this book focus on the identification of these normative rules of engagement and the individual and situational factors that lead to their acceptance and violation within a particular context.

The Prevalence of Interpersonal Violence in the United States

Rates of interpersonal violence in the United States are consistently higher than in other Western democracies and most industrialized countries of the world. This national propensity toward interpersonal violence is a major feature of U.S. history and remains a core aspect of contemporary society.[8] Official rates of homicide, rape, robbery, and aggravated assaults increased dramatically in the United States throughout the 1960s and 1970s, vacillated but remained high in the 1980s, dropped throughout most of the 1990s, and have remained relatively low compared to the previous decade in the early years of the twenty-first century (see figures 1.1 and 1.2 for the number of known offenses).

Figure 1.1   Number of Forcible Rapes and Murders, 1960–2000

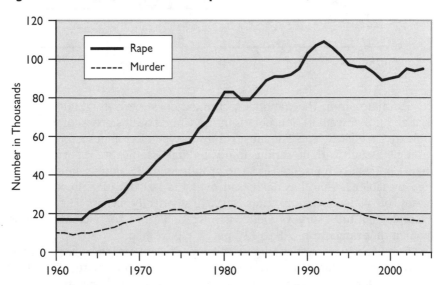

Based on FBI incident reports, there were about 16,100 murders and nonnegligent manslaughters known to the police in 2004. Over the last 40 years, the number of lethal assaults ranged from a low of about 8,500 in 1962 to a high of nearly 25,000 in 1991. Over 94,600 forcible rapes were known to the police in 2004; the low for these incidents was about 17,000 in 1960 and the high about 109,000 in 1992. There were over 400,000 known robbery incidents in 2004, growing from about 106,000 in 1961 to a peak of almost 700,000 in 1991. The number of aggravated assaults ranged from 153,000 to nearly 1.1 million in this same period, representing about 855,000 incidents in 2004.[9] Both in absolute numbers of known violent incidents and rates per capita, the last twenty-five years of the twentieth century was one of the most violent times for interpersonal violence in U.S. history.

Figure 1.2   Number of Aggravated Assaults and Robberies, 1960–2000

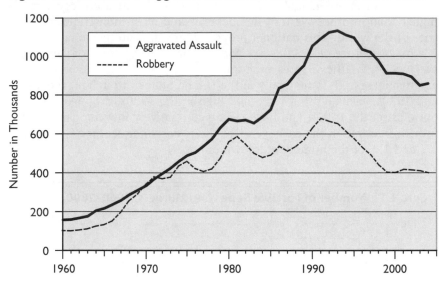

Estimates from the national victimization surveys for 2004 indicate that about 3 percent of households in the United States are victimized by a violent crime each year. The most common type of violent victimization is a simple assault with no serious injury. Sexual assaults are reported in less than 1 percent of households.[10] The proportion of U.S. households victimized by violent crime has decreased over the last decade. However, estimates of violent victimization vary dramatically across surveys. For example, national surveys yield victimization rates for violence against women that range from 7.5 to 117 per 1,000 women.[11]

Comprehensive and national self-report data on the prevalence of interpersonal violence are available only in a few major studies of high school students. For example, estimates from youth risk surveys indicate that about 33 percent of high school students in 2003 have been in a physical fight in the previous 12 months; almost 17 percent said they had carried a gun or other weapon.[12] Nearly 10 percent of students report that they have been bullied at school.[13]

The prevalence of interpersonal violence in the U.S. is probably far greater than revealed in these statistics. For example, it is widely known that both police data and victimization surveys underestimate criminal offenses committed by acquaintances and family members. When incidents of domestic violence among intimate partners, physical attacks among siblings, and corporal punishment practices of parents are considered, it is clear that interpersonal violence is a major fact of modern life in this country.[14] The wide availability of lethal weapons like handguns, the glorification of violence in film and by the mass media, and the historical legacy of using violence as a method of dispute resolution are some of the social forces that provide the context for high levels of interpersonal violence in U.S. culture.

Although opportunities for interpersonal violence and its frequency of occurrence are common in contemporary U.S. society, it is important to recognize that most acts of violence involve only minor physical injuries.[15] The relative rarity of serious physical harm or lethal consequences in violent incidents in the face of the widespread availability of lethal hardware suggests that much of the potential severity of violence is channeled or controlled through various mechanisms. In this book we will try to identify the individual and situational factors that distinguish between less and more serious acts of violence. In other words, what are the personal and situational dynamics that lead to the escalation and de-escalation of violence?

The Social Distribution of Interpersonal Violence

Crimes of violence do not occur in a vacuum. Rather, most violent crimes are situational events that represent the convergence of characteristics of the offender, victim, and offense in a particular time and space. Previous research has repeatedly shown that the risks of violent offending and victimization are not uniform across social groups, time, or location.

Offender Characteristics. Males account for the vast majority of the arrestees for each major form of violent crime, and similar patterns are found in self-report and victimization surveys.[16] The predominance of males as violent offenders is found across U.S. history and various Western cultures.[17]

Another strong demographic correlate of violent crime is the age of the offender. Criminologists for years have been interested in the disproportionate overrepresentation of juveniles and young adults in violent crime and the group context of much of this violence.[18] Over the last two decades, there have been increasing public concerns about an "epidemic" of youth violence within and outside the context of schools.[19] However, youth violence (especially among young males) has been a persistent theme throughout U.S. history.

Table 1.1   Profile of Violent Offenders (Persons Arrested in 2004)

	% Male	% < 25	% Black
Murder	88	48	47
Forcible Rape	98.5	46	32
Robbery	89	60	53
Aggravated Assault	79	40	33
All Known Offenses	76	45	27

Source: FBI-UCR (2004) Tables 41, 42, 43

Among arrestees for violent crime, African Americans are clearly over-represented relative to their population distribution. About half of the persons arrested for homicide or robbery are Black, and Blacks account for over one-third of those arrested for rape and aggravated assault. Similar patterns are found in historical studies of persons arrested throughout the twentieth century.[20]

A variety of ethnographic and ecological studies have documented social class differences in violent offending. Beginning with the early Chicago ecologists (e.g., Robert Park, Robert Burgess, Clifford Shaw, and Henry McKay), researchers have found disproportionately high levels of violence and other types of deviance within socially disorganized, transitional, lower class areas of central cities.[21] Later research discussed a predominance of "hot spots" for violent incidents within lower income areas.[22] Detailed ethnographic studies of daily life in areas of concentrated disadvantage provide further evidence of the high risks of violent offending in lower income neighborhoods.[23] The link between concentrated disadvantage and violence is also found in more macro-level studies of community dynamics.[24]

Victim Characteristics.   The victims of violent crime share many of the same characteristics as offenders; they are disproportionately male, young, Black, and poor.[25] Based on crime and victimization data, males are over 3.5 times more likely than females to be homicide victims. Although the number of Black murder victims is almost the same as White murder victims, the numbers in proportion to representation in the population mean that Blacks are 4 times more likely to be victims of homicide.[26] Males are over 2 times more prone to be victims of robbery and aggravated assault than their female counterparts. Risks of victimization by any type of violent crime for persons aged 16 to 19 are over 27 times higher than the risks for senior citizens over 65 years old. Victimization rates for rape, robbery, and aggravated assault are at least 1.5 times higher for Blacks than for Whites. Persons from low income families (i.e., <\$7,500 per year) are at least 4 times more likely to be victimized by an aggravated assault or robbery than persons from higher income households (i.e., >\$75,000 per year).[27]

The high risk of violent victimization for these groups is often attributed to factors related to group differences in routine activities and lifestyles. From this perspective, opportunities for violent victimization are enhanced by physical proximity to motivated offenders, exposure to risky and dangerous situations (e.g., participation in public activities at night), lower protection or guardianship, and greater perceived attractiveness as a crime target.[28]

Offense and Ecological Characteristics.   Aside from the attributes of victims and offenders, violent acts are also associated with a particular ecology or micro-environment of the crime event. Common elements include the type of victimization (e.g., physical assault, robberies, sexual attacks), weapon use, number of offenders and victims in the incident, the relationship between the victim and offender (e.g., family members, strangers, acquaintances), provocative or instigative actions by either party or bystanders, drug and/or alcohol use, and the motive or circumstance surrounding the crime (e.g., lover's quarrel, dispute over money). Physical aspects of the setting for violence include its location (e.g., home, street, commercial business) and time (e.g., daytime or nighttime, day of the week). The characteristics of the offenders, victims, and offenses combine to form the situational context of crime events.[29]

Over two-thirds of the violent incidents in national victimization surveys are threatened or attempted acts of personal violence (rather than completed acts), and assault victims suffer serious injuries in less than 7 percent of the incidents.[30] Homicides are committed with a firearm 70 percent of the time, and this weapon is used or threatened in over one-fourth of the robberies and aggravated assaults.[31] While the group context of violence is often emphasized in public commentaries and academic research, the typical violent offense involves a single victim and a single offender.

The proportion of violent offenses involving victims and offenders who are strangers varies widely across types of violent incidents. Victimization by strangers represents approximately one-half of all violent incidents. Strangers are the perpetrators in almost one-third of rapes, nearly three fourths of robbery victimizations, and in about one fourth of the homicides in which the victim-offender relationship could be determined.[32]

Acts of interpersonal violence are also more common during nighttime hours and weekends. Offenders are perceived by their victims to have been under the influence of either drugs or alcohol in 55 percent of sexual assaults and 35 percent of aggravated assaults.[33] A strong link between alcohol and homicide has also been made in past research.[34]

Given the amount of time spent in or near the home, it should not be surprising to find that most violent crimes occur within or near the victim's residence. Personal robbery, however, is somewhat different in terms of its greater prevalence in public areas (like streets and parks) and its lower perceived likelihood of drug or alcohol use by offenders.[35]

Based on various methods of inquiry (e.g., field observations, narrative accounts, and interviews), there are numerous motivations and circumstances surrounding violent offenses. What are often considered by others as "trivial" altercations and disputes become the basis for many acts of nonlethal and lethal violence. Fights and brawls are often motivated by feelings of masculine competitiveness and disrespect, evolving into character or honor contests to preserve and perpetuate aspects of one's social identity.[36] A retaliatory effort to "save face" in the aftermath of verbal or physical provocation are elements of the sequential dynamics that underlie a wide array of violent encounters. The active roles of victims and bystanders in precipitating and escalating violent events have also been identified as crucial components in the situational context of violence.[37]

Theories of Interpersonal Violence

A wide assortment of biological, psychological, and sociological theories have been used to explain the etiology and distribution of interpersonal violence. For our purposes, these theories are grouped into three general categories: (1) theories of violent propensities, (2) social structural and cultural theories of the macro-ecology of violence, and (3) theories of crime events.

Theories of Violent Propensities.   Most biological and psychological theories of violence focus attention on the identification of predispositions and risk factors to determine propensities toward violence. Some of the behavioral traits and biochemical conditions associated with violent propensities include the following: impulsivity, sensation seeking and risk taking, childhood aggression and bullying, low academic achievement and learning disabilities, maturational retardation, attention deficiency and hyperactivity, lack of empathy, high baseline testosterone levels, and low serotonin levels.

Learning and social process theories are other approaches associated with the identification of predispositions. From this perspective, violent propensities are developed and channeled through mechanisms of behavioral modeling, differential association, weakened bonds to mainstream institutions, and/or the learning of cognitive neutralizations.[38]

These individual-level risk factors have been well documented in the enormous literature on the causes and correlates of interpersonal violence. Unfortunately, these theories are unable to account for basic features of violent events, such as situational context, why injuries are rare, and variation in precipitating factors for different social groups.

Macro-Structural and Cultural Theories.   Macro-structural theories describe how rates of violence in particular geographical areas or among particular social groups are a reflection of social conditions that enable and constrain the opportunity and motivation for violence. For example, high rates of violence in low income areas are attributed to social disorganization caused by low economic opportunity, high population mobility, and ethnic diversity.[39] These conditions of social disorganization are linked to higher crime rates because they impede the collective efficacy of these neighborhoods to control and monitor deviance.[40] Concentrated disadvantage in lower class neighborhoods are social conditions that fuel frustration, despair, and anger.

Cultural and subcultural values have been the central focus of various theories of interpersonal violence and its distribution. High rates of violent crime are often attributed to frustrations that emanate from the inability to achieve the cultural goal of material success through legitimate means, cultural legacies of using violence for purposes of social control and dispute settlement, and subcultural values among particular groups that may lead to differential perceptions of anger-provoking stimuli. Other cultural approaches emphasize paternalistic values and masculine competitiveness as explanations for high levels of violence among males. According to these theoretical perspectives, the causes of gender, race, and class differences in violence are located in both cultural and structural forces that enable and constrain its expression.

Similar to biological and psychological approaches, macro-structural and cultural theories offer explanations for the differential propensity toward violence. However, the focus of sociological theories is in understanding differences across social groups and geographical areas (e.g., why are violent crime rates higher among males than females and in central cities rather than rural areas?). Current macro-sociological theories are unable to account for the differences in the location and timing of violent encounters, variation in the lethality of disputes, and other aspects of their situational context.

Theories of Crime Events. The theoretical focus on crime as events has evolved from the integration of theories of offender motivations and criminal opportunities. Routine activities and lifestyle theories attribute crime and victimization risks to the convergence in time and space of motivated offenders, suitable victims, and the lack of guardianship.[41] Other theories within this general framework focus on the episodic dynamics of violent transactions and the role of facilitating places, hardware, and facilitating others in the commission of deviant acts.[42]

An emphasis on crime events requires an examination of the predisposing and precipitating factors that not only increase the propensity toward violence but also affect the outcome of the event itself. Accordingly, the analysis of violent events is necessarily contextual, involving elements of structure and process that underlie the escalation and desistance of violent encounters. By focusing on the crime event as the unit of analysis, researchers within this tradition are able to more directly identify offender, victim, and offense elements that distinguish between different types of violent acts and variation in their resolution.

OUR APPROACH

Drawing on various theoretical approaches, we will explore the normative rules of engagement that pattern the nature, intensity, duration, and outcome of acts of interpersonal violence. Our primary goal is to address three related aspects of violence and aggression: (1) describe the routines, rituals, and rules that underlie various types of physical aggression in various contexts, (2) show how existing theories account for the social distribution of violence and the typical behavioral patterns that underlie it, and (3) identify the social constraints and facilitators of violence that affect its nature and severity beyond normative thresholds.

Theoretical developments in the study of violence and aggression are described in chapter 2. Social learning theories, subcultural theories, and theories of crime events that explain individual and group differences in violent propensities are emphasized because they are most relevant to the understanding of the normative rules associated with human aggression. Rather than reviewing all theories of deviance and conformity, our discussion is limited to those theories that offer the most insight into the patterning of the rules and rituals surrounding the preemption and commission of incidents of violent behavior.

Our description of the rules of aggression and violence begins with a brief overview of animal studies and the patterned behavioral responses to violence within this context. In chapter 3, we discuss different types of agonistic behaviors (e.g., territoriality defense, preemptive actions, fighting strategies) and the rules and routines surrounding animal aggression. These rules and ritualized behaviors are examined within the context of predatory aggression, inter-male aggression, fear-induced aggression, and courtship-related aggression. The patterned rules of engagement for aggression among animals provides a starting point for the investigation of similar rules and routines within the context of human interpersonal aggression.

The next four chapters provide a descriptive account of various normative rules of violence throughout history and contemporary society. Chapter 4 explores legal and extrajudicial forms of violence within the historical context of duels, the Western gunfight, and the imposition of state-sponsored corporate punishments. The normative rules that regulate and control the nature and magnitude of different types of street violence (e.g., "fair" fistfights, verbal banter among males that escalates into violent character contests, drive-by shootings, sexual assaults, street muggings and other robberies) are described in chapter 5.

The typical action patterns and behavioral sequences underlying physical assaults among intimate partners and family members are discussed in chapter 6. The rules and routines of domestic violence are examined within a comparative and historical framework.

Chapter 7 extends the context of normative rules of violence to athletic contests. Our discussion of the rules of acceptable violence within sporting events focus on the "fair" fight in blood sports like boxing, professional team sports (e.g., hockey, football, basketball, roller derby), and violent encounters among and between sports fans and athletes. The rules of violence in sports are used to illustrate types of violent behavior within otherwise legitimate contexts that exceed normative thresholds. All these applications of interpersonal violence focus on describing the typical behavioral sequences in the violent encounter and its situational contexts.

Chapter 8 explores the constraints and facilitators that help generate the normative rules of engagement for acts of aggression. This chapter pays particular attention to how the normative rules of engagement and disengagement shape and account for the dominant offender, victim, and situational contexts underlying interpersonal violence.

The final chapter examines the sources of control of interpersonal violence. It begins with a description of the most common situational contexts for simple assaults, aggravated assaults, and homicides in contemporary U.S. society. Next we discuss intervention strategies to control differential propensities toward violence and the situational crime prevention approaches to reduce the physical opportunity for aggressive behavior. Finally we look at how the construction and reestablishment of normative rules of violence may restrict and minimize the physical injuries from violence-inducing situations in a changing social world.

The practical aspects of this book involve developing strategies to deter and de-escalate potentially violent situations. The best way to accomplish this goal is through increasing public awareness of the normative rules and routines that underlie most incidents of human aggression. By increasing awareness of dangerous situations and anger-provoking actions, citizens should be better able to directly minimize their own risks of victimization by acts of interpersonal violence.

Notes

[1] Federal Bureau of Investigation (FBI). 2005. Crime in the United States, 2004. Uniform Crime Reports. Washington, DC (see especially the Supplemental Homicide Reports).

[2] David G. Myers. 1999. *Social Psychology.* 6th Edition. Boston: McGraw-Hill, p. 384.

[3] Edward O. Wilson. 2000. *Sociobiology: The New Synthesis.* 25th Anniversary Edition. Cambridge, MA: The Belknap Press of Harvard University, p. 578.

[4] For relatively nontechnical syntheses of the literature on biological influences and crime, see David C. Rowe. 2002. *Biology and Crime.* Los Angeles: Roxbury Publishing Company; Diana Fishbein. 2001. *Biobehavioral Perspectives in Criminology.* Belmont, CA: Wadsworth.

[5] See Irving Horowitz. 2002. *Taking Life: Genocide and State Power.* 5th Edition. New Brunswick, NJ: Transaction Publishers.

[6] R. L. Sivard. 1991. *World Military and Social Expenditures.* Washington, DC: World Priorities.

[7] See Gordon C. Barclay and Cynthia Tavares. 2000. *International Comparisons of Criminal Justice Statistics, 1998.* London: British Home Office.

[8] For a review of the history of violence in the United States, see Ted Robert Gurr. 1981. "Historical Trends in Violent Crime: A Critical Review of the Evidence." In M. Tonry and N. Morris (eds.), *Crime and Justice: An Annual Review of Research.* Chicago: University of Chicago Press, pp. 295–353; Ted Robert Gurr. 1979. "On the History of Violent Crime in Europe and America." In H. D. Graham and T. R. Gurr (eds.), *Violence in America: Historical and Comparative Perspectives.* Beverly Hills, CA: Sage; Roger Lane. 1997. *Murder in America: A History.* Columbus: Ohio State University; Eric H. Monkkonen. 1991. *Crime and Justice in American History: The Colonies and Early Republic,* Vol. 1 and 2. Edited by E. H. Monkkonen. Westport, CT: Meckler Publishing.

[9] See Federal Bureau of Investigation (FBI). 1960–2004. *Crime in the United States: Uniform Crime Reports. Select Years.* Washington, DC.

[10] See Shannan Catalano. 2005. *Criminal Victimization, 2004.* Based on the number of violent crimes and number of households referenced in table 2, p. 3. U.S. Department of Justice. Bureau of Justice Statistics. Washington, DC.

[11] For a review of data used to generate these estimates, see Richard J. Gelles. 2000. "Estimating the Incidence and Prevalence of Violence Against Women: National Data Systems and Sources." *Violence Against Women* 6(7):784–804.

[12] See Centers for Disease Control and Prevention. 2004. *Surveillance Summaries*. MMWR 2004: 53 (No. SS-2), p. 5.

[13] J. F. DeVoe, K. Peter, M. Noonan, T. D. Snyder, and K. Baum. 2005. *Indicators of School Crime and Safety: 2005* (NCES 2006-01/NCJ 210697). U.S. Departments of Education and Justice. Washington, DC: U.S. Government Printing Office, p. 38.

[14] The level of direct exposure to aggression would increase dramatically if other forms of agonistic behaviors were included (e.g., physical threats, submission and retreat from aggressive situations, verbal taunting). Under this wider definition, it is not unreasonable to assume that direct exposure to aggression is a daily life experience for most people living in the United States.

[15] For example, according to the National Crime Victimization Survey, over one-quarter of victims of robbery and assault received physical injuries. However, only about 7 percent of these victims of violent offenses incurred medical expenses for their injuries, suggesting that the nature of the injuries was relatively mild. See National Crime Victimization Survey. 2005. *Criminal Victimization in the United States, 2003*. Tables 75 and 77. U.S. Department of Justice. Bureau of Justice Statistics. Washington, DC.

[16] See Federal Bureau of Investigation (FBI). 2005. *Crime in the United States: Uniform Crime Reports, 2004*. Washington, DC; Shannan Catalano. 2005. *Criminal Victimization, 2004*. U.S. Department of Justice. Bureau of Justice Statistics. Washington, DC.

[17] See Terance D. Miethe and Wendy C. Regoeczi. 2004. *Rethinking Homicide: Exploring the Structure and Process Underlying Deadly Situations*. Cambridge, UK: Cambridge University Press; Rosemary Gartner, K. Baker, and Fred Pampel. 1990. "Gender Stratification and the Gender Gap in Homicide Victimization." *Social Problems* 37:593–612; Timothy Hartnagel. 1982. "Modernization, Female Social Roles, and Female Crime: A Cross-National Comparison." *The Sociological Quarterly* 23(4):477–490; Michael P. Ghiglieri. 1999. *The Dark Side of Man: Tracing the Origins of Male Violence*. Reading, MA: Perseus Books; Roger Lane. 1997. *Murder in America: A History*, Columbus: Ohio State University.

[18] See James F. Short., Jr. and Fred L. Strodtbeck. 1965. *Group Process and Gang Delinquency*. Chicago: University of Chicago Press; Mark Warr. 2002. *Companions in Crime: The Social Aspects of Criminal Conduct*. Cambridge, UK: Cambridge University Press.

[19] See Mark H. Moore and Michael Tonry. 1998. "Youth Violence in America." In M. Moore and M. Tonry (eds.), *Crime and Justice: An Annual Review of Research*, Vol. 24. Chicago: University of Chicago Press, pp. 1–24; Philip J. Cook and John H. Laub. 1998. "The Unprecedented Epidemic in Youth Violence." *Crime and Justice: A Review of Research* 24:27–64.

[20] See Harold C. Brearley. 1932. *Homicide in the United States*. Chapel Hill: University of North Carolina Press; Marvin Wolfgang. 1958. *Patterns of Criminal Homicide*. Philadelphia: University of Pennsylvania Press.

[21] See, for example, Clifford Shaw and Henry McKay. 1942. *Juvenile Delinquency and Urban Areas*. Chicago: University of Chicago Press.

[22] See Lawrence W. Sherman, Patrick R. Gartin, and Michael E. Buerger. 1989. "Hot Spots of Predatory Crime: Routine Activities and the Criminology of Place." *Criminology* 27:27–55.

[23] See, for example, Elijah Anderson. 1998. "The Social Ecology of Youth Violence." *Crime and Justice: A Review of Research* 24:64–103; Elijah Anderson. 1999. *Code of the Street: Decency, Violence, and the Moral Life of the Inner City*. New York: W. W. Norton.

[24] See Robert J. Sampson, Stephen W. Raudenbush, and Felton Earls. 1997. "Neighborhoods and Violent Crime: A Multilevel Study of Collective Efficacy." *Science* 277:918–920; Robert J. Sampson and William Julius Wilson. 1995. "Toward a Theory of Race, Crime, and Urban Inequality." In John Hagan and Ruth D. Peterson (eds.), *Crime and Inequality*. Stanford, CA: Stanford University Press; William Julius Wilson. 1996. *When Work Disappears: The World of the New Urban Poor*. New York: Knopf; William Julius Wilson. 1991. "Studying Inner-City Social Dislocations: The Challenge of Public Agenda Research." *American Sociological Review* 56:1–14.

[25] The exception is sexual assault, where women are over 16 times more likely to be victimized by this offense than males. See National Crime Victimization Survey. 2005. *Criminal*

Victimization in the United States, 2003, table 2. U.S. Department of Justice. Bureau of Justice Statistics. Washington, DC.

[26] See Federal Bureau of Investigation (FBI). 2005. *Crime in the United States: Uniform Crime Reports, 2004.* Table 2.4. Washington, DC.

[27] National Crime Victimization Survey. 2005. *Criminal Victimization in the United States, 2003. Tables 3, 5, 20.* U.S. Department of Justice, Bureau of Justice Statistics. Washington, DC.

[28] For discussions of various criminal opportunity theories (e.g., routine activity theory, lifestyle-exposure, structural-choice perspectives), see Lawrence E. Cohen and Marcus Felson. 1979. "Social Change and Crime Rate Trends: A Routine Activity Approach." *American Sociological Review* 44: 588–608; Michael S. Hindelang, Michael Gottfredson, and James Garofalo. 1978. *Victims of Personal Crime.* Cambridge, Massachusetts: Ballinger; Terance D. Miethe and Robert F. Meier. 1990. "Criminal Opportunity and Victimization rates: A Structural-Choice Theory of Criminal Victimization." *Journal of Research in Crime and Delinquency* 27: 243–66;Terance D. Miethe and Robert F. Meier. 1994.*Crime and Its Social Context: Toward an Integrated Theory of Offenders, Victims, and Situations.* State University of New York Press: Albany, New York; Robert F. Meier, Leslie W. Kennedy, and Vincent F. Sacco. 2001. *The Process and Structure of Crime: Crime Events and Crime Analysis. Advances in Criminological Theory,* Vol. 9. New Brunswick, NJ: Transaction.

[29] See Terance D. Miethe and Wendy C. Regoeczi. 2004. *Rethinking Homicide: Exploring the Structure and Process Underlying Deadly Situations.* Cambridge, UK: Cambridge University Press; Terance D. Miethe and Robert F. Meier. 1994. *Crime and Its Social Context: Toward an Integrated Theory of Offenders, Victims, and Situations.* State University of New York Press: Albany, New York; Robert F. Meier, Leslie W. Kennedy, and Vincent F. Sacco. 2001.*The Process and Structure of Crime: Crime Events and Crime Analysis. Advances in Criminological Theory,* Vol. 9. New Brunswick, NJ: Transaction; Leslie W. Kennedy and Vincent F. Sacco. 1996. *Crime Counts: A Criminal Event Analysis.* Nelson Canada. Scarborough, Ontario.

[30] National Crime Victimization Survey. 2005. *Criminal Victimization in the United States, 2003.* Table 77. U.S. Department of Justice. Bureau of Justice Statistics. Washington, DC.

[31] Federal Bureau of Investigation (FBI). 2005. *Crime in the United States: Uniform Crime Reports, 2004,* p. 18.

[32] See National Crime Victimization Survey. 2005. *Criminal Victimization in the United States 2003,* table 66. U.S. Department of Justice. Bureau of Justice Statistics. Washington, DC. Federal Bureau of Investigation (FBI). 2005. *Crime in the United States: Uniform Crime Reports, 2004,* p. 18. Washington, DC.

[33] National Crime Victimization Survey. 2005. *Criminal Victimization in the United States, 2003,* table 32. U.S. Department of Justice. Bureau of Justice Statistics. Washington, DC.

[34] Robert Nash Parker. 1995. "Bringing 'Booze' Back in: The Relationship between Alcohol and Homicide." *Journal of Research in Crime and Delinquency* 32:3–38; Robert Nash Parker and Linda Rebhun. 1995. *Alcohol and Homicide: A Deadly Combination of Two American Traditions.* Albany: State University of New York Press.

[35] National Crime Victimization Survey. 2005. *Criminal Victimization in the United States, 2003,* tables 32 and 65. U.S. Department of Justice. Bureau of Justice Statistics. Washington, DC.

[36] See Kenneth Polk. 1994. *When Men Kill: Scenarios of Masculine Violence.* Cambridge, UK: Cambridge University Press; Terance D. Miethe and Wendy C. Regoeczi. 2004. *Rethinking Homicide: Exploring the Structure and Process Underlying Deadly Situations.* Cambridge, UK: Cambridge University Press; David F. Luckenbill. 1977. "Criminal Homicide as a Situated Transaction." *Social Problems* 25:176–186.

[37] See James T. Tedeschi and Richard B. Felson. 1994. *Violence, Aggression, and Coercive Actions.* Washington, DC: American Psychological Association.

[38] See Albert Bandura. 1973. *Aggression: A Social Learning Analysis.* Englewood Cliffs, NJ: Prentice Hall; Edwin H. Sutherland. 1947. *Principles of Criminology.* 4th Edition. Philadelphia: Lippincott; Travis Hirschi. 1969. *Causes of Delinquency.* Berkeley: University of California Press; Gresham Sykes and David Matza. 1957. "Techniques of Neutralization: A Theory of Delinquency." *American Journal of Sociology* 22:664–670.

[39] See Clifford Shaw and Henry McKay. 1942. *Juvenile Delinquency and Urban Areas.* Chicago: University of Chicago Press; Robert J. Sampson and W. Bryon Groves. 1989. "Community Structure and Crime: Testing Social-Disorganization Theory." *American Journal of Sociology* 94:774–802.

[40] Robert J. Sampson, Stephen W. Raudenbush, and Felton Earls. 1997. "Neighborhoods and Violent Crime: A Multilevel Study of Collective Efficacy." *Science* 277:918–920; Robert J. Sampson and William Julius Wilson. 1995. "Toward a Theory of Race, Crime, and Urban Inequality." In John Hagan and Ruth D. Peterson (eds.), *Crime and Inequality*. Stanford, CA: Stanford University Press.

[41] See Lawrence E. Cohen and Marcus Felson. 1979. "Social Change and Crime Rate Trends: A Routine Activity Approach." *American Sociological Review* 44:588–608; Michael S. Hindelang, Michael Gottfredson, and James Garofalo. 1978. *Victims of Personal Crime*. Cambridge, MA: Ballinger; Terance D. Miethe and Wendy C. Regoeczi. 2004. *Rethinking Homicide: Exploring the Structure and Process Underlying Deadly Situations*. Cambridge, UK: Cambridge University Press; Terance D. Miethe and Robert F. Meier. 1994. *Crime and Its Social Context: Toward an Integrated Theory of Offenders, Victims, and Situations*. Albany: State University of New York Press.

[42] See John Lofland. 1969. *Deviance and Identity*. Englewood Cliffs, NJ: Prentice Hall.

Theories of Interpersonal Violence and Its Context

An impressive research literature exists on the causes and social distribution of violence over groups, time, and space. The literature covers acts of collective violence (e.g., wars, labor strikes), interpersonal violence (e.g., homicides, sexual assaults), and self-inflicted violence (e.g., suicide). Theories of violent propensities and the social distribution of violence span the full spectrum of evolutionary, physiological, psychological, and sociological explanations. These perspectives identify facilitating and inhibiting factors that when considered simultaneously should account for the social profile and situational dynamics underlying the preemption, onset, and escalation of violence incidents.

This chapter summarizes various theories of violent propensities and the nature of aggression. Biochemical, social learning, subcultural, and criminal opportunity theories are discussed as they relate to explaining differences in violent propensities, the structural profile of violent incidents, and the patterned response sequences associated with their commission, escalation, and de-escalation.

THEORIES OF VIOLENT PROPENSITIES

A longstanding concern in the study of human behavior involves the "nature-nurture" debate. The current view is that human behavior is a product of both forces. Substantial evidence exists on the genetic influences on behavior (e.g., the inheritability of particular traits) and the commonality of neural and biochemical responses to aversive stimuli (e.g., reflexes, physiological reactions to threat, the pain-attack response). An equally impressive literature demonstrates the strong impact of shared environmental and cultural experiences on the learning of social behavior.

Neurobiological Controls and Facilitators

Biological laws of human nature provide a basic foundation for the regulation and control of our behavior. Many reactions to threatening or aversive stimuli are automatic—"hard wired" or programmed through the nervous system and its information pathways. For example, fear-inducing threats automatically trigger various physiological responses (e.g., changes in heart rate, blood pressure, respiration) and the following action sequence: we stop what we were doing, turn toward the source of the threat, pause from taking action while processing information about the threat, and then respond by fight, flight, or submission. In both humans and other vertebrates, fear-induced action patterns are remarkably similar across different contexts and cues (e.g., a police officer's command to "freeze"; animals' use of the smell, sight, or sound of predators and rivals). Research in the last half century has greatly enhanced our understanding of the patterns of physiological responses to external stimuli and the biological pathways that lead to human aggression.[1]

Neurotransmitters

One of the basic communication systems within the body involves neurotransmitters—the essential messengers that trigger chemical reactions across a nerve pathway that ultimately result in a change in the way we think, feel, or behave. Of at least 50 known neurotransmitters, most research on aggressive behavior has focused on a relatively small number of them, especially dopamine and serotonin.[2] Dopamine triggers emotional responses that provide the fuel for fight-or-flight responses, exploration of something novel, avoidance of something unpleasant, and the ability to experience pleasure and pain.[3] In contrast, serotonin is normally involved in temperature regulation, sensory perceptions, and mood control (a factor associated with emotional disorders such as depression, suicide, impulsive behavior, and aggression). Both dopamine and serotonin are strongly and consistently linked to aggressive behavior.[4]

Neurotransmitters prime the individual to respond to particular stimuli. While they provide the foundation for understanding patterned response sequences to external threats, the process of learning and life experiences also affect how humans interpret and attach meaning to particular physiological states and how they respond. From this perspective, different agonistic responses may emanate from a basic biochemical reaction, but the nature, magnitude, and form of these behavioral patterns are socially constructed through shared experiences and reinforcement. A similar argument applies to the role of testosterone and other hormones in human aggression.

Hormonal Factors

The most commonly identified hormones associated with agonistic behavior are testosterone and other androgens. Elevated levels of testosterone are found in male violent offenders, and another hormone (estradiol) seems important in maternal aggression.[5] Animal studies indicate that the response topography is similar for both types of hormone-dependent aggression (e.g., both male and female animals use lateral attacks and exhibit piloerections—hair-raising). Testosterone levels in humans peak in the mid-teens and decline over the life course.

The effect of high levels of testosterone on aggression is highly context-specific and depends on both characteristics of the individual and social circumstances. It is difficult to isolate the effect of testosterone on human behavior because of the possibility of reciprocal causation. In other words, elevated testosterone levels may predispose some individuals to behave in dominant and aggressive ways, but behaving in these specific ways may also increase testosterone levels.[6] Testosterone may be one of the core biological factors that account for the prevalence of male aggression.[7] However, hormonal factors, in and of themselves, are unable to account for the highly patterned rules of engagement that underlie human aggression in particular contexts.

Social Learning Theories

The idea that violent propensities are learned has been a central assumption of many theories of criminal behavior. In fact, the most influential criminological theory of the twentieth century—Edwin Sutherland's theory of differential association—is a learning theory.[8] Other cultural and subcultural explanations of violent behavior also emphasize the principles of learning, even though the specific learning mechanisms are only vaguely described in these theories.[9] It took the efforts of Albert Bandura and subsequent theorists to articulate a social learning theory of aggression more fully.[10]

The basic assumption of social learning theory is that aggressive response tendencies are acquired and maintained through experience. These experiences shape the expected rewards and punishments that derive from different agonistic behaviors (i.e., threat, aggression, submission, escape). Accordingly, social learning theory contends that the specific elements of aggressive behavior (i.e., its frequency and forms, evoking situations, target selection) are the product of learning experiences.[11]

The fundamental principles underlying the social learning approach to aggression are relatively straightforward. Humans acquire aggressive responses through observation and behavioral modeling and maintain them as behavioral choices in subsequent situations through reinforcement. These principles have been elaborated on more fully in theories of social cognition and information processing. The basic ideas from these theories that are relevant to the learning of aggression include the following:[12]

- Humans have the capacity to exercise control over their thought processes, motivation, affect, and actions to produce certain results; they are not simply reactive organisms shaped and driven by external events. Proactive human agency means we selectively perceive, process, and react to potentially violent cues and other aversive conditions.

- Humans observe agonistic behavior throughout the life cycle in various forms. They observe aggression in real-life settings (e.g., at home, in schools, at work, on the street) and vicariously in the visual world of the media (e.g., television, video, and motion pictures). Previous exposure to violence in real life or media portrayals is a necessary but not sufficient condition for an individual's subsequent commission of violent behavior.

- By observing the consequences of aggression to others, children gradually acquire a rudimentary knowledge of certain "rules of conduct" (e.g., that one may sometimes obtain something desirable by using physical force). As children gain experience with aggression and its consequences, they acquire a wider repertoire of aggressive behaviors.

- Whether or not aggressive behaviors are acted out depends on the anticipated rewards and punishments for various action plans. The likelihood of aggression is higher when suitable incentives for aggression are present and violence has been rewarding to the person in similar situations in the past. Expectations of rewarding outcomes and enhanced feelings of self-efficacy for successful commission of violence perpetuate aggressive responses in future situations.

- Through repeated experiences with aggression, children develop a more elaborate sense of the rules of aggressive conduct prescribed by society and tend to incorporate these rules as guides for their own behavior. These normative beliefs and personal experiences become integrated into internal cognitive representations that people form of their environment. The scenarios and scripts of aggression that derive from these processes are encoded into memory, maintained through rehearsal, and retrieved as guides for subsequent behavior.

When a learned script is applied to a particular interaction, it provides a general framework for understanding the nature and patterns of violent episodes. Specifically, the retrieval of scripts provides an immediate cognitive appraisal of anticipated actions and consequences that influence (1) how to attack or counteract and its form, (2) the selection of a person or group as the appropriate target, (3) the proper reaction based on whether the provocation justifies or requires aggressive retaliation, and (4) interpreting the situation or context as one in which aggression is either appropriate or inappropriate.[13]

It should be clear that theories of social learning, cognition, and information processing are directly relevant to our understanding of the normative rules of aggressive behavior. For example, the cognitive integration of direct experiences with violence and shared normative beliefs about its appropriateness in particular contexts should result in common patterns in the prevalence of interpersonal violence, triggering events, action sequences, and targets selected. These theories also predict substantial variation across different social groups and situational contexts in terms of the normative scripts learned and applied.

Direct Experiences with Violence

As documented in chapter 1, people in the United States have a relatively high risk of direct exposure to interpersonal violence and aggression in their daily lives. To review, over one-half of U.S. residents are predicted to be victims of violent crimes in their lifetime, about 3 percent of households reportedly are "touched" by a violent crime each year, and about one-third of high school students indicate that they have been in a physical fight in the last year. Particular social groups (e.g., males, the young, Blacks, urban residents) are also found to have far greater exposure to different types of violent victimization than others.

Given the enormous undercounting of violent offenses and threats among family members (e.g., domestic violence assaults, fights among siblings), these national estimates provide only a gross assessment of the public's direct exposure to violence. They also fail to recognize the extensive exposure to violence in the form of corporal punishment by parents during childhood, bullying behavior by older or bigger classmates, wrestling matches among adolescent siblings, and the various forms of physical roughhousing that often characterizes play among adolescent males. When other types of agonistic behavior are also considered (e.g., aggressive driving, gestures, or verbal taunts), exposure to violence or its threat is a daily occurrence for most people in the United States.

According to Bandura's social learning theory of aggression, direct experiences are especially important for behavioral modeling because they involve the major agents of socialization (i.e., family members, peers). The action sequences, the outcomes of these direct life experiences, and the relative rewards associated with particular actions shape the ongoing cognitive processes of script formulation, modification, and rehearsals that provide humans with their own "rule book" on aggressive conduct. When confronted with potentially aggressive situations, these cognitive scripts serve as information-processing "shortcuts" that prime the individual to anticipate particular outcomes and to enact learned responses.

Mass Media and Violence

Social science research has extensively explored the relationship between violence and its portrayal in mass media.[14] Research has explored the cultivation of violence in U.S. society, the direct impact of viewing violence in television and other media (like film, videos, music) on violent behavior, and the extent to which depictions of violence in media sources result in modeling. As discussed below, there is no doubt that violence is a major theme and source of enormous revenue in the news and entertainment industries. It is less clear, however, how exposure to violence in media affects violent propensities in viewers.

The average person in the United States spends about 9½ hours each day watching television, going to movies, renting videos, reading magazines, listening to music, or surfing the Internet.[15] Violence is a major theme in each of these media sources. In fact, before their eighteenth birthday, the typical child will witness over 200,000 acts of violence on television, including 16,000 murders.[16] Well over half of all major characters on television are involved each week in some form of violent action.[17] The most popular video games for adolescent boys have violence as a major theme (e.g., fighting, war games). One researcher thinks the constant barrage of violent images will have consequences.

> Today, the combination of ready access to real guns, videogame practice at shooting human beings, a general loosening of social controls, and increasingly frequent violent imagery on television and in movies poses a new danger.[18]

Criticisms of the mass media's preoccupation with and portrayals of violence are wide and varied. Media sources have long been criticized for presenting images of violence that result in the vulgarization of culture—cheapening human life, promoting undesirable role models, sanitizing the pain and suffering associated with violence, and the trivialization and minimization of alternative, nonviolent methods of dispute resolution. Industry efforts to address these criticisms have been directed primarily at developing rating and warning systems for potential viewers, rather than minimizing the amount of violence portrayed.

Consistent with popular beliefs about the harmful effects of media violence, some research has shown a strong association between interpersonal violence and media exposure to it. However, the impact of media violence on violent behavior depends on its form, context, duration, and intensity. Some of the context-specific effects of media violence on the propensities for individuals to engage in interpersonal violence include the following:

- Exposure to pornographic materials is only slightly related to risks of sex offending. However, pornography within a violent context is strongly associated with sexual predation.[19]
- Longitudinal studies have found that 8-year-old boys who viewed the most violent programs growing up were most likely to engage in aggressive and delinquent behavior by age 18 and serious criminal behavior by age 30.[20]

• Exposure to violent video games increased aggressive behavior in both the short and long term.[21]

There are various theoretical explanations for how violent messages in media sources translate into violent behavior in viewers. Some learning theories focus on how violence becomes a conditioned response to anger-provoking stimuli through social processes of imitation and behavioral modeling. Other theories of media effects examine how images of media violence lead to diffuse forms of brutalization, desensitization, and the cultivation or inculcation of values that embrace destruction, retribution, and violence as a culturally acceptable way of life.

Researchers in mass communication over the last two decades have devoted considerable theoretical and empirical attention to the media as a major force in the cultivation and mainstreaming of U.S. culture. From this perspective, television and modern communication delivery systems (e.g., cable, satellite, the Internet) have become an increasingly homogenized source of socialization and everyday information for otherwise diverse population groups.[22] Modern television programming has retained some elements of a multi-dimensional ideological orientation to cater to particular viewers (e.g., particular genres or programs are shown during particular time slots), but profit margins require media industries to provide content that attracts the largest and most heterogeneous audiences. By producing a coherent set of unified images and messages that often reflect themes that have already proved to be profitable, the modern media have emerged as a primary source for the cultivation of a shared conception of reality, the mainstreaming of diverse groups, and the subsequent development of a shared national culture.[23] Violence has remained a dominant and lucrative theme of the media's projection of culture.

While fashion styles, language, and plot lines have changed over time, themes and cultural messages surrounding the appropriateness of violence have exhibited both change and stability. For example, industry standards within the early history of television required "bad guys" to be brought to justice by the legitimate authorities, and similar images of legal retribution are espoused in current media coverage. However, an increasingly common message within prime-time television programming and motion pictures is the portrayal of "street justice" as a cultural value of equal or even greater social acceptability.[24] The related notion of "the ends justify the means" is another cultural message that is often promoted within the current context of violence in the mass media.

Other cultural themes distributed through media sources involve images of when violence is and is not justified. For example, violence against "bad guys" is portrayed as totally acceptable and almost a righteous thing to do in most contemporary media accounts of violence.[25] Negative images of gratuitous and nonutilitarian acts of violence are often expressed in prime-time television, but these forms of violence are also portrayed in a somewhat glorified fashion in particular genres of motion pictures (e.g., marital arts films). At the same time, exhibiting self-control in the face of anger-provoking situations represents an antiviolence message that is sometimes presented in film and television.

The mass media's role in cultural "mainstreaming" derived from its vilification and negative portrayal of various types of extremist attitudes and behavior. For example, public displays of extreme masculinity, violent rage, and the lack of self-control have long been chastised and conveyed as silly or stupid in news programs and prime-time television.[26] At the same time, however, the latest genre of "reality" television often presents these extreme views as a true reflection of the tough and gritty existence of real life on the streets. Frequent viewers of this type of material may develop a "mean world" view of life that promotes rather than changes stereotypical images of different social groups.[27] These stereotypes include the expected responses of particular groups to potentially violent situations (e.g., "real" men fight, the impulsivity of youth, images of angry and rage-filled Black males).

Research from the field of mass communication strongly suggests that media images of violence contribute to the social reality of violence. When coupled with everyday life experiences, the media cultivates shared normative beliefs about violence and its legitimacy under general and specific conditions. It is within these life experiences and the media's portrayals of interpersonal violence that the normative rules of aggressive conduct are developed, spread throughout diverse groups, and ultimately reinforced in the home and on the street.

Cultural and Subcultural Theories of Violence

Cultural and subcultural theories of violent propensities have a long history in U.S. criminology. Various theories fall within this general perspective. For example, Walter Miller argued that higher rates of violence and crime were found among lower class boys because of their endorsement of various "focal concerns" (i.e., values like toughness, excitement, trouble, fate, and autonomy).[28] Hyman Rodman described a "lower class value stretch" that increases their exposure to violence.[29] Albert Cohen wrote about the negativistic and nonutilitarian purpose of crime among lower class youth.[30] Similarly, James Short and Fred Strodtbeck's study of group process and gang delinquency explored the subcultural basis of violence.[31] Two formulations of cultural theories related to criminal behavior are especially useful for our purposes of understanding normative rules of aggressive conduct: the "subculture of violence" by Marvin Wolfgang and Franco Ferracuti and Elijah Anderson's "code of the street."

The Subculture of Violence. Of the theoretical developments that focus on the learning and cultural transmission of violence, Wolfgang and Ferracuti's thesis has received the most attention and notoriety. Originally conceived to explain subcultural differences in violence among Italians and Sicilians, this general perspective has been extended to account for regional differences in violence in the United States (e.g., a Southern subculture of violence), racial and class differences in male violence, and even differences within sports (e.g., hockey). Ideas generated from their theory have been incorporated into more recent subcultural theories (e.g., Elijah Anderson's "code of the street").

Wolfgang and Ferracuti contend that six features characterize violent subcultures.[32] These features include:

- Violence is a potent theme in its values, norms, and conduct.

- Although violence is not continual, it is endemic.

- There is a general willingness to use violence, especially in response to certain stimuli.

- Although differences in opinion exist, there is a general sanction, based on pragmatic and moral justifications, for the violent victimization of those categorized as adversaries.

- While there may be sporadic challenges in the use of violence, those who participate in the violence exhibit little ambivalence and do not view their conduct as morally illicit.

- Nonviolence is a counter norm, and those reluctant to endorse or participate in violence face penalties or the threat thereof.

The subculture of violence theory is an explanation of violence that draws on basic differences in values and norms. Its primary contention is that within particular pockets of society (subcultures) there is a way of life or value system in which violence is an expected, tolerated, and even demanded response to anger-provoking stimuli. There is also differential perception of what is anger-provoking within these subcultural settings. For example, a derogatory comment about one's mother may be laughed off in mainstream culture or other subcultures, but the insult is considered "fighting words" within a subculture of violence. The quick resort to violence to resolve conflict is another fundamental element of this subculture. Pro-violence values are learned at home in parental disciplinary approaches, in schoolyards, and in childhood play—and ultimately reinforced on the streets.

The subculture of violence theory has been criticized on a number of grounds (e.g., what are the origins of this subculture), but its major limitation is the lack of empirical support for the contention that particular groups have unique pro-violence values. In fact, rather than exhibiting unique values for different groups, public surveys consistently find little differences in the reported "value" placed on violence by males and females, Blacks and Whites, and lower- and middle-class people.

Rather than saying there are group differences in pro-violence values, other subcultural explanations for violence have focused on more structural aspects of the context for violence. For example, William Harvey attributes high rates of violence among young, African-American, urban males to a "subculture of exasperation" in which the sense of frustration and powerlessness felt by many African Americans manifests itself through violence and aggression.[33] With limited resources and alternatives, the use of violence within this context becomes a necessary form of "self help" and a mechanism for resolving conflict. Under this formulation, violence is not necessarily "valued"; it simply becomes an expected or even necessary response in the absence of other resources.

Elijah Anderson's "Code of the Streets." Based on ethnographic observations of life in inner city communities, Elijah Anderson discovered the presence of various rules that regulate public interpersonal behavior and especially violent interactions in such settings. This "code of the street" is said to have evolved as a "cultural adaptation to a profound lack of faith in the police and the judicial system, and in others who would champion one's personal security."[34] Within marginalized neighborhoods, residents develop a willingness to defend themselves and their loved ones by whatever means necessary. The ability of individuals to "take care of themselves" becomes a source of status.

Anderson contends that two disparate types of normative systems coexist in the inner city of Philadelphia. One system reflects middle-class values (the so-called "decent" families) and is followed by the majority of residents in the inner city. The other normative structure—the "street" orientation—is in opposition to mainstream values. However, spatial proximity in inner city communities demands that even adolescents from "decent" families acquire a working knowledge of the code of the street in order to negotiate their way through public space. "Code switching" (i.e., the ability to be "street" when needed) is especially important for young males for survival and co-existence within these two normative systems. In this manner, all inner city adolescents become versed in the ways of the street, including the need to defend oneself through displays of toughness or violence.

Similar to our idea of rules of aggressive conduct, the code of the street is an unwritten and informal set of rules that has emerged in inner-city communities as a response to various social problems (e.g., lack of "living wage" jobs, racial prejudice and discrimination, isolation, and alienation). The rules of appropriate behavior concerning violence are learned early in life and reinforced by the pervasiveness of violence and conflict in these communities. Children learn the code by observing how older kids resolve disputes through cursing and abusive talk or direct physical violence. "Street-oriented" adults and parents also help shape and reinforce understanding of the code through verbal messages such as: "watch your back," "protect yourself," "don't punk out," "respect yourself," and "if someone disses you, you got to straighten them out."[35] "Decent" inner-city parents reinforce the same code but they also emphasize to their children the value of getting "out of stuff" by outwitting adversaries and standing one's ground only as a last resort.[36]

Rather than a normative system that endorses the value of violence per se, the code of the street is actually more representative of a set of functional imperatives and adaptations for survival in a world of despair and limited legitimate opportunities. Within this wider physical environment, various staging areas (e.g., street "hangouts" including the areas outside bars, multiplex theatres, sporting events, or concerts) exist where campaigns for demonstrating, maintaining, or enhancing one's reputation and ability to handle oneself are carried out. In these staging areas, violence or the threat of violence serves as a status-enhancing resource for individuals—"representing" who they are to a public audience. In short, fighting and other forms of violence become the physical manifestations of campaigns for status and self-respect.

The pursuit of respect and status through physical threats and acts of violence are central themes in other research on the causes and distribution of violence. For example, parallel factors are found to underlie violence in research that focuses on "character contests," "honor contests," and public displays of masculine competitiveness as forums for self-enhancement.[37] Although these alternative formulations are not necessarily restricted to the violence of inner-city youths, they are similar to a code of the street in their portrayal of violence as a type of self-help used by individuals with limited resources and few avenues to resolve disputes and simultaneously enhance their social status.

THEORIES OF CRIMINAL AND VIOLENT ACTS

There has been a longstanding debate about the proper focus of criminological inquiry. As reflected in theories of criminal propensity, many researchers focus their study on criminality (i.e., persistent patterns of offending over one's criminal career). The alternative has been the study of crime (i.e., discrete criminal acts) and the physical requisites for the opportunity to commit these acts. Obviously, any comprehensive theory should be able to explain both motivations (i.e., the differential criminal propensities of individuals and groups) and the physical, spatial, and temporary properties of criminal acts.

Two general theoretical orientations offer some integration of motivation and opportunity within the study of violent acts: criminal opportunity theories and the interactionist's framework of symbolic interactionism and ethnomethodology.

Criminal Opportunity Theories

Theories of criminal opportunity involve an assortment of approaches that place the causes of crime within the symbiotic relationships between conventional and illegal activities of everyday life.[38] Daily routine activities and conventional lifestyles affect criminal opportunities because they affect the convergence in time and space of three necessary elements of predatory offenses: (1) exposure to motivated offenders, (2) suitable targets, and (3) the absence of guardianship.

Criminal opportunity theories have wide appeal among criminologists because they can be applied across a variety of units of analysis and contexts. For example, the initial "routine activities" formulation was directed at explaining post-World War II changes in crimes in the United States, whereas the "lifestyle-exposure" approach focused primarily on explaining group differences in victimization risks. The research on "hot spots" for criminal activity, in contrast, uses these theories to account for the social, spatial, and temporary clustering of crime incidents.[39]

Although receiving empirical support in different contexts, we find criminal opportunity theories to be most useful as a general orientation for the micro-level study of criminal acts. From this perspective, violent acts are concentrated within particular dominant settings because of the convergence of motivated offenders and the available criminal opportunities. For example, it is the offender's familiarity with the social space, the accessibility of a crime target, and the lack of public scrutiny or guardianship that contributes to recurrent acts of domestic violence within the victim's home. In contrast, the street provides an attractive and visible public arena for status-enhancement through character contests and other demonstrations of one's physical prowess. It is the union of motivated offenders, suitable targets, and the absence of guardianship that are the basic structural features of the home and street environments that enhance their attractiveness as physical locations for different kinds of violent acts.

The Interactionist's Framework

The interactionist's perspective is a dominant conceptual framework for studying violent situations within the field of microsociology. This general intellectual tradition includes symbolic interactionism (i.e., George Herbert Mead's theory of the self), the work on interaction rituals and the presentation of self in everyday life by Erving Goffman, and labeling theories of deviant behavior.[40]

Interactionists emphasize the subjective aspects of social life and how humans continually adjust their behavior in interpersonal encounters in accordance with the anticipated or real actions of other people. Humans are able to make these adjustments because of the unique capacity to interpret acts symbolically and to rehearse alternative lines of action mentally before acting. The process of "minding" (i.e., the inner dialogue used to test alternatives, rehearse action, and anticipate reactions before overt action) allows for reflective thought and the framing of actions in ways that maximize or maintain one's social self.

Many of the basic concepts used by Erving Goffman in the study of social interaction are especially relevant for understanding the nature and process underlying violent situations. In particular, his idea that self-presentation or "face work" is a primary motive of social behavior is a dominant theme underlying most studies of confrontational violence that employ the language of status threats and character contests. Similarly, studies of violence as situated transactions or events also rely on Goffman's dramaturgical metaphor of the theatre and key elements underlying it (i.e., performances, frames, staging, plots, acting parts, rehearsals, taking roles, rituals, and social audiences).[41]

Homicide as a Situated Transaction. A good illustration of the application of an interactionist's perspective to the understanding of interpersonal violence is David Luckenbill's study of homicide transactions.[42] This study used various official documents (e.g., police reports, court testimony, offender statements) to reconstruct the chronology of dialogue and actions underlying seventy homicides. Transactions that ended in homicide occurred within a variety of loosely structured social occasions (e.g., drinking alcoholic beverages, watching television, cruising the streets).[43]

Luckenbill's analysis reveals several general trends about the situated transactions of lethal encounters. First, most of them escalated from what Goffman called "character contests" (i.e., a confrontation in which at least one participant, but usually both, attempt to establish or save face at the other's expense by standing steady in the face of adversity).[44] Second, almost half of the lethal transactions had historical roots (i.e., previous rehearsals between the participants). Third, as events that occur in the presence of a social audience, these "face games" are viewed as situated performances within time-ordered stages. The basic properties of the six stages of the homicide transaction are:

- STAGE 1: The victim makes an opening move that is considered by the offender as an offense to "face." This action by the victim typically involves a direct verbal expression, the refusal to cooperate or comply with the offender's request, or a nonverbal, physical gesture.
- STAGE 2: The offender interprets the victim's previous move as personally offensive. The offender learns the meaning of the victim's move (e.g., was it insulting and intentional?) from inquiries made of the victim or audience.
- STAGE 3: The apparent affront could evoke different responses (e.g., excuse the violation, flee the scene, or ignore it), but in these lethal transactions it initiates a retaliatory move aimed at restoring face and demonstrating strong character. Most of these retaliatory moves begin with the offender issuing a verbal or physical challenge.
- STAGE 4: The victim and offender come to a "working" agreement with the proffered definition of the situation as one of violence. The working agreement to use violence is reached by the victim's direct actions or by the offender's misinterpretation of their actions.

- STAGE 5: The offender and, in many cases, the victim become committed to battle. Both parties have stakes in this battle (e.g., saving face, building or maintaining reputation). Commitment to battle is enhanced by the availability of weapons to support verbal threats and challenges. The actual physical interchange is often brief and precise (e.g., a single lethal shot, stab, or blow).
- STAGE 6: The transaction terminates once the victim has fallen. During this final stage, the offender either flees the scene, remains voluntarily, or is physically subdued by audience members until the police arrive.

Although Luckenbill's portrayal of the stages and elements of these character contests has been widely criticized, it nonetheless serves as a clear illustration of how Goffman's theatrical metaphor of the stage, performances, actors, and audiences can be applied to the study of social interactions that turn deadly.[45] In fact, the dramaturgical idea that social scripts (i.e., expectations that apply in particular social occasions) are formed and subsequently guide various stages in public performances is directly comparable to our premise that basic normative rules of engagement underlie the onset, escalation, and termination of aggressive conduct.

Facilitating Conditions for Closure on Deviant Acts. Drawing upon symbolic interactionism as the theoretical framework, John Lofland's book *Deviance and Identity* is primarily concerned with the social self and the processes involving identity formation and maintenance. However, he also presents an interesting model of the situational cues and interpretive processes associated with an individual's decision to commit deviant acts. This aspect of the book and his emphasis on defensive acts of deviance (i.e., acts done to preserve one's sense of self or save face) are directly applicable to understanding of the situational context for aggressive behavior.

Lofland contends that all actors have the capacity for commission of both conventional and deviant acts, but the specific conditions of threat and then encapsulation increase the risks of face-saving acts of deviance. These risks are further enhanced by the presence of facilitating places, facilitating hardware, and facilitating others. Consistent with symbolic interactionism, it is also the actor's subjective life experiences and interpretations of potential facilitating conditions that strongly affect the likelihood of deviant acts.

The initial impetus for the production of defensive deviant acts involves actions or objects that are perceived by the actor as a clear and present threat. This threat may involve basic defenses of the physical body or types of social defacement or disgrace (e.g., threats to masculine identity or social rank). Elements of the situational context that are most likely to lead to the escalation of deviant acts include perceived threats in combination with feelings of encapsulation, the availability of facilitating places, hardware, and facilitating others.

According to Lofland, "facilitating" places involve physical locations that provide only limited protection from others. Walls, limited public access and traffic flow, and night-time locations with restricted lighting are examples of facilitating places for violent offenses. The home is also considered an attractive site for violent acts because it is bounded by physical walls and social norms of privacy that minimize intervention by others. Other locations like streets in the offender's neighborhood are also facilitating places because they are accessible and offer familiar pathways for escape.

Facilitating hardware involves visible, accessible, and available objects that are used in the threat or commission of violent acts. These objects include an assortment of everyday household items (like knives, bottles, hammers, and bricks) and more specialized hardware like guns. Firearms are often considered an especially facilitative hardware because they do not require extensive training before use, are widely available, do not require physical strength or even direct contact with the victim, and have higher risks of lethality than most other weapons.

The idea of facilitating others in Lofland's approach applies to situations in which the actions of others offer encouragement for the offender to commit the act or provide little resistance for engaging in deviant conduct. Some types of behaviors on the part of the victim and others that may serve as facilitative actions include leaving doors unlocked or keys in the ignition and walking alone in a dangerous neighborhood at night.

From our perspective, the value of Lofland's framework is that it identifies three basic situational factors that underlie violent offenses. These necessary conditions for violence (i.e., facilitating places, facilitating hardware, and facilitating others) structure the nature of interpersonal encounters and affect the actor's assessment of situations as being conducive or non-conducive to the commission of violent acts.

SUMMARY

Biochemical factors serve as basic physiological messengers for aggressive responses, but social cognition and learning experiences affect the actual risks, nature, intensity, and target of human aggression. Normative scripts about expected conduct and elements of the criminal opportunity structure (e.g., motivated offenders, suitable targets, guardianship patterns, facilitating places, facilitating hardware, facilitating others) provide the social context for the onset, commission, and possible escalation of violent acts.

If these basic theoretical perspectives offer an accurate representation of human violence, then the empirical study of violent events should reveal clear and discernable patterns about the situational context, the characteristics of the participants, and the normative rules of engagement that underlie them. We begin to explore these rules of aggressive conduct more deeply in the next chapter by examining the action patterns and typical response sequences found in different types of agonistic behavior in nonhuman animals.

Notes

[1] Most biobehavioral researchers contend that genes strongly affect an individual's range of responses and behaviors, but the environment influences the variability in the timing and expression of these behaviors. See Diana Fishbein. 2001. *Biobehavioral Perspectives in Criminology*. Belmont, CA: Wadsworth, p. 35.

[2] See Albert J. Reiss, Jr. and Jeffrey A. Roth. 1993. *Understanding and Preventing Violence*. Washington, DC: National Academy Press, pp. 119–120. Other neurotransmitters linked to aggression include norepinephrine and GABA (i.e., Gamma-Amino Butyric Acid). As a neurotransmitter produced from dopamine, norepinephrine regulates arousal, dreaming, and moods. It is also is associated with the fight-or-flight responses by causing the release of stress hormones from the adrenal glands that trigger the subsequent physiological manifestations of stress (i.e., increases in blood pressure, constriction of blood vessels, and increases in heart rate). GABA neurons are found in many brain regions; in addition to neurotransmission, they are needed by the body for the metabolism of food and producing energy.

[3] For examples of empirical studies of biochemical influences, see Terrie E. Moffitt, G. L. Brammer, A. Caspi, J. P. Fawcett, M. Raleigh, A. Yuwiler, and P. Silva. 1998. "Whole Blood Serotonin Relates to Violence in an Epidemiological Study." *Biological Psychiatry* 43:446–457; O. Cases, I. Seif, J. Grimsby, P. Gaspar, K. Chen, S. Pournin, U. Muller, M. Aguet, C. Babinnet, J. C. Shih, and E. De Maeyer. 1995. "Aggressive Behavior and Altered Amounts of Brain Serotonin and Norepinephrine in Mice Lacking MAOA." *Science* 268:1763–1766; S. Gabel, J. Stadler, J. Bjorn, R. Shindledecker, and C. J. Bowen. 1995. "Homovanillic Acid and Monamine Oxidase in Sons of Substance-Abusing Fathers: Relationship to Conduct Disorders." *Journal of Studies on Alcohol* 56:135–139. See also Albert J. Reiss, Jr. and Jeffrey A. Roth. 1993. *Understanding and Preventing Violence*. Washington, DC: National Academy Press, p. 120.

[4] For reviews of this literature, see Diana Fishbein. 2001. *Biobehavioral Perspectives in Criminology*. Belmont, CA: Wadsworth, pp. 36–41; Lee Ellis and Anthony Walsh. 2000. *Criminology: A Global Perspective*. Boston: Allyn and Bacon, pp. 287–306; Albert J. Reiss, Jr. and Jeffrey A. Roth. 1993. *Understanding and Preventing Violence*. Washington, DC: National Academy Press, pp. 119–123. These sources also indicate some contradictory findings across studies on the effects of particular neurotransmitters. These differences are attributed in large part to the populations studied (e.g., type of species, clinical verses "normal" populations), model specification (e.g., examining main or direct effects versus interactions with other neurotransmitter systems), and type of aggression or anti-social behavior investigated.

[5] See Diana Fishbein. 2001. *Biobehavioral Perspectives in Criminology*. Belmont, CA: Wadsworth; James T. Tedeschi and Richard B. Felson. 1994. *Violence, Aggression, and Coercive Actions*. Washington, DC: American Psychological Association; Kenneth E. Moyer. 1987. *Violence and Aggression: A Physiological Perspective*. New York: Paragon House.

[6] Allen Mazur and Allen Booth. 1998. "Testosterone and Dominance in Men." *Behavior and Brain Sciences* 21:353–363.

[7] Some authors go even further by asserting that testosterone "is the natural chemical of male aggression." Michael P. Ghiglieri. 1999. *The Dark Side of Man: Tracing the Origins of Male Violence*. Reading, MA: Perseus Books, p. 50.

[8] Nearly all of the basic principles of differential association theory include specific references to learning, for example: (1) criminal behavior is learned, (2) criminal behavior is learned in interactions with other persons in a process of communication, (3) the principal part of the learning of criminal behavior occurs within intimate personal groups, (4) when

criminal behavior is learned, the learning includes (a) techniques of committing the crime, which are sometimes very complicated, sometimes very simple; (b) the specific direction of motives, drives, rationalizations, and attitudes, and (5) the process of learning criminal behavior by association with criminal and anti-criminal patterns involves all of the mechanisms that are involved in any other learning. For all of the principles underlying differential association theory, see Edwin H. Sutherland and Donald R. Cressey. 1966. *Principles of Criminology.* 7th Edition. Philadelphia: J.B. Lippincott, pp. 81–83.

[9] For examples of other theories in which learning principles are a basic component see David Matz. 1964. *Delinquency and Drift.* New York: John Wiley; Elijah Anderson. 1999. *Code of the Street: Decency, Violence, and the Moral Life of the Inner City.* New York: W. W. Norton; James F. Short, Jr. and Fred L. Strodtbeck. 1965. *Group Process and Gang Delinquency.* Chicago: University of Chicago Press; Marvin Wolfgang and Franco Ferracuti. 1967. *The Subculture of Violence: Toward an Integrated Theory in Criminology.* London: Tavistock.

[10] Albert Bandura. 1973. *Aggression: A Social Learning Theory Analysis.* Englewood Cliffs, NJ: Prentice Hall.

[11] While a person's genetic and biological composition provides the potential for aggressive behavior, the idea of innate predispositions and biological structures plays no significant causal role in social learning theory. See Albert Bandura. 1983. "Psychological Mechanisms of Aggression." In Russell G. Geen and Edward I. Donnerstein (eds.), *Aggression: Theoretical and Empirical Reviews,* Vol. 1. New York: Academic Press, pp. 1–40; Russell G. Geen. 1998. "Aggression and Antisocial Behavior." In Daniel T. Gilbert, Susan T. Fiske, and Gardner Lindzey (eds.), *The Handbook of Social Psychology.* 4th Edition. Vol. 2. Boston: McGraw-Hill, p. 317.

[12] These ideas derive from the discussion of social learning theory in Russell G. Geen. 1998. "Aggression and Antisocial Behavior." In Daniel T. Gilbert, Susan T. Fiske, and Gardner Lindzey (eds.), *The Handbook of Social Psychology.* 4th Edition. Vol. 2. Boston: McGraw-Hill, pp. 324–326. For a comprehensive treatment of social cognitive theory, see Albert Bandura. 1999. "Social Cognitive Theory of Personality." In Lawrence A. Pervin and Oliver P. John (eds.), *Handbook of Personality: Theory and Research.* 2nd Edition. New York: The Guilford Press, pp. 154–218.

[13] See Robert A. Baron and Donn Byrne. 1994. *Social Psychology: Understanding Human Interaction.* 7th Edition. Boston: Allyn and Bacon, p. 439. The expectations about how people in a specific social situation will behave are referred to as dramaturgical roles. This concept is similar to scripts in that both are interpretative frameworks for the formulation of expectations.

[14] For a critical review of the literature on media violence, see Jonathan Freedman. 2002. *Media Violence and Its Effect on Aggression: Assessing the Scientific Evidence.* Toronto: University of Toronto Press.

[15] See Media Use in America. 2003. *Issue Briefs.* Universal City, CA: Mediascope Press; N. Gross. 1998. "The Entertainment Glut." *Business Week.* February 16.

[16] See "Facts about Media Violence." 1996. American Medical Association. Cited in Media Use in America. 2003. *Issue Briefs.* Universal City, CA: Mediascope Press.

[17] George Gerbner. 1998. "Cultivation Analysis: An Overview." *Mass Communication and Society* 1(3/4):184.

[18] James Garbarino. 2000. *Lost Boys: Why Our Sons Turn Violent and How We Can Save Them.* New York: Anchor, p. 115.

[19] See Edwin Meese. President's Commission on Causes and Prevention of Violence. Mass Media Effects.

[20] See L. Eron. 1995, June 12. Testimony before the Senate Committee on Commerce, Science, and Transportation, Subcommittee on Communications. Cited in Media Use in America. 2003. *Issue Briefs.* Universal City, CA: Mediascope Press.

[21] See Craig A. Anderson and Karen E. Dill. 2000. "Video Games and Aggressive Thoughts, Feelings, and Behavior in the Laboratory and in Life." *Journal of Personality and Social Psychology* 78(4):772–790.

[22] George Gerbner. 1998. "Cultivation Analysis: An Overview." *Mass Communication and Society* 1(3/4):178. For additional sources on cultivation analysis, see N. Signorielli and M. Morgan. 1990. *Cultivation Analysis: New Directions in Media Effects Research.* Newbury Park, CA: Sage; M. Morgan and J. Shanahan. 1996. "Two Decades of Cultivation Analysis: An Appraisal and a Meta-Analysis." In B. Burleson (ed.), *Communication Yearbook 2020,* pp. 1–45. Thousand Oaks, CA: Sage.

[23] It has been argued that, compared to other media sources, television is unique in its ability to reflect and generate a shared national culture because its visual message is widely available and its form of delivery is not impeded by historical barriers to print media such as literacy, social stratification, and geographical isolation. See George Gerbner. 1998. "Cultivation Analysis: An Overview." *Mass Communication and Society* 1(3/4):177.

[24] Under the cultivation framework of mass media effects, shared cultural messages of "street justice" are generated by television and evolve from social life. The "chicken vs. egg" question about causal ordering is not necessarily problematic for this perspective because it assumes a strong and symbiotic relationship between ongoing behavioral patterns and portrayal of violence and other cultural messages in the mass media.

[25] The villain is either shot, blown up, or eliminated by some other dramatic means (e.g., pushed off a building, eaten by some creature) in the closing scenes of action movies, horror films, and television dramas. The hero in these scenes usually exhibits some slight hesitancy about whether or not to kill the temporarily incapacitated villain. The villain's ultimate demise is often precipitated by another fleeting effort to attack the hero or the hero's recognition that taking the life of the "bad guy" is a just and righteous action. These themes are present in nearly all movies and television programs. Films like *Dirty Harry, Lethal Weapon, Rambo,* or the Chuck Norris films about rescuing Vietnam vets "missing in action" offer classic examples of the conditions under which the extrajudicial executions of the villain by the hero are scripted as morally righteous and justifiable.

[26] In a similar vein, prime-time television characters in various historical periods like Archie Bunker (in *All in the Family*), Al Bundy (in *Married with Children*), and Andy Sipowicz (in *NYPD Blue*) have been mocked for their extreme racial or sexist prejudice and a key storyline often involves the character's ultimate realization of the harmfulness of their extreme views and the subsequent display of a "softer" or more sensitive side.

[27] For a discussion of this "mean world" syndrome and the development of an index to measure it, see N. Signorielli. 1990. "Television's Mean and Dangerous World: A Continuation of the Cultural Indicators Perspective." In N. Signorielli and M. Morgan (eds.), *Cultivation Analysis: New Directions in Media Effects Research.* Newbury Park, CA: Sage, pp. 85–106.

[28] Walter B. Miller. 1958. "Lower Class Culture as a Generating Milieu of Gang Delinquency." *Journal of Social Issues* 14:5–19.

[29] Hyman Rodman. 1963. "The Lower Class Value Stretch." *Social Forces* 42:205–215.

[30] Albert Cohen. 1955. *Delinquent Boys.* New York: Free Press.

[31] James F. Short, Jr. and Fred L. Strodtbeck. 1965. *Group Process and Gang Delinquency.* Chicago: University of Chicago Press.

[32] Marvin Wolfgang and Franco Ferracuti. 1967. *The Subculture of Violence: Toward an Integrated Theory in Criminology.* London: Tavistock.

[33] William R. Harvey. 1986. "Homicide among Young Black Adults: Life in the Subculture of Exasperation." In D. F. Hawkins (ed.), *Homicide among Black Americans.* Lanham, MD: University Press of America, pp. 153–171.

[34] Elijah Anderson. 1999. *Code of the Street: Decency, Violence, and the Moral Life of the Inner City.* New York: W. W. Norton, p. 81.

[35] Elijah Anderson. 1999. *Code of the Street: Decency, Violence, and the Moral Life of the Inner City.* New York: W. W. Norton, p. 70.

[36] Elijah Anderson. 1999. *Code of the Street: Decency, Violence, and the Moral Life of the Inner City.* New York: W. W. Norton, p. 72.

[37] See David F. Luckenbill. 1977. "Criminal Homicide as a Situated Transaction." *Social Problems* 25:176–186; Kenneth Polk. 1994. *When Men Kill: Scenarios of Masculine Violence.*

New York: Cambridge University Press; James F. Short, Jr. and Fred L. Strodtbeck. 1965. *Group Process and Gang Delinquency.* Chicago: University of Chicago Press.

[38] For variations within criminal opportunity theories, see Lawrence Cohen and Marcus Felson. 1979. "Social Change and Crime Rates: A Routine Activity Approach." *American Sociological Review* 44:588–608; Michael Hindelang, Michael Gottfredson, and James Garofalo. 1978. *Victims of Personal Crime.* Cambridge, MA: Ballinger; Terance D. Miethe and Robert F. Meier. 1994. *Crime and Its Social Context.* Albany: State University of New York Press; Pamela Wilcox, Kenneth Land, and Scott Hunt. 2003. *Criminal Circumstances: A Dynamic Multicontextual Criminal Opportunity Theory.* New York: Aldine de Gruyter.

[39] See Lawrence W. Sherman, Patrick R. Gartin, and Michael E. Buerger. 1989. "Hot Spots of Predatory Crime: Routine Activities and the Criminology of Place." *Criminology* 27:27–55.

[40] For descriptions of these different interactionist traditions, see George Herbert Mead. 1934. *Mind, Self, and Society.* Chicago: University of Chicago Press; Randall Collins. 2005. *Interaction Ritual Chains.* Princeton, NJ: Princeton University Press; John P. Hewitt. 1997. *Self and Society: A Symbolic Interactionist Social Psychology.* 7th Edition. Boston: Allyn and Bacon; Erving Goffman. 1959. *The Presentation of Self in Everyday Life.* Garden City, NY: Doubleday Anchor Books; Erving Goffman. 1963. *Behavior in Public Places: Notes on the Social Organization of Gatherings.* Glencoe, IL: Free Press; Erving Goffman. 1967. *Interaction Rituals: Essays on Face-to-Face Behavior.* Garden City, NY: Doubleday; Edwin M. Lemert. 1951. *Social Pathology: A Systematic Approach to the Theory of Sociopathic Behavior.* New York: McGraw-Hill; Walter R. Gove. 1975. *The Labeling of Deviance: Evaluating a Perspective.* New York: Halsted.

[41] See David F. Luckenbill. 1977. "Criminal Homicide as a Situated Transaction." *Social Problems* 25:176–186; Robert F. Meier, Leslie W. Kennedy, and Vincent F. Sacco. 2001. *The Process and Structure of Crime: Crime Events and Crime Analysis.* Volume 9 of *Advances in Criminological Theory.* New Brunswick, NJ: Transaction; Vincent F. Sacco and Leslie W. Kennedy. 2002. *The Criminal Event: Perspectives in Space and Time.* 2nd Edition. Belmont, CA: Wadsworth; Lonnie Athens. 1985. "Character Contests and Violent Criminal Conduct: A Critique." *Sociological Quarterly* 26:419–431.

[42] See David F. Luckenbill. 1977. "Criminal Homicide as a Situated Transaction." *Social Problems* 25:176–186.

[43] Luckenbill's use of the terms "situated transaction" and "social occasions" are based on Goffman's work. A situated transaction is a chain of interaction between two or more people that ends when the participants no longer are in one another's immediate physical presence. In contrast, a social occasion involves a wider social context in which many situated transactions may form, dissolve, and re-form. For our purposes, what is important is that social occasions carry with them various rules and boundaries that establish what kinds of transactions are appropriate and inappropriate. Rules of aggressive conduct become routinized and shared among individuals within particular situational contexts. See David F. Luckenbill. 1977. "Criminal Homicide as a Situated Transaction." *Social Problems* 25:177–178; Erving Goffman. 1963. *Behavior in Public Places: Notes on the Social Organization of Gatherings.* Glencoe, IL: Free Press, especially pp. 167, 198–215; Erving Goffman. 1967. *Interaction Rituals: Essays on Face-to-Face Behavior.* Garden City, NY: Doubleday.

[44] See David F. Luckenbill. 1977. "Criminal Homicide as a Situated Transaction." *Social Problems* 25:177–178; Erving Goffman. 1963. *Behavior in Public Places: Notes on the Social Organization of Gatherings.* Glencoe, IL: Free Press, pp. 218–219, 238–257.

[45] For criticisms of various aspects of this work, see Lonnie Athens. 1985. "Character Contests and Violent Criminal Conduct: A Critique." *Sociological Quarterly* 26:419–431; Gini R. Deibert and Terance D. Miethe. 2003. "Character Contests and Dispute-Related Offenses." *Deviant Behavior* 24:245–267.

Attack and Defense
Routines in Animals

Animals adapt and employ various strategies for their survival. Specific skills and tactics evolve under particular environmental circumstances. These adaptations can be identified by the variation in physical size, shape, color, diet, and reproductive practices (e.g., courting rituals, caretaking of eggs and the young) among members of the same species across different environmental contexts. Various environmental threats (e.g., drought, fires, floods, cold weather) lead to other adaptive behaviors (e.g., the development of greater burrowing skills, the establishment of alternative migration routes, and changes in the number of offspring to reduce competition over scarce resources).

The use of aggression and its threat is another adaptive skill within the context of survival strategies. Predators develop greater stealth and physical prowess for aggression against their prey, whereas many potential sources of prey avoid lethal attack through similar adaptive mechanisms. Both humans and other animals develop numerous preemptive strategies for protecting property or territory, offspring, hierarchical or social position, and other resources from predators.

This chapter provides a brief overview of the typical action patterns and response sequences underlying agonistic behavior among animals. We describe the type and context of aggression in animals and the highly stereotyped and ritualized action patterns associated with it. By describing the various behavioral responses of nonhuman animals associated with physical threats and predation, we will attempt to demonstrate the numerous parallels that exist with human aggression. The common and distinct rules and routines in human aggression are described more fully in subsequent chapters.[1] Here we will look at the more general patterns and routines of territorial defense, preemptive actions, fighting strategies, and retreat and submission observed when animals attack.

TERRITORIALITY AND THE DEFENSE OF SPACE

Animals are extremely territorial and establish clear boundaries for their physical space and possessions. Most vertebrate animals tenaciously defend their offspring, food supply, reproductive mates, resting places, and other physical territory and property. The deposit of species-specific chemical substances marks the boundaries of an animal's home range.[2] Other animals use vocalizations against intruders of the same species. For example, chipmunks make a "chipping" sound to inhibit the approach of conspecifics (i.e., other chipmunks) around their burrow entrance, lions roar to signal other lions to stay away, and larger male sea lions bark to restrict the movements and vocalizations of other, smaller male sea lions.[3] Hummingbirds defend their territory through vigilante surveillance and aggressive posturing within their home range.

Across a variety of species, there are both typical (i.e., normative) and deviant responses to threats to space and resources.[4] Fixed-action patterns characterize the behavioral sequences in many aggression-inducing situations related to space or resources (e.g., inter-male fights, courtship or sex-related aggression). For example, inter-male fighting situations involve clear and consistent patterns of pre- and post-fight rituals and movements. Although the complexity of the expected behavioral patterns is specific to particular species and types of aggression, the "standard operating procedures" in prefight rituals often involve preemptive vocalizations (e.g., snarls, growls, hisses) and physical posturing (e.g., rhythmic raising or lowering of the head or front legs in an attack position, "bluff" charges) that are usually sufficient to deter physical injury to both combatants.

Results from animal experiments suggest that the typical response to threat depends on the animal's familiarity with the environment. For example, a mouse in a home cage is more likely to initiate and win a fight against an introduced intruder, primarily because the stranger spends most of the time investigating the unfamiliar cage rather than focusing on fighting. In general, animals tend to investigate or escape unfamiliar situations rather than initiating a full-blown aggressive response. Various aggressive responses, however, are the most common reaction when animals retreat to their familiar, core territory.[5]

Parallel rules in the protection of private territory and property are found among humans. Specifically, spatial norms clearly exist in different cultures, and humans lay claim over particular physical areas and expect others to respect their claims. Clear rules are established in most U.S. households about private territory (e.g., adolescents tell their parents to "stay out" of their rooms) and the use of others' property (e.g., don't borrow someone's stuff without asking first). Defense and monitoring of one's "turf" is also a well entrenched part of U.S. gang culture. Many potentially violent encounters among humans are preempted by following basic rules about physical space. Violations of territorial norms invoke anger in many humans, but physical violence is also avoided in most cases by the same defense mechanisms used by other animals (e.g., vocal utterances, physical posturing).

VARIABILITY IN PREEMPTIVE ACTIONS

For purposes of survival, the most effective adaptive responses to threat for any species are preemptive actions, because direct attack against the intruder runs the risks of serious injury or death. Accordingly, most animals have evolved specific preemptive responses to aversive stimuli. Rattlesnakes, for example, use their rattle to send a distinct, auditory message to ward off intruders. Other animals (e.g., mammals, birds) also use sound to warn others and to repel unwanted guests. Mammals will display teeth and take a fighting posture to deter intrusion into their space. Some birds (e.g., robins, larks, jays, geese) threaten other birds and animals with physical displays (e.g., puffing up their breasts, flapping wings aggressively); some fish also display offensive and defensive posturing (e.g., puff up the bodies, make their fins more erect).[6] These behavioral responses are highly stereotyped patterns within different species.

Observations of humans in prefight staging activities reveal preemptive strategies that are similar in form and effect to those used by animals. For example, talking tough and other vocalizations (e.g., outraged screaming) are threatening sounds in human interactions that may deter actual violence. Attempts to look bigger or more powerful by puffing up the chest are particularly common preemptive moves to deter violent attacks. However, in contrast to other animals, these verbal and physical actions may actually trigger violence in humans in some situations, especially when they are perceived as a public affront to one's status or social identity.

The "bluff" attack or charge is similar to posturing in its potential deterrent value. Many animals will simply feign an attack by showing their teeth, raising their primary fighting instruments (e.g., horns, feet/hooves, tail), or making a forward thrust or movement. Bluff charges by larger animals (e.g., elephants, rhinos, bears) are particularly effective actions against smaller intruders and adversaries.

Preemptive fighting behaviors within human interactions take the form of physical posturing and displays of prowess. The mere physical movement into a fighting position (e.g., raised and clenched fists in a boxing stance, taking a marital arts defensive position) may be sufficient to elicit immediate retreat responses from opponents. The quick appearance of friends and fellow combatants may have a similar chilling effect. The brandishing of a lethal weapon like a knife or gun is a particular prefight action that may inhibit the onset of physical violence, or at least dramatically change the course and outcome of conflict situations.[7]

RETREAT AND SUBMISSION

Acts of aggression within the animal kingdom can be met with various responses, including indifference, retreat, submission, or fighting. When resources are plenty and the threat is minor (e.g., when brown bears are gorging themselves on spawning salmon while humans are watching), a temporary state of coexistence and indifference may exist between potential challengers. Challenges to hierarchical arrangements are often met with physical displays of aggression that may result in actual fights, but other alternatives are also available for conflict resolution.

Acts of retreat and submission are the modal responses to aggression in most threatening encounters; basic explanations for these responses include instinctive reactions to preserve the species or the principle of least effort. For example, members of the *Canidae* family (e.g., wolves, domestic dogs, jackals) will submit to stronger opponents by exposing their jugular vein on the underside of the neck. These submissive acts have apparently evolved to establish the hierarchy within the pack and to preserve the life of its members. Deference and submission within primates and other animals are established through gazing or staring behavior directed at an opponent. The first party that turns away during these "stare downs" is submitting to the other's dominance. Such gazing hierarchies are found within both human and nonhuman primates.[8] The anger and intimidation that is often invoked by staring at someone (called "grilling" or "mad-dogging" in U.S. street culture) may be a human manifestation of this basic principle.

FIGHTING STRATEGIES

If responses have not deterred or de-escalated threatening situations, fighting is an available alternative for all animals. However, even when this option is exercised, the particular response patterns regulate the damage and injuries suffered in these aggressive encounters. Specific examples of some action sequences and typical response patterns for different animals in fighting situations are shown in table 3.1.

During the early stages of aggressive encounters, the "flight" reaction is often considered a strong survival strategy for all animals. This reaction may be triggered by a physiological response to pain or it may simply be conditioned through centuries of adaptation. Whatever their origins, many fights among co-species are preempted by flight.

Defensive body posturing is another patterned response to aversive stimuli that minimizes serious injury to the combatants. Observations of animal fights reveal numerous efforts to protect vital body parts during prolonged attacks. The most obvious defensive posture involves the use of a shell for protection in animals like a tortoise or armadillo. Quills, spikes, fur, and blubber also provide exterior protection from physical attacks. For example, elephant seals are like other mammals that attack the neck

Table 3.1 Examples of Patterned Rules of Engagement for Different Types of Aggression for Different Animals

A squirrel that is about to attack pulls its ears back and produces a chattering sound with its front teeth. The reaction is quite different, however, if the animal is cornered and on the defensive. In that case it squeals and raises its ears.[9]

The initial reaction of cats to a threatening agent is the disruption of ongoing activities and flight when that is possible. If escape is not an available option, the cat faces the enemy and hisses with an open mouth while showing piloerections (hair-raising) and pupil dilation. This response structure of fear-induced aggression is quite different from behavior patterns exhibited when cats attack. Hissing is replaced by a low growl in attack situations and hair raising and pupil dilation is frequently absent.[10]

Inter-male fights among baboons involve bites directed at the shoulder or neck of the opponent. These animals fence rapidly with open jaws without really touching each other, and the head is held back. During a fight, each opponent also hits out at the face of the other with his hand, usually without making contact. The biting and hitting ritual goes on with tremendous speed for a few seconds, silently, with the opponents facing each other. Then, one of them turns to flee. There can be vigorous chasing, interrupted by some more fencing, but the interaction usually lasts no longer than 10 seconds. Most fights come to an end when one opponent flees.[11]

When a dog approaches a strange dog or human in a savage or hostile frame of mind, it walks upright and very stiffly; its head is raised slightly, or not much lowered; the tail is held erect and quite rigid; the hairs bristle, especially along the neck and back; the prickled ears are directed forward, and the eyes have a fixed stare.[12]

A common aggression-inhibiting response of submissive behavior in inter-male conflict among a number of subhuman primates involves sexual presentation. The submissive animal in these situations turns and presents his hindquarters to the dominant male. This presentation posture then elicits a perfunctory mounting response and the conflict is subsequently terminated.[13]

Fear-induced response sequences for New Zealand rabbits include the following components: an oriented jump toward the side of the body that was touched with a blunt probe; hind limb thrust; vocalization; stabbing out with the forelimb; striking the ground with the hind limb; directed escape; and biting attack. Biting attacks and vocalizations occur when the animals are cornered or when poked in the presence of their young. Similar behavior is found in other rabbits (e.g., antelope jackrabbits, European hare).[14]

region of their prey and rivals. However, extreme and intense fighting among male elephant seals rarely results in serious injuries due to tough skin and large fat pads in the neck region.

Except when their rivals and offspring are considered a food supply in times of scarcity, physical fights among large animals of the same species are usually deterred by bluff attacks and other threats (e.g., snarls, grunts). If posturing is ineffective in discouraging attack, the actual fight is often of short duration and ends quickly with the slightest injury to one of the combatants. Animals with lethal bodily instruments (e.g., long and sharp claws, powerful jaws, sharp teeth) threaten but rarely use these weapons of destruction against their foes and offspring. Instead, their "bark" is usually sufficient to reduce the necessity of their "bite."

Defense posturing and fighting protocols have many parallels in human aggression. For example, the ability to look tough, stare down, and show no fear has long been the *modus operandi* for the typical schoolyard bully and the street thug. This "representing" or posturing is often a public proclamation to others to stay away. Although the reputations that develop from this posturing are sometimes challenged in actual physical combat, retreat and submission appear to be the more common response.[15] This seems especially true among humans when the risks of violent action in a particular situational context are high and the potential rewards are limited.

Humans also resemble other animals in their actions during the physical fight. For example, many animals direct their attacks at the neck and other critical, anterior portions of the body.[16] Human boxers and street fighters have learned to attack and defend vital and vulnerable body parts. Comparable environmental adaptations and structured rules of conduct may also regulate the nature, duration, and intensity of aggressive responses in both humans and other mammals. From this perspective, the brandishing of guns and knives is the human equivalent to big claws and snarling teeth as weapons of threat reduction and predation.

RULES AND RITUALS IN TYPES OF ANIMAL AGGRESSION

Animals in their natural habitat engage in different forms of aggression. In fact, ethological studies indicate that specific rituals and routines of engagement are often context-specific for different types of aggression.[17]

Predatory Aggression

One of the most basic types of animal aggression involves predation. It is attack behavior that is directed at the animals' natural prey, elicited by the appearance and movement of prey, stimulated by food deprivation, and inhibited by fear. Predation among mammals is almost always between different species, conducted in silence, and done with no prior display of threatening behavior (i.e., it's a "blitz" attack without warning).[18] It is these elements that give predation its uniqueness as a type of aggression.[19]

Aggression that occurs in the context of predation is often highly ritualized and structured in mammals. This includes search and stalking tactics like specific bodily movements and posturing prior to the attack. Hunting routines in pack animals reflect hierarchical structures among group members and often involve the development of strategic and synchronized rules for stalking and attacking prey (e.g., turning back or funneling prey toward the rest of the pack). Similar notions of routines and rituals are used to describe the stalking behaviors of serial killers and sexual predators among humans.[20]

The preys of predators have also developed various strategies of flight and fight to enhance their chances of survival. Preemptive defenses by potential prey include warning systems (e.g., distress calls by fellow prey), physical posturing (e.g., visible displays of weapons for self-defense, such as teeth, claws, tails, quills), and other defensive movements (e.g., encircling the vulnerable young by groups of adults).[21] The proverbial "laws of nature" between predator and prey enhance the likelihood of survival for both species by culling the weak and reducing overcrowding.

Inter-Male Aggression

For most mammals and under most conditions, males are more aggressive than females, and the target of their aggression is often other males within their species.[22] The higher prevalence of inter-male aggression is observed in the rough-and-tumble play of most juvenile mammals, and much of it among adult animals is directed at competition and access to females.[23] Most of these encounters are ritualized demonstrations of superiority over another without serious physical injury. Submission and escape are defensive responses to this aggression, especially when the dominant male has previously rebuffed the challenger.

Acts of inter-male aggression establish hierarchical social order within colonies or groups of animals through an interconnected pattern of dominant-submissive relationships among male members. Once this pecking order is in place, deference or submission becomes the rule, and the prevailing order is maintained by threats or posturing behaviors without resort to actual fighting. In fact, inter-male aggressive behavior decreases dramatically through processes of habituation in established colonies of animals. This type of aggression, however, will immediately increase with the introduction of a new male stranger.

Available evidence suggests that the ritualized fighting routines between males of the same species are largely innate. In particular, laboratory studies indicate that behavioral sequences and displays of posturing, tussling, and biting between male conspecifics are essentially the same for animals with and without prior learning experiences. Other researchers have also shown that learning is not essential to the manifestation of aggressive responses.[24] However, cultural variability in what constitutes anger-provoking stimuli and the diverse behavioral responses to it suggest that learning experiences play a major role in inter-male conflict among humans.

Experimental studies and naturalistic observations suggest that the patterned behavioral responses in inter-male fighting contests of nonhuman animals have evolved in such a way that superiority is demonstrated with little physical damage to the loser. Contrary to the rules and routines in predatory aggression, inter-male conflict is quickly resolved by fleeing and retreat without lengthy pursuit by the victor and by submissive posturing by the defeated animal. The chances of serious injury are further reduced by aiming attacks at portions of the opponent's anatomy that minimize physical harm (i.e., posterior regions with less vital organs or areas protected by tougher skin, thicker fur, or more muscle and fat).[25]

Rival males also fight in less lethal ways than is true of their behavior in predatory situations. For example, many antelope use their sharp horns for defense against predators, but they employ these lethal instruments only to facilitate the locking of heads in inter-male pushing contests.[26] Other horned animals charge and push rival males in a head-to-head manner, reducing the risk of serious or lethal stabbing injuries through the less protected undersides of the body. While deaths and serious injuries sometimes happen in these challenges, inter-male fights are qualitatively different in behavioral patterns before, during, and after the attack from predation and other types of aggression.

Fear-Induced Aggression

When animals are unable to escape a threat or find themselves in an unfamiliar circumstance, fear may elicit an aggressive response. Fear-induced aggression is always preceded by attempts to escape and involves an emotional component that includes specific patterns of autonomic arousal.[27] Maternal aggression in vertebrates against intruders who approach their young is often a fear-induced reaction that is extremely ferocious and unrelenting. Aside from aggression, fear may also elicit other reactions, including flight, "freezing," fainting, and submissive posturing. Except in cases of brood defense, the modal action pattern for cornered animals is often flight rather than fight.

The proximity of the threatening source is an important situational factor in the fear-flight response. Studies of different types of wild animals reveal the existence of critical "flight distance" rules that necessitate flight reactions.[28] Unabated flight before the intruder reaches this distance successfully preempts aggression. In contrast, immediate bursts of fear-induced aggression are often provoked when an animal is surprised and recognizes that its "safe zone" has been breached in a sudden invasion by a predator or rival.

Irritable Aggression

Another type of animal aggression is called "irritable" aggression. This type of aggression is unique because it is nonspecific in its target (i.e., it may be directed at any available organism or inanimate object). In this capacity, it is similar to displaced aggression among humans. Irritable aggression varies dramatically in its intensity of response, ranging from annoyance threats, to half-hearted attacks against the target, to destructive, uncontrollable rage.[29]

Irritable aggression is elicited by a variety of internal and external stimuli, including frustration, pain, or the deprivation of food, water, sleep, or social contact.[30] Other types of aggression (e.g., predatory, inter-male, maternal aggression) are triggered by a narrower set of particular stimuli. Irritable aggression is also unique in that extreme violent frenzies of rage in animals may sometimes result in self-mutilation when other targets are not available. Physical aggression toward oneself or others, however, is only one of many possible responses to anger-provoking stimuli.

Sex-Related Aggression

Various types of agonistic behavior also occur in the context of courtship and mating. Male animals sometimes threaten or attack females for purposes of mating with them. Many bodily movements and physical actions during courtship and mating are potentially lethal (e.g., some mammals like bears and lions bite the necks of their mates). However, serious injuries during courtship and mating are rare.

Courtship and mating rituals, rules, and routines have been widely observed and studied across a variety of species. In terms of their behavioral patterns and interaction rituals, aggressive courtship displays can be distinguished from fighting by their consequences. However, sex-related aggression in animals sometimes exceeds normative rules or boundaries, as it does in sexual assaults and sexual murders among humans. Sex-related aggression is found primarily but not exclusively in the male animal, and it exhibits the most variable and bizarre forms in humans.[31]

SUMMARY

Animal aggression takes various forms, and its duration and lethality are related to these forms. Predation, for example, is the only context for aggression that routinely involves lethal consequences for the prey. In contrast, agonistic behavior involving territorial defense, inter-male rivals, mating and courtship, and fear-induced attacks are often preempted by defensive posturing and other adaptive responses (e.g., submission, attacks on less crucial body parts). Highly structured and patterned behavioral sequences are commonly observed in the agonistic responses associated with these different contexts for aggression.

As noted in various parts of this chapter, there are numerous parallels in the agonistic behaviors of humans and other animals. Patterns of behavior surrounding different contexts for aggression (e.g., territoriality, inter-male rivals, sex-related attacks) are the most obvious generalizations across species. However, many scholars (especially those within the symbolic interactionist's tradition) contend that human behavior is unique because of our language structure and our cognitive ability for self-reflection and rehearsal of alternative scripts before we act. While we share this view about the differential human capacity, it is also the case that the nature and response patterns in human aggression are incredibly consistent with the stereotyped behavioral sequences that underlie aggressive situations among other animals.

Notes

[1] Some of the readers of this chapter will be bothered with our assertions of various parallels between nonhuman and human aggression. Given the larger size of our mammalian brain and our distinct ability to use a symbolic language, apply cognitive scripting to future actions, and to engage in self-reflection, we share a similar concern about over-generalizing across species. However, even if our violent actions are less predictable and motivated by an assortment of idiosyncratic factors and not just sexual selection and protection of other resources, it is the way we act before and during potentially violence-invoking situations that has many parallels to our nonhuman counterparts. We suspect that most people who have witnessed aggressive encounters among nonhuman animals in acts of predation or defense make immediate comparisons to human aggression. It is this tendency to see animal behavior through the human lens that sparked the authors' interests in the rules and routines of human aggression.

[2] Scent marking, however, may serve other purposes besides territorial marking to deter intruders. These other purposes of marking include defining a safe area to promote colony cohesion, sexual communication, or as a trail or path marker for migration. See Kenneth E. Moyer. 1976. *The Psychobiology of Aggression.* New York: Harper and Row, p. 220.

[3] See Kenneth E. Moyer. 1976. *The Psychobiology of Aggression.* New York: Harper and Row, p. 221.

[4] The words "normative" and "deviant" are used here in a statistical sense. Normative responses are those that represent typical reactions in given situations of violence; they can be innate or learned.

[5] For a discussion of these response patterns and the research studies that support them, see Kenneth E. Moyer. 1976. *The Psychobiology of Aggression.* New York: Harper and Row, pp. 222–224.

[6] For a wider description of animal behavior related to fighting, see N. Tinbergen. 1990. *Social Behaviour in Animals.* London: Chapman and Hall; K. E. Moyer. 1976. *The Psychobiology of Aggression.* New York: Harper and Row.

[7] There are alternative viewpoints about whether the presence of a weapon deters or escalates violence. Some contend that weapons escalate violence by eliciting defense responses, whereas others suggest that weapon possession serves as a deterrent for potential attackers. For a discussion of these perspectives and empirical evidence to support them, see Gary Kleck. 1991. *Point Blank: Guns and Violence in America.* Hawthorne, NY: Aldine; Leonard Berkowitz and A. LePage. 1967. "Weapons as Aggression-Eliciting Stimuli." *Journal of Personality and Social Psychology* 7:202–207.

[8] See, for example, Alan Mazur. 1985. "A Biosocial Model of Status in Face-to-Face Primate Groups." *Social Forces* 64:377–403; S. A. Altmann. 1967. "The Structure of Primate Communication." In S. A. Altmann (ed.), *Social Communication Among Primates.* Chicago: University of Chicago Press, pp. 235–262; James T. Tedeschi and Richard B. Felson. 1994. *Violence, Aggression, and Coercive Actions.* Washington, DC: American Psychological Association.

[9] I. Eibl-Eiebesfeldt. 1961. "The Fighting Behavior of Animals." *Scientific American* 205:112–122.

[10] Kenneth E. Moyer. 1976. *The Psychobiology of Aggression.* New York: Harper and Row, p. 177.

[11] H. Kummer 1968. *Social Organization of Hamadryads Baboons: A Field Study.* Chicago: University of Chicago Press.

[12] Charles Darwin. 1896. *The Expression of Emotions in Man and Animals.* New York: D. Appleton.

[13] Kenneth E. Moyer. 1976. *The Psychobiology of Aggression.* New York: Harper and Row, p. 168.

[14] Kenneth E. Moyer. 1976. *The Psychobiology of Aggression.* New York: Harper and Row, pp. 177–178.

[15] The common utterance by friends and family to "just walk away" from anger-provoking situations is an example of this retreat norm.

[16] Studies of prey-catching behavior of a variety of carnivores suggest that the precise aiming of the biting response is developed through learning, but the response itself appears to be the result of an innate tendency for animals to strike slightly ahead of a moving prey. There is also some evidence that the killing protocol used by many animals of grabbing the prey by the back of the neck and shaking it derives from the efforts of predators to counterattack their prey. See J. F. Eisenberg and P. Leyhausen. 1972. "The Phylogenesis of Predatory Behavior in Mammals." *Zeitschrift fur Tierpsychologie* 30:59–93; Kenneth E. Moyer. 1976. *The Psychobiology of Aggression.* New York: Harper and Row, pp. 141–142.

[17] For a more detailed description of these types of animal aggression, see Kenneth E. Moyer. 1976. *The Psychobiology of Aggression.* New York: Harper and Row; Jan Volavka. 1995. *Neurobiology of Violence.* Washington, DC: American Psychiatric Press, pp. 22–31. Our discussion of types of animal aggression is based on these sources.

[18] Several mammals (e.g., lions, bears) will eat others of their own species when food supplies are limited, whereas others (e.g., spotted hyena) are usually just "passive" cannibals (i.e., feeding on dead members of their species rather than stalking live ones). Cannibalism is far more common among lower animals (e.g., fish, birds, mice) for various reasons (e.g., they can't distinguish their young from other food sources, they kill due to crowding and to reduce overpopulation). See Edward O. Wilson. 2000. *Sociobiology: The New Synthesis.* Cambridge, MA: Belknap Press of Harvard University Press, p. 246.

[19] Predatory aggression is largely unrelated to the use and effectiveness of other types of aggression. For example, male cows (i.e., bulls) and the hippopotamus are very aggressive in inter-male encounters but are herbivores and have no predatory tendencies. See Kenneth E. Moyer. 1976. *The Psychobiology of Aggression.* New York: Harper and Row, pp. 135–136.

[20] The predatory behavior of human serial killers has parallels to animal predation in the within-species variability of characteristics of their "natural" prey. Specifically, serial killers, pr may select particular targets because of the way they look (e.g., young, brown-haired women), where they live or work, or there may be no preference in victim selection. For a discussion of the target selection processes involved in human serial killers, see Eric W. Hickey. 1997. *Serial Murderers and their Victims.* 2nd Edition. Belmont, CA: Wadsworth. Among other mammals, predatory responses are released by olfactory (i.e., smell), visual, and/or auditory sensations. Rats are one animal in which no particular sensory channel is essential for a predatory response. Kenneth E. Moyer. 1976. *The Psychobiology of Aggression.* New York: Harper and Row, p. 138.

[21] As another defense strategy to protect offspring, some birds like the killdeer will feign a broken wing to draw predators away from their nesting area.

[22] Hamsters and gibbons are exceptions to this pattern of greater aggressiveness of males. Field observations indicate no sex differences in agonistic behavior in either species. Maternal aggression in the protection of offspring is a particular context in which the display and intensity of aggression is more common among females across a variety of species. Jan Volavka. 1995. *Neurobiology of Violence.* Washington, DC: American Psychiatric Press, p. 23; Kenneth E. Moyer. 1976. *The Psychobiology of Aggression.* New York: Harper and Row, p. 151.

[23] See Michael P. Ghiglieri. 1999. *The Dark Side of Man: Tracing the Origins of Male Violence.* Reading, MA: Perseus Books.

[24] See J. B. Calhoun. 1962. "The Ecology and Sociology of the Norway Rat." U.S. Department of Health, Education, and Welfare, Public Health Service Publication No. 1008. Washington, DC: U.S. Government Printing Office; I. Eibl-Eibesfeldt. 1961. "The Fighting Behav-

ior of Animals." *Scientific American* 205:112–122; E. C. Grant. 1963. "An Analysis of the Social Behaviour of the Male Laboratory Rat." *Behaviour* 21:260–281. These studies are cited in Kenneth E. Moyer. 1976. *The Psychobiology of Aggression*. New York: Harper and Row, p. 154.

[25] Kenneth E. Moyer. 1976. *The Psychobiology of Aggression*. New York: Harper and Row, pp. 157–158.

[26] Kenneth E. Moyer. 1976. *The Psychobiology of Aggression*. New York: Harper and Row, p. 158.

[27] Kenneth E. Moyer. 1976. *The Psychobiology of Aggression*. New York: Harper and Row, p. 176.

[28] For a summary table of flight distances for a number of animals, see H. Hediger. 1950. *Wild Animals in Captivity: An Outline of the Biology of Zoological Gardens*. London: Butterworth's Scientific.

[29] Kenneth E. Moyer. 1976. *The Psychobiology of Aggression*. New York: Harper and Row, p. 187.

[30] Displays of irritable aggression toward inanimate objects are often somewhat amusing to outsider observers. These include situations in which humans are seen hurting their hands by punching walls after stubbing their toes, dogs biting and tearing up grass or newspapers for no apparent reason, and bears totally destroying any available object in an uncontrollable rage. However, the amusement value of viewing this type of aggression is quickly lost when the observer thinks about the consequences of the level of rage and anger being directed at animate objects.

[31] See Kenneth E. Moyer. 1976. *The Psychobiology of Aggression*. New York: Harper and Row, pp. 204–205; Edward O. Wilson. 2000. *Sociobiology: The New Synthesis*. Cambridge, MA: Harvard University Press.

Rules and Rituals of Aggression in Human History

Our review of ethological studies in chapter 3 highlighted routines and rituals in agonistic behavior among animals. These behavioral patterns are found in the response sequences for different types of aggression. Male aggression against rival males in various species, for example, is highly stereotyped and ritualized, involving fixed-action patterns of posturing, attack sequence, retreat, and submission. Similarly, preemptive actions in territorial or brood defense also exhibit enormous regularity of response patterns within particular species (e.g., marking patterns, snarling, exposing teeth, hair-raising, specific defensive posturing, and attack sequences).

This chapter explores the normative rules and routines of human aggression within a historical context. We describe the functions of normative rules of engagement and "proper" protocol in the implementation of structured forms of violence. The rules surrounding legal and extrajudicial types of violence are illustrated within the historical context of dueling, Western gunfights, and state-sponsored corporal punishment. Before discussing these historical examples, however, we take a slight detour to describe types of human violence and events that trigger it.

AGGRESSION-TRIGGERING ACTS AND CUES

Acts of human aggression require the basic elements of motivation and opportunity. The motivation may be instrumental (i.e., goal-directed) or expressive (i.e., spontaneous or unintentional acts of rage and anger).

The opportunity structure for acts of aggression involves physical proximity or accessibility to an available target or potential victim.

Under various drive models of human aggression, environmental stimuli trigger arousal states that cause aggressive behavior toward available targets.[1] The motivating stimuli for most mammals are particular external cues that invoke behavioral responses to satisfy basic biological needs (e.g., the sight or smell of prey elicits predation; signs of predators elicit acts of brood defense or flight among prey).

Human aggression may be sparked by similar biological needs, as is often expressed in claims of self-defense and having to fight to "protect myself or my family." However, humans are also unique in that much of our aggression is linked to status threats (e.g., threats to masculine identity, perceived power/entitlements) and the defense of moral imperatives (e.g., honor, retributive justice).

Threat to Masculinity

Much of the previous research on character contests and confrontational violence emphasizes the role of masculinity.[2] Threats to one's masculine identity are seen in various verbal taunts about being weak or lacking backbone (e.g., be tough, be a man). Other verbal provocations about masculinity include public affronts about one's sexual identity and virility. For evolutionary psychologists and other Darwinians, the roots of male aggression are tied directly to adaptive strategies of sexual selection.[3]

It is somewhat difficult to articulate the normative rules of the appropriate response to threats to one's masculinity because the range of reactions exhibits wide variability across cultures, situational contexts, and individuals. Under the general rule of reciprocity, the proper normative response would be retaliatory verbal banter of equal offensiveness. In contrast, under the premise that any verbal or physical reaction offers some legitimacy to the message of the original verbal taunt, another normative response is to ignore the threat. The response of "doing nothing" is considered in some contexts to be the most admirable or honorable action, but it may be interpreted as a sign of weakness (i.e., low masculinity) in other contexts.

Based on the criminal law and the court of public opinion, the use of extreme physical violence against verbal taunts is considered unjustified retaliation, regardless of how abusive or offensive it is to one's masculinity.[4] However, the fact that lethal violence is often precipitated by challenges to one's masculinity suggests that some people clearly do not subscribe to these normative beliefs about appropriate conduct. This may be especially true of poor, urban, minority youth who are often denied access to traditional avenues of expressing masculinity (e.g., through achievements in work and educational institutions).[5] Under these conditions, the "code of the street" may dictate a violent response to any verbal threat to one's masculinity or sexual identity.

Threats to Entitlements and Property

Various situations that escalate into violent encounters are often sparked by a threat to one's perceived or real entitlements. Fights over money (e.g., money loaned, unpaid debts), property taken or borrowed, and one's social standing (e.g., challenges to a claim of superiority or authority) are the triggering events in many acts of aggression.

There are numerous instances of entitlement-invoked aggression in contemporary U.S. society. For example, challenges to one's authority are often the distal and proximate causes of domestic violence among spouses and the physical abuse of children by their parents. A distorted sense of entitlement also underlies many acts of sexual assault, especially within the context of dating situations. Even armed robbers invoke some notion of entitlement as motivation for their acts by claiming that their nefarious thefts are actually justified by the previous injustices done to them by the victim or wider society.

Similar to types of territoriality defense among other mammals (e.g., the protection of food supplies, shelters, and mating partners), humans in most Western cultures are highly protective of their personal property and often go to extraordinary lengths of lethal force to defend it. In fact, those who attempt to steal property (e.g., carjackers, burglars, armed robbers) are often stopped by lethal force or by the threat of such force by their victims. While U.S. criminal laws prohibit the use of lethal force to protect property per se, current legal rules do permit civilians to use lethal force in cases involving imminent or immediate threat of serious bodily injury or death. In violent situations initiated by the actions of a third party (e.g., a male making sexual advances to another male's girlfriend, lover's triangles), the code of chivalry may call for the defense of honor. However, retaliatory actions that exceed the provocative act are legally prohibited. Legal codes and normative rules offer different prescriptions about the appropriate course of action in such situations.

Defense of Moral Imperatives

A clearly distinct human motivation for violent behavior involves a wide variety of aggressive actions that are invoked and subsequently justified on the grounds of a larger moral imperative. Certain acts of violence are considered "righteous" in their ultimate purposes, as were the actions of Robin Hood in stealing from the rich to feed the poor.

Violent situations that are motivated by a moral imperative have a long history. Acts of collective violence during the religious crusades of the Middle Ages, the lynching of Blacks and their supporters in the postbellum South, the Jewish Holocaust, the massive executions of civilians in the conflict among various tribes in Africa (e.g., Hutus and Tutsis in Burundi), and other cases of "ethnic cleansing" (e.g., the gassing of Kurds in Iraq) are just a few examples of lethal violence conducted under this often nebulous façade or rubric of a moral imperative. At the interpersonal level, serious assaults against various undesirable characters (e.g., the neighborhood thug, the schoolyard bully, the snitch, the drug dealer, the child molester) are often justified as "street justice." Whether or not these actions are actually justifiable as a moral imperative is not important. What matters is the actor's perception that assaulting this person is the righteous thing to do.

Even when an assault against another is deemed morally appropriate, an assortment of different interaction rituals surrounds the retaliatory actions. Depending on the gravity of the initial wrongdoing, "justice" may be dispensed through a largely public degradation ceremony that vilifies the violations of the accused and results in their death (e.g., the Salem witch trials).[6] Alternatively, the moral balance may also be restored by a relatively quick, direct, and private response (e.g., the proverbial punch in the nose). Other actions (e.g., ostracism, banishment, restitution, penal servitude) are alternatives to physical aggression in these situations.

Self-Initiated Proactive and Displaced Aggression

Rather than being a reactive response to various threats, human aggression is often a proactive, instrumental attack for purposes of achieving some desired ends (e.g., state-sponsored retribution, the social control of deviants, making money, enhancing one's social status or reputation). Other violent acts derive from more generic sources (e.g., irritability, high impulsivity, low self-control) or from the displacement of anger from one target to another.[7]

Contrary to acts of defensive aggression, normative expectations about appropriate conduct are more ambiguous in situations of proactive and displaced aggression. This is the case because proactive aggression, by definition, places greater emphasis on the instrumental "ends" at any "means" rather than the proper "means" of accomplishing the goals. However, both proactive and displaced aggression are similar to other types of aggression in that particular rules, rituals, and action patterns are found in the process of committing these offenses. For example, street muggers often share a similar *modus operandi* in their target-selection search, their pre-contact routines, and the method of immobilizing their victim.[8] In the case of displaced violence, the aggression sequence begins with an unexpected target who is visible, accessible, and acts in some way that is interpreted as offensive to the aggressor.

RULES OF HUMAN VIOLENCE IN A HISTORICAL CONTEXT

Both historical and anecdotal evidence suggest that rules of engagement have been widely established in the onset and commission of physical aggression. These implicit and explicit rules cover all aspects of aggressive behavior, including defining what is considered sufficient verbal or physical provocation, principles of reciprocity, the specific sequence of behavioral responses, and proper etiquette throughout the dispute. Depending on one's theoretical orientation, the origins of these patterns may emanate from natural laws of human physiology, evolutionary adaptations, or socially constructed rules of conduct to create order, predictability, and/or civility in human societies.

Whatever the origins of these rules, however, there are clear interaction rituals associated with human violence in a variety of cultural contexts. Dueling, the gunfights of the Western frontier, and state-sponsored corporal punishment provide clear examples of the nature, purposes, and structural elements of the rules and rituals of violence.

The Dueling Tradition

The practice of dueling is an excellent illustration of fighting rules throughout Western history. The dueling tradition evolved from practices among European nobles in the Middle Ages. It became relatively common in the United States during the American Revolution and grew in popularity until the mid-nineteenth century. Even in its early forms, the response sequence in dueling was shrouded in normative rules and rituals that dictate appropriate protocol before, during, and after the battle or "contest."[9]

Most scholars agree that the custom of dueling and other violent ritualized combat developed as a method of settling disputes that fell outside the purview of the law.[10] Compared to unregulated brawls and vengeance feuds, dueling was effective at preserving social order in tumultuous times because it provided a structured context for confining and directing men's passions. The "civilizing" of the dueling tradition was eventually replaced in the late nineteenth and early twentieth centuries in Europe and the United States by extensions of state power and control in the form of a comprehensive criminal justice system.[11]

For most of Western history, duels were highly staged and ritualized acts of mutual combat among aristocrats and gentlemen. The precipitating event was typically an affront to one's honor or dignity. The affront was then followed by a formal challenge delivered by a "second" (a friend of the offended) to rescind the insult or to agree to mutual combat. The following is a synopsis of the dueling process:

> Pistols at dawn! The challenge is issued. To turn it down would leave you marked as a coward for life. You meet at the chosen spot, facing your opponent at a distance of 20 paces. Your dueling pistols are loaded. One or both of you could be seriously wounded or killed today. Doctors are standing by to mend the damage if possible, while your friends eye each other warily.[12]

Although variability existed in the particular procedures and protocol, the gentleman's code for dueling involved the articulation of specific rules regarding the time and place of the event, the action sequence, the type of weapon, and when and how the duel was terminated (e.g., was it a fight to the death or did it end with the first wound?). A neutral party often served as a judge or referee to make sure that proper protocol was maintained. This third party also functioned as an external legal witness to the mutual agreement to resolve the dispute through these violent means.

The *Code Duello*, a set of rules drafted by Irish gentlemen in 1777 (see table 4.1), clearly reveals the highly stylized and ritualized rules of engagement in dueling. The code became essentially the "official" rule book for dueling in the United States and elsewhere.[13] The rules that covered the practice of dueling and the "points of honor" include how apologies are rendered and accepted (rules #1 and #5), dueling etiquette (rules #13 and #15), the role of seconds (rules #18 and #21), and the termination of the duel (rule #22).

Aside from the rules in the *Code Duello*, certain specifications structured the nature and process of the ritualized fights. For example, most duels occurred in secluded areas to avoid prosecution under existing laws, and they often involved procedures that decreased the risks of lethality (e.g., having participants back-to-back before pacing off the agreed-upon distance and then turning quickly to shoot plus the use of smooth-bored guns that were less accurate than rifles). Dueling etiquette also gave the winner the authority to spare or to slay the loser. The victor was further given the informal right to desecrate the body of his rival in any manner of his choice. Decapitation and the posting of the head of the loser in a public place was one form of public desecration in many countries.

Although dueling rules were firmly entrenched in the code of gentlemen, various types of cheating and other rule violations also characterized the tradition. Rule violations included the rigging of dueling pistols to misfire, deliberately shooting in the air to avoid the target (i.e., "dumb" shooting, despite rule 13), wearing baggy and oversized clothing to obscure the target's body, using others (i.e., "seconds") as the equivalent of a stunt double, and even cutting the foe's hamstrings before the duel to restrict his thrusting motion or ability to turn and fire accurately.[14] The seconds for duelists also served the role of bodyguards to guarantee that their primaries would not be harmed prior to the duel or in the aftermath by hired assassins of the opponent.

On first glance, cheating would seem to conflict with the honor-bound tradition of dueling. However, cheating was extremely functional in these contests. For example, the preemptive attack by hired strangers allowed the champion to receive public accolades as an honorable man for his willingness to participate in a duel—and to do so without any threat to his own personal injury. In these and other cases, rule violations before or during the duel allowed people to build reputations as principled and fearless adversaries without participation in an event that could have serious physical consequences.

Table 4.1   The Code of Duello

Rule 1:   The first offense requires the first apology, although the retort may have been more offensive than the insult. Example: A tells B he is impertinent, etc. B retorts that A lies; yet A must make the first apology because he gave the first offense, and then (after one fire) B may explain away the retort by a subsequent apology.

Rule 2:   But if the parties would rather fight on, then after two shots each (but in no case before), B may explain first, and A apologize afterwards.

Rule 3:   If a doubt exists as to who gave the first offense, the decision rests with the seconds; if they won't decide or can't agree, the matter must proceed to two shots, or to a hit, if the challenger requires it.

Rule 4:   When the direct lie is the first offense, the aggressor must either beg pardon in express terms; exchange two shots previous to apology or three shots followed by an explanation; or fire until one party or the other is severely hit.

Rule 5:   As a blow is strictly prohibited under any circumstances among gentlemen, no verbal apology can be received for such an insult. The alternatives, therefore—the offender handing a cane to the injured party, to be used on his own back, at the same time begging pardon; firing on until one or both are disabled; or exchanging three shots, and then asking pardon without proffer of the cane.

           If swords are used, the parties engage until one is well blooded, disabled, or disarmed; or until, after receiving a wound, and blood being drawn, the aggressor begs pardon.

Rule 6:   If A gives B the lie, and B retorts by a blow (being the two greatest offenses), no reconciliation can take place until after two discharges each, or a severe hit; after which B may beg A's pardon humbly for the blow and then A may explain simply for the lie; because a blow is never allowable, and the offense of the lie, therefore, merges in it (see preceding rules).

Rule 7:   But no apology can be received, in any case, after the parties have actually taken ground, without exchange of fires.

Rule 8:   In the above case, no challenger is obliged to divulge his cause of challenge (if private) unless required by the challenged so to do before their meeting.

Rule 9:   All imputations of cheating at play, races, etc., to be considered equivalent to a blow; but may be reconciled after one shot, on admitting their falsehood and begging pardon accordingly.

Rule 10:   Any insult to a lady under a gentleman's care or protection to be considered as, by one degree, a greater offense than if given to the gentleman personally, and to be regulated accordingly.

Rule 11:   Offenses originating or accruing from the support of ladies' reputations, to be considered as less unjustifiable than any others of the same class, and as admitting of slighter apologies by the aggressor: this to be determined by the circumstances of the case, but always favorable to the lady.

Rule 12: In simple, unpremeditated recontres with the small sword, or *couteau de chasse,* the rule is—first draw, first sheath, unless blood is drawn; then both sheath, and proceed to investigation.

Rule 13: No dumb shooting or firing in the air is admissible in any case. The challenger ought not to have challenged without receiving offense; and the challenged ought, if he gave offense, to have made an apology before he came on the ground; therefore, children's play must be dishonorable on one side or the other, and is accordingly prohibited.

Rule 14: Seconds to be of equal rank in society with the principals they attend, inasmuch as a second may either choose or chance to become a principal, and equality is indispensable.

Rule 15: Challenges are never to be delivered at night, unless the party to be challenged intends leaving the place of offense before morning; for it is desirable to avoid all hot-headed proceedings.

Rule 16: The challenged has the right to choose his own weapon, unless the challenger gives his honor he is no swordsman; after which, however, he can decline any second species of weapon proposed by the challenged.

Rule 17: The challenged chooses his ground; the challenger chooses his distance; the seconds fix the time and terms of firing.

Rule 18: The seconds load in presence of each other, unless they give their mutual honors they have charged smooth and single, which should be held sufficient.

Rule 19: Firing may be regulated—first by signal; secondly, by word of command; or thirdly, at pleasure—as may be agreeable to the parties. In the latter case, the parties may fire at their reasonable leisure, but second presents and rests are strictly prohibited.

Rule 20: In all cases a miss-fire is equivalent to a shot, and a snap or non-cock is to be considered as a miss-fire.

Rule 21: Seconds are bound to attempt reconciliation before the meeting takes place, or after sufficient firing or hits, as specified.

Rule 22: Any wound sufficient to agitate the nerves and necessarily make the hand shake, must end the business for that day.

Rule 23: If the cause of the meeting be of such a nature that no apology or explanation can or will be received, the challenged takes his ground, and calls on the challenger to proceed as he chooses; in such cases, firing at pleasure is the usual practice, but may be varied by agreement.

Rule 24: In slight cases, the second hands his principal but one pistol; but in gross cases, two, holding another charged case in reserve.

Rule 25: Where seconds disagree, and resolve to exchange shots themselves, it must be at the same time and at right angles with their principals, thus: if with swords, side by side, with five paces interval.

Source: Hamilton Cochran. 1963. *Noted American Duels and Hostile Encounters.* Philadelphia: Chilton Books.

The demise in dueling in U.S. society has been associated with several historical events. These include the growing sophistication and stability of the U.S. legal system, the emergence of libel and slander laws as an alternative method of recourse for honor violations, and public outrage over the death of Alexander Hamilton, a major statesman, at the hands of Vice President Aaron Burr in 1804. Compared to other regions of the country, the chivalrous code of dueling had a longer history in the South.

The Western Gunfight

Although less stylized and regimented than duels among gentlemen, the Western gunfight in the nineteenth century was another context where historical records reveal fighting rules. Descriptive accounts indicate the following sequencing of events: one party makes what is interpreted as an antagonistic move, the offended party then assumes a defensive posture, and the crowd quickly disperses, followed by additional physical posturing and possible verbal challenges, and the ultimate termination of the dispute by retreat, third party intervention, or gunfire. The "quick draw" and the "bushwhack" attack were alternative scenarios of gunfight violence on the Western frontier that were less honorable in form and had a more diverse action pattern.

There were many gunfighters on the Western frontier, but "Wild Bill" Hickok was one of the most famous and notorious.[15] His legendary exploits as a scout, hunter, lawman, gambler, and gunfighter were immortalized in newspapers, dime novels, and numerous biographies. Eastern writers, whose urban audiences longed for adventure but had no idea about life on the Western frontier, exaggerated and embellished the escapades of Wild Bill as the "civilizer" of the savage and lawless territories.[16]

It is difficult to separate the myth from the reality in Hickok's life, but several things seem clear about his contribution to the stereotypical image of the Western gunfighter. First, he was described as a "dandy" (someone overly attentive to clothes and appearance) and genteel in both language and manner. Wild Bill's image as a well-groomed, finely dressed gentleman with ivory-handled pistols became the stereotypical portrait of the professional gunfighter in U.S. literature and cinema. Second, his dubious moral qualities and shortcomings were often ignored in media accounts.[17] This primary focus on his real and alleged acts of heroism and fair play shaped public images of appropriate conduct for the frontiersman and bolstered his reputation as a Western hero.

Viewed as functionally equivalent to dueling among gentlemen and nobles, the "proper" rules of engagement in the Western gunfight were aptly demonstrated and immortalized in the gunfight between Hickok and Davis Tutt in Springfield, Missouri. According to several accounts, the two men had a history of "bad blood" over issues of gambling debts, military services, and women. On this particular occasion, Hickok had lost considerable money to Tutt in a card game and could not cover his losses. Tutt presumably took Hickok's pocket watch as payment, Hickok objected, and an argument ensued. The *Springfield Weekly Patriot* described the subsequent gunfight:

> On the evening of July 21,1865, Hickok and Tutt faced each other across Springfield's huge public square. They walked toward each other and drew their pistols. Wild Bill placed the barrel of his pistol across his left forearm to level his spot. He and Tutt fired at almost the same time. Tutt's shot echoed harmlessly across the huge town square, but Wild Bill's bullet struck Tutt in the chest, killing him almost instantly.[18]

Similar to the protocol of the *Code Duello,* the gunfights of Hickok and other Western folk heroes are widely portrayed as chivalric affairs that proceeded in an orderly, cool, and dispassionate manner. This glamorized view of the gunfight in action novels and newspaper accounts, and the high moral integrity bestowed on the motives of its champions, helped cultivate a progressive image of increasing civility in the expansion of the Western frontier.[19]

Most authoritative historical accounts would seriously challenge these stereotypical, glorified portrayals of the gunfight and gunfighter. Instead, the typical gunfight was far more spontaneous, brutal, and clearly less honorable than many duels between gentlemen. Men killed other men for a host of reasons, including money, women, personal insults, and drunken brawls. Some contemporary movies and television programs have moved away from the glamorized and sanitized image of the gunfight, portraying a much grittier, violent reality.[20]

Rules in Corporal Punishment

Corporal punishment is imposed in a variety of different contexts with an assortment of methods and consequences to the recipient. It is a unique form of aggression in that it is (1) used almost exclusively in a retaliatory context (e.g., as punishment for criminals, to extract confessions from the guilty) and (2) it may be legal even when lethal if the punishment is imposed according to the rule of law. Contrary to other types of retaliatory violence, there is also an implicit understanding that state-sponsored corporal punishment should be delivered in a dispassionate or detached manner. The different contexts for corporal punishment, and the explicit and implicit rules of implementing it, are summarized below.

Capital Punishment and Its Imposition. As punishment for especially nefarious and severe misconduct, executions in the United States and elsewhere have long been characterized by rules, rituals, and routines. The execution process begins with the criminal trial and public dramatization of the evil of the prohibited conduct and the offender. During a sometimes lengthy appeal process, the condemned person remains imprisoned until the lethal punishment is imposed. The method of execution is time- and place-specific, but in all settings it is highly ritualized with specialized roles and fixed-action sequences.

Executions in England during the seventeenth and eighteenth centuries were public events, often conducted in a carnival-like atmosphere Popular descriptions such as a "hanging match," "sheriff's ball," or "hanging fair" reveal the public spectacle surrounding executions.[21] London gained special notoriety during this period for the nature of its execution practices and rituals. Gibbets (steel cages in which bodies of the executed were hung) and gallows were common sights and often widely known landmarks in the city. A culture of hanging evolved. Judges dressed in wigs and scarlet robes sat up high and pronounced death sentences along with a booming, resonant speech designed to impress the audience. The condemned was led by cart through a cheering or jeering mob in a long procession from Newgate prison to the triple gallows tree at Tyburn, speaking freely to the crowd in belligerent defiance or solemn remorse. The multiple purposes of the public execution seemed clear: it provided a dramatic, visual impression of the power of the King's law and the lethal consequences of its violation. Ironically, the rowdy spectacle surrounding public executions (and the volatility and unpredictability of the mob reaction) often detracted from these explicit purposes, eventually resulting in the abolition of the procession in favor of public executions inside Newgate prison. Public executions in England were abolished in 1868.

For state-sponsored executions in the United States, the rules and rituals have remained fairly stable over the last half century. The condemned is transferred to a holding cell or other physical setting close to the execution site, receives the last meal, visits by friends and family, and spiritual guidance and comfort by religious leaders. Prison staff test equipment and procedures, and the prisoner is prepared for the execution method (strapped on a hospital gurney for lethal injections, blindfolded in most hangings and firing squads, head and right leg shaved for most electrocutions). At a specified time, the execution commences, medical officials check the body for signs of life, and ultimately a prison spokesperson makes a public announcement of the death. This execution process has changed little over the last fifty years, although lethal injection results in less physical disfigurement of the body than was true of hanging, firing squads, and electrocutions.

The rules of proper protocol for state-sponsored executions in the United States do not apply to how legal executions are conducted in other countries or in cases of extrajudicial executions. Brief descriptions of legal executions in contemporary China and Saudi Arabia illustrate national variability. In particular, when compared to U.S. practices, China has an extremely short appeal process (final appeals are accepted or declined within 12 days of the original trial), a greater range of offenses are capital crimes (e.g., economic, public order, and violent offenses), and the primary lethal method involves a single bullet shot in the back of the head.[22] In Saudi Arabia, the nature of criminal trials and prosecutions is shrouded in secrecy. However, the following account of a public beheading provides a graphic illustration of the differences in the execution process and execution methods.

> Policemen clear a public square of traffic and lay out a thick blue plastic sheet about 16 feet by 16 feet on the asphalt. The condemned, who has been given tranquilizers, is led from a police car dressed in his own clothing. His eyes are covered with cotton pads, bound in plaster and covered with a black cloth.
>
> Barefoot, with feet shackled and hands cuffed behind his back, the prisoner is led by a police officer to the center of the sheet and made to kneel. An Interior Ministry official reads out the prisoner's name and crime before a crowd of witnesses.
>
> A soldier hands a long, curved sword to the executioner. He approaches the prisoner from behind and jabs him with the tip of the sword in the back so that the prisoner instinctively raises his head.
>
> It usually takes just one swing of the sword to sever the head, often sending it flying about three feet. Paramedics bring the head to a doctor, who uses a gloved hand to stop the fountain of blood spurting from the neck. The doctor sews the head back on, and the body is wrapped in the blue plastic sheet and taken away in an ambulance.[23]

Violations of the rules of lethal corporal punishment are most evident in the case of extrajudicial executions by paramilitary forces and other vigilante groups. These "death squads" in various countries impose a type of "street justice" that is often swift and severe. Contrary to the image of total anarchy, some rules about the appropriate targets (e.g., death to all family members or only to the alleged perpetrator), immunity, evidentiary requirements, and a proper adjudicative process often operate even within these extrajudicial executions. However, these rules are followed largely in a perfunctory manner in the extrajudicial context of mock trials and summary judgments.

Flogging and Physical Torture. All societies employ some form of nonlethal corporal sanctions for purposes of punishment and social control. Flogging (the beating of a person with a whip, strap, or rope) is still a legal form of punishment in many countries and a method of discipline within some military organizations. Flogging and other types of physical torture are also legally permitted in many countries for purposes of extracting information and confessions. Regardless of the method or purpose, flogging is similar to other types of interpersonal aggression in that it is a highly ritualized and rule-bound behavior.

The normative rules of flogging are most clearly seen in the imposition of criminal punishments under Islamic law. Under this legal tradition, flogging is the mandatory and nondiscretionary punishment for persons convicted of particular *hudud* ("acts against God") offenses. Adultery by an unmarried person receives 100 lashes; defamation by a free person, 80 lashes; and the use of alcohol by a free person, 80 lashes.[24] Flogging is also used as a discretionary, extrajudicial punishment in Saudi Arabia by the *mutawa'een* (the religious police) against political dissenters and foreign nationals, traffic offenders, and anyone suspected of harassing women.

Given Muslim customs about dress and the exposure of the body, the normative rules of flogging require that the convicted person be lightly attired with clothing when they are whipped. Special conditions also apply to how the whipping is done: it is inflicted by scholars well versed in Islamic law; blows are spread over the body but not to the head or face; males are flogged while standing and women are seated; the whipping should not lacerate the skin.[25] Violation of these sacred rules may result in punishment to the flogger.

Similar to public executions, nonlethal corporal punishments are often justified on the grounds of their deterrent value. In particular, the spectacle of a severe public beating administered by the state is designed to send a clear message to others who may be contemplating a similar deviant act. The humiliation and degradation associated with a public flogging and the ceremonial stripping of the accused of their clothing, rank, and/or social identity is an important component of the presumed deterrent effect on future wrongdoing by the offender and others in the community.

Numerous international organizations (e.g., the United Nations, Amnesty International, Human Rights Watch) prohibit or monitor excessive torture and physical abuse of inmates and others in confinement. Nonetheless, these types of violent acts have a long, checkered history and continue in the modern world. Although somewhat less grisly and brutalizing than the methods of the Medieval Inquisition, "standard operating procedures" for extracting confessions and obtaining information still exists in many countries. Severe physical pain and injuries to those being interrogated is usually condoned as long as the corporal punishment yields accurate and useful information. In other words, the normative rules of torture are often guided by the principle "the ends justify the means." Accounts of torture and abuse of inmates at the Abu Ghraib prison by American military guards is a contemporary application of these principles (i.e., the information gleaned from coercive interrogations is perceived as justifying its use).

SUMMARY

The purpose of this chapter was to describe the nature and context of some of the rules of violence in Western history. Although they occur in widely different contexts, codes of dueling, the Western gunfight, and state-sponsored corporal punishment share a common purpose of social control and order maintenance through the use of highly structured and ritualized forms of aggression.

There are numerous other contexts and examples of rules and rituals in human aggression in contemporary society. These include situations of domestic violence, rules of acceptable violence within sporting events, and violence associated with the commission of street-level criminal behavior. The interaction rituals associated with codes and rules of violence in these contexts are described in the next three chapters.

Notes

[1] For examples of drive theories of aggression, see Konrad Lorenz. 1966. *On Aggression.* New York: Harcourt, Brace, and World; Sigmund Freud. 1950. *Beyond the Pleasure Principle.* New York: Liveright. (J. Strachey, translation); J. Dollard, N. Doob, N. E. Miller, O. H. Mowrer, and R. R. Sears. 1939. *Frustration and Aggression.* New Haven, CT: Yale University Press; Kenneth E. Moyer. 1987. *Violence and Aggression: A Physiological Perspective.* New York: Paragon House.

[2] See, for example, Kenneth Polk. 1994. *When Men Kill: Scenarios of Masculine Violence.* New York: Cambridge University Press; William Oliver. 1994. *The Violent Social World of Black Men.* New York: Lexington; Jeffrey Fagan and Deanna L. Wilkinson. 1998. "Guns, Youth Violence, and Social Identity in Inner Cities." In Mark Moore and Michael Tonry (eds.), *Crime and Justice: An Annual Review of Research.* Vol. 24. Chicago: University of Chicago Press, pp. 105–188.

[3] For applications of this perspective to human violence, see Michael P. Ghiglieri. 1999. *The Dark Side of Man: Tracing the Origins of Male Violence.* Reading, MA: Perseus Books; Martin Daly and Margo Wilson. 1988. *Homicide.* New York: Aldine de Gruyter; Martin Daly and Margo Wilson. 1999. "An Evolutionary Psychological Perspective on Homicide." In M. Dwayne Smith and Margaret A. Zahn (eds.), *Studying and Preventing Homicide: Issues and Challengers.* Thousand Oaks, CA: Sage.

[4] Under all homicide laws in the United States, verbal insults about one's sexual identity or other social status are not considered adequate victim provocation to reduce a criminal homicide to a noncriminal homicide (e.g., justifiable homicide) or to reduce a murder to manslaughter. However, when we asked a sample of 175 male college students about situations in which physical attacks are justified, about 25 percent of them said that it was acceptable to hit someone with your fist if they had threatened your masculinity or sexuality. This latter finding suggests that some men view nonlethal physical force as an appropriate response to verbal threats.

[5] For a review of the literature on this topic, see Terance D. Miethe and Wendy C. Regoeczi. 2004. *Rethinking Homicide: Exploring the Structure and Process Underlying Deadly Situations.* Cambridge, UK: Cambridge University Press.

[6] See Harold Garfinkel. 1956. "Conditions of Successful Degradation Ceremonies." *American Journal of Sociology* 61:420–424.

[7] Regardless of whether it is proactive or displaced, aggression that is self-initiated and without victim provocation is often judged as less socially acceptable. The street mugger or the "road rage" offender, for example, garner little public support or approval for their violent actions even when little physical injury is imposed on their victims. Political terrorists who use bombings and other violent acts for instrumental motives are viewed in a similar vein. Even claims of acting in self-defense (e.g., retaliatory bombings) are not usually sufficient for public approval of these acts. Rules of common decency may operate in a general sense in these cases (e.g., political attacks should be directed at government authorities and structures rather than civilians, arsonists should burn only unoccupied buildings), but offenders often ignore such restraints when they impede the achievement of their specific goals.

[8] For previous research on the *modus operandi* of various types of criminals, see Derek B. Cornish and Ronald V. Clarke. 1986. *The Reasoning Criminal: Rational Choice Perspectives on Offending.* New York: Springer-Verlag.

[9] The word "contest" to describe dueling derives from its historical usage as a sporting event or contest among noblemen. The best example of dueling as a sporting contest involved the jousting among knights on horses in the Middle Ages (see chapter 7, endnote 1 for

information on contemporary jousting). Modern-day fencing matches are another contemporary example of dueling as a sporting "contest."

[10] See, for example, Pieter Spierenburg. 1998. *Men and Violence: Gender, Honor and Rituals in Modern Europe and America*. Columbus: Ohio State University Press.

[11] The argument about the change in the civilizing processes and the nature of social control in the nineteenth and twentieth centuries is consistent with the works of Norbert Elias on civilizing sensibilities and Michel Foucault's thesis on systems of control of the mind and body. See Norbert Elias. 1982. *The Civilizing Process II: Power and Civility*. New York: Pantheon; Michel Foucault. 1977. *Discipline and Punish*. New York: Pantheon.

[12] Ed Grabianowski. "How Duels Work." Available online at: http://people.howstuffworks.com/duel.htm.

[13] For a full description of the rules of dueling underlying the *Code Duello*, see Hamilton Cochran. 1963. *Noted American Duels and Hostile Encounters*. Philadelphia: Chilton Books. The *Code Duello* of 1777 was influenced by and essentially replaced several earlier Italian codes of the fourteenth and fifteenth centuries. Within the new American Republic, the principal rules of the *Code Duello* were followed with some deviations. A U.S. version of this code was written by South Carolina Governor John Lyde Wilson in 1838. For discussion of these codes, see Barbara Holland. 2003. *Gentlemen's Blood: A History of Dueling from Swords at Dawn to Pistols at Dusk*. London: Bloomsbury Publishing; John Lyde Wilson. 1838. *The American Code: Code of Honor; or, Rules for the Government of Principals and Seconds in Dueling*. Available online at: www.cbc2.org/faculty/dabbott/duAmericanCode.html.

[14] For a description of these cheating practices, see Barbara Holland. 2003. *Gentlemen's Blood: A History of Dueling from Swords at Dawn to Pistols at Dusk*. London: Bloomsbury Publishing.

[15] This list of the most famous and notorious gunfighters also includes Clay Allison (1840–1887), Wyatt Earp (1848–1929), Doc Holiday (1852–1887), Bat Masterson (1853–1921), Luke Short (1854–1893), and Ben Thompson (1843–1884). For a descriptive account of their exploits, see Dale T. Schoenberger. 1971. *The Gunfighters*. Caldwell, ID: The Caxton Printers.

[16] See Kent Ladd Steckmesser. 1965. *The Western Hero in History and Legend*. Norman: University of Oklahoma Press.

[17] For example, rather than using his six-guns for the "correct" purpose of maintaining order and civility in a lawless land, Wild Bill also killed people for less honorable reasons, including politics, gambling disputes, drunken brawls, and fights over women. Southern and Confederate writers of the times were generally far more critical of Wild Bill's image as a hero and public defender of the chivalric code, describing him in one newspaper account as "nothing more than a drunken, reckless, murderous coward, who is treated with contempt by true border men, and who should have been hung years ago for the murder of innocent men." Cited in Kent Ladd Steckmesser. 1965. *The Western Hero in History and Legend*. Norman: University of Oklahoma Press, p. 151.

[18] *Springfield Weekly Patriot*. July 27, 1865.

[19] For further discussion of this "civilizing effect," see Kent Ladd Steckmesser. 1965. *The Western Hero in History and Legend*. Norman: University of Oklahoma Press, especially pp. 105–159.

[20] A good example of this trend is the HBO series *Deadwood*. This series takes place in the late 1800s in the town (Deadwood, South Dakota) where Wild Bill Hickok was actually shot during a card game. The saloon owner and other persons in the program are represented as largely vile, disgusting, uncouth, amoral, and despicable individuals. Little value is placed on human life, and there is little honor or interpersonal integrity. In the movie *Unforgiven,* the lead character, William Munny, is a gunfighter and a ruthless killer. Contrast these images with the gunfighters portrayed in earlier movies (e.g., *High Noon; Gunfight at the OK Corral; The Good, the Bad, and the Ugly; Silverado*). Until recently, the gunfights in most movies resembled the idealized image of the fair-play duel in both form and structure.

[21] Graeme Newman. 1978. *The Punishment Response*. Philadelphia: J.P. Lippincott, p. 125.

[22] Lethal injection has increased in the last decade as a method of execution in China. In the rural provinces, there are actually mobile execution vans that drive out to the remote loca-

tions to impose lethal injections. For a fuller description of the methods and history of punishment in China, see Terance D. Miethe and Hong Lu. 2005. *Punishment: A Comparative Historical Perspective*. Cambridge, UK: Cambridge University Press.

[23] This account by Associated Press correspondent Anwar Faruqi appeared in an article from the Human Rights Watch. "Human Rights in Saudi Arabia: A Deafening Silence." AP April 24, 2000. See also Terance D. Miethe and Hong Lu. 2005. *Punishment: A Comparative Historical Perspective*. Cambridge, UK: Cambridge University Press.

[24] Under the *Shari'a* (i.e., Islamic law), the mandatory punishment for adultery is death by stoning if the person is married. The formal rule of law in these cases depends on the marital status of the offender. For other offenses, the particular *hudud* punishments depend on other social statuses of the offender (e.g., gender, "free man" versus slave). For a discussion of *hudud* punishments, see Terance D. Miethe and Hong Lu. 2005. *Punishment: A Comparative Historical Perspective*. Cambridge, UK: Cambridge University Press; Matthew Lippman, Sean McConville, and Mordechai Yerushalmi. 1988. *Islamic Criminal Law and Procedure: An Introduction.* New York: Praeger.

[25] Matthew Lippman, Sean McConville, and Mordechai Yerushalmi. 1988. *Islamic Criminal Law and Procedure: An Introduction.* New York: Praeger, p. 43.

The Rules of Street Violence

The term "street violence" is often used to describe acts of interpersonal violence that occur in public places. These violent, public encounters may involve collective acts (e.g., riots or gang-related rumbles) or physical confrontations between a single offender and a victim. Depending on the nature of the confrontation and a variety of situational factors, many of these potentially violent situations are quickly diffused and de-escalate without injury or further incident. However, some of them escalate into serious criminal acts of simple and aggravated assault, robbery, sexual assaults, and homicide.

For most readers of this book, the notion of street violence implies a certain level of raw, uncontrolled, and unregulated physical aggression. In support of this stereotypical view, the media use military rhetoric to describe some of the physical locations in which the violence takes place: "war zones" or "combat zones." However, even within inhospitable public places, there is often a "code of the street" that provides some regulation and control of human aggressive responses. In some cases, the code of the street may prescribe a course of action that runs contrary to the legal rules of mainstream culture.

This chapter examines the normative rules and action sequences in situations of street violence in U.S. society. It explores these rules in the context of fistfights, verbal banter among males in character contests and confrontational disputes, gang violence and drive-by shootings, sexual assaults, and personal robberies (street muggings). We begin with estimates of the prevalence of different types of street violence.

THE PREVALENCE OF PHYSICAL ASSAULTS IN PUBLIC PLACES

The most comprehensive information on the characteristics of the offenders, victims, and situations of physical assault in public places involve crime data collected under the Federal Bureau of Investigation's National Incident-Based Reporting System (NIBRS).[1] The NIBRS data used in this analysis include over 130,000 physical assaults known to the police in 2001 that occurred in public locations (i.e., in a location other than the home of the victim or offender). Because NIBRS data is based on incidents known to the police, our inferences about street assaults derived from this data will be restricted to those physical assaults that have been deemed serious enough to warrant the filing of a police report.[2]

Our analysis focuses on those incidents in which the most serious charge was either a simple assault (a completed battery involving no or minor injuries), aggravated assault (a battery with serious injury or threatened battery with a dangerous weapon), or murders (the nonnegligent killing of one person by another). After excluding cases with missing data on any major offender, victim, or offense characteristic, the most serious offenses in our sample of 129,941 incidents of "street" assaults were: 97,893 simple assaults, 31,697 aggravated assaults, and 351 murders.[3]

Before exploring the attributes associated with street assaults, it is important to recognize that most physical assaults known to the police *do not* occur in public places. Instead, they occur in the homes of the victim and/or offenders. About two-thirds of all physical assaults reported in NIBRS data occurred in the home, and there is little variation across types of assaults (e.g., 69 percent of simple assaults took place in the home, 61 percent of aggravated assaults, and 67 percent of homicides). The nature of home or domestic assaults will be discussed in the next chapter. Here, we will exclusively focus on the profile of street assaults. The offender, victim, and offense characteristics associated with different types of street assaults are summarized in table 5.1.

There are several basic features about the nature of serious street assaults revealed by the data in table 5.1.

- Nearly all serious street assaults known to the police are resolved through nonlethal means. Far less than 1 percent of these assaults are lethal; major physical injuries or threat of serious bodily injury are found in less than one-fourth of all serious assaults in public places. When reporting biases are taken into account (i.e., offenses with more serious injury are more likely to be reported to the police), the low prevalence of serious injury in the typical street assault suggests that this type of violence quickly de-escalates before it approaches the threshold of serious injury or death. The primary factors associated with the nonlethal termination of most street assaults may be cultural rules of disengagement, intervention by third parties, internal monitoring or self-control, defensive

Table 5.1 Structural Elements of Street Assaults

Variables	Simple Assault	Aggravated Assault	All Street Homicide	Assaults
Offender Attributes:				
Sex (Male)	71.8%	78.7%	88.3%	73.5%
Race (Black)	37.0%	41.6%	57.5%	38.2%
Age (< 20)	34.5%	28.1%	26.5%	32.9%
Victim Attributes:				
Sex (Male)	48.4%	63.3%	76.4%	52.1%
Race (Black)	28.2%	33.9%	49.0%	29.7%
Age (< 20)	34.5%	27.6%	17.1%	34.0%
Offense Attributes:				
Multiple Offenders	16.9%	20.4%	32.5%	17.8%
V-O Strangers	20.2%	32.0%	28.8%	23.1%
	n= 97,893	n= 31,697	n= 351	n= 129,941

Source: NIBRS (2001)

posturing/actions, or an assortment of other individual or situational elements.

- As the gravity of assaults increase, the profile of offenders and victims becomes increasingly male. This is especially true for victims. The proportion of male victims increased from less than half in simple assaults to over three-fourths of homicide victims.

- The proportion of street assaults involving adults, multiple offenders, or Blacks as offenders and victims also rose as the severity of the street assaults increased. For example, the proportion of victims who were teenagers dropped from about one-third of simple assaults to less than one fifth of homicides. The proportion of incidents involving multiple offenders was nearly twice as high among homicides as it was for simple assaults.

Another way to assess the social profiles of various street assaults is by exploring the joint distribution of the attributes of the offenders, victims, and offenses. Table 5.2 illustrates this approach by summarizing the 5 most prevalent combinations of attributes found in simple assaults, aggravated assaults, and homicides.

The results in table 5.2 demonstrate several additional features about the nature of different types of street assaults. For example, regardless of the type of street assault, the most common situations in which these criminal acts occur always involve male offenders and victims of the same race and age group as their offenders. The most prevalent cases of street assaults rarely involve multiple offenders, teenage offenders, or attacks among strangers. Instead, they are primarily male-on-male disputes among adult acquaintances of the same race.

Table 5.2 Most Common Profiles for Simple Assaults, Aggravated Assaults, and Homicides that Occur in Public Places

Offender Attributes	Victim Attributes	Offense Attributes	Number of Cases
Simple Assaults:			
1. Male White >20 yrs old	Female White > 20 yrs old	Acq/Fam SingOff	10,235
2. Male White > 20 yrs old	Male White > 20 yrs old	Acq/Fam SingOff	6,567
3. Male Black > 20 yrs old	Female Black > 20 yrs old	Acq/Fam SingOff	6,149
4. Male White < 20 yrs old	Male White < 20 yrs old	Acq/Fam SingOff	5,679
5. Male White > 20 yrs old	Male White > 20 yrs old	Stranger SingOff	4,241
Aggravated Assaults:			
1. Male White > 20 yrs old	Male White > 20 yrs old	Acq/Fam SingOff	2,774
2. Male White > 20 yrs old	Male White > 20 yrs old	Stranger SingOff	2,244
3. Male White > 20 yrs old	Female White > 20 yrs old	Acq/Fam SingOff	2,135
4. Male Black > 20 yrs old	Male Black > 20 yrs old	Acq/Fam SingOff	1,605
5. Male White < 20 yrs old	Male White < 20 yrs old	Acq/Fam SingOff	1,259
Homicide:			
1. Male White > 20 yrs old	Male White > 20 yrs old	Acq/Fam SingOff	39
2. Male Black > 20 yrs old	Male Black > 20 yrs old	Acq/Fam SingOff	39
3. Male White > 20 yrs old	Female White > 20 yrs old	Acq/Fam SingOff	30
4. Male Black > 20 yrs old	Male Black > 20 yrs old	Acq/Fam MultOff	18
5. Male Black > 20 yrs old	Female Black > 20 yrs old	Acq/Fam SingOff	14

Notes: Acq/Fam = victim and offender are acquainted or family members; SingOff = single (one) offender; Multoff= multiple offenders.

Source: NIBRS 2001.

The types of street violence in these data—interpersonal assaults in public places among males—resemble in form and structure what previous literature has referred to as confrontational assaults and character contests.[4] Within this context, particular public places (e.g., street corners, bars, parking lots, playgrounds) serve as staging areas for status enhancement and public declarations of masculinity.

RULES AND ROUTINES IN DIFFERENT TYPES OF STREET VIOLENCE

The primary forms of street violence in contemporary U.S. society involve fistfighting, verbal banter among males that escalates into physical assaults, gang violence and drive-by shootings, sexual assaults, and street muggings and other robberies. Each of these types of street violence, and the rules of engagement that underlie them, are described below.

Rules in Fistfights

The "fair" fistfight is a widely entrenched situational context of aggression that is highly regulated and controlled by rules of proper conduct.

Whether done in a boxing ring or on the street, these fights are literally contests, often involving shared rules of appropriate conduct for the fight participants, the audience, and the aftermath. Normative rules of fair play are applicable to most forms of fighting (e.g., dueling, gunfighting), but they seem especially germane to the fistfight. In fact, even in an "ends justify the means" world, the "low blow" and the "sucker punch" are clear breaches of proper conduct that elicit social condemnation from friends of both the winners and losers.

Aside from the context of prize fighting (see chapter 7), the bare-knuckles fistfight has been a primary method of dispute settlement among males throughout U.S. history. When motivated by a perceived threat to one's honor or reputation, the fistfight between two combatants has served as the poor man's equivalent to dueling throughout history, and it was also regulated by normative rules of engagement.

During much of the twentieth century, there was a normative code for fistfighting. Some of these rules include principles of fair play (e.g., no sucker punching, no brass knuckles), appropriate body areas to hit (e.g., no punching below the belt line), the role of bystanders (e.g., no outside assistance), and the appropriate point of termination of the fight (e.g., at the first sight of blood, when the opponent is totally incapacitated). Similar to the boxing match, many fistfights would take place at a pre-arranged time and place, occur in front of a public audience, and the fighters would often shake hands at both the onset and completion of their battle.

Over the last quarter century, however, the rules of fighting have dramatically changed. The concept of a fair fight is now nebulous at best, and the process and outcome of street fights are far less consistent and predictable. Some interaction rituals still underlie these violent encounters, but the normative expectations of appropriate conduct are far more context-specific. For example, the normative expectation for fistfights among close friends and family members is that you terminate the fight at any sign of serious injury. However, the degree of injury, the possible assistance of outsiders, and the proper resolution of the dispute are more difficult to anticipate in fights among strangers.

The mixed scenarios of appropriate fighting behavior are a product of the diverse messages about fighting in contemporary U.S. society. Within this context, some parents and educators may preach the virtues of seeking nonviolent solutions to particular problems, whereas others may condone various types of aggression. In addition, various media sources (e.g., televised events of *Extreme Fighting;* videos like *Street Fighter*) and popular books (Chuck Palahniuk's *Fight Club*) provide audiences with a diverse array of strategic moves and fighting techniques. This cultural climate of mixed messages about the who, what, when, where, and why of fighting makes it more difficult to ascertain and follow the appropriate normative course of action.

Although stereotypical images of fistfighting and its rules have changed over time, the increased popularity of martial arts and self-defense training have also altered the normative expectations surrounding fighting behavior. When these new fighting skills are coupled with changing cultural beliefs about the ends justifying the means, the "anything goes" mentality may nullify previous normative rules. Further erosion of traditional fighting norms may arise from greater uncertainty about how others may react to anger-provoking situations. Under these conditions, the anticipation of potentially lethal attacks and counteracts in even the most benign situations may have generated new normative rules for both fight and flight.

Verbal Banter, Character Contests, and Playing the Dozens

From the perspective of crime as events, physical assaults in public locations have a beginning, middle, and end. They are often precipitated by some degree of verbal banter or insult that is interpreted by the recipient as a threat to one's status or social identity. When verbal taunts among males of relatively low social standing (e.g., young men, the economically disadvantaged) occur in front of a public audience, they become a staging area for character contests.

Most verbal confrontations in public places are quickly defused by particular acts of omission or commission by the potential combatants. The major act of omission is the simple refusal of one party to continue to participate in the dispute by walking away or showing signs of contrition or deference. Acts of physical threat (e.g., bodily movements into offensive or defensive postures, displays of a lethal weapon) may also be sufficient to terminate the dispute without physical injuries. However, face-saving verbal exchanges escalate into violent encounters under conditions of threat, encapsulation, and the confluence of facilitating places, hardware, and other people. Some researchers assert that a mutual agreement to resort to violence is a necessary element of violent character contests, but others contend that these public displays of masculinity or assertions of social status do not require mutual consent.[5]

A good example of ritualized forms of verbal banter that sometimes erupt into physical violence is variously called *"playing the dozens," "doin' the dozens,"* or more simply *"the dozens."* This verbal character contest has its historical roots in traditional West African culture, where verbal sparring helped resolve tribal disputes in nonviolent ways.[6] The original norms of this highly spirited verbal banter involved rival tribes shouting threats and insults at each other across an open field from a distance sufficient to prevent violent reactions. If these verbal exchanges result in an agreement among the parties, the village leaders meet in a neutral space, embrace or display other physical signs of approval, and depart without physical violence.[7] In other instances, the verbal barrage becomes the precursor to a tribal battle.

The *dozens* within the context of African-American street culture involves a mutual exchange of "trash talking" or "snaps" (one-liners or rhyming sentences like "yo' mamma's so . . ."). The two competitors take turns making increasingly insulting comments about the adversary's mother, sister, or other family member. The banter among friends, associates, and others who know the game is often outlandish, highly exaggerated, sexually loaded, and humorous. The goals of this competitive game are to demonstrate verbal and mental superiority over the adversary by getting the most laughs from the public audience, not losing emotional control, and leaving the opponent without a worthy comeback.[8]

Playing the dozens is often viewed as a light-hearted, good-natured street game between adolescents and young men that is linked to developing and affirming one's self-control, verbal ability, mental agility, and mental toughness. However, these public contests may easily degenerate into physical violence when encouraged by third parties or when a derogatory retort is especially offensive because it hits a sensitive nerve or contains an element of truth. While a fundamental rule of the dozens is that the insults are not literally true, the code of appropriate conduct is often breached in the heat and emotion of the verbal battle.

Drive-By Shootings

A somewhat amorphous category of street violence involves the drive-by shooting. The typical image of a drive-by shooting is an urban street assault by young minority males. However, the drive-by shooting was also a relatively common method of retaliatory violence among Italian and Sicilian mobsters throughout the twentieth century and the various gangsters who robbed armored trucks and other mobile vehicles in a blaze of gunfire for financial gain. Bandits on horseback who robbed Western stagecoaches and trains in the nineteenth century are another example. The common practice in rural areas of shooting animals and inanimate objects (e.g., signs, mail boxes) out of moving vehicles constitutes another type of drive-by shooting.

Although both the context and motive vary in these violent situations, different types of drive-by shootings nonetheless share several basic structural features. First, drive-by shooters in each context are primarily young males. Second, these acts involve multiple offenders who have specialized roles (e.g., drivers, copilots, shooters). Third, some level of planning and cognitive rehearsal underlie these offenses, but the primary *modus operandi* is a quick blitz attack of the target. Fourth, as attacks in public places, collateral damage and injury to bystanders are a clear possibility in all of these situations. Fifth, for purposes of escaping detection by the authorities, drive-bys often occur in remote locations and under the cover of nightfall. However, the intrinsic motivations for these attacks (e.g., payback, showing courage, loyalty, toughness) often requires an audience for public confirmation of the shooter's "bad ass" identity, contributing to the frequency of such attacks in highly public situations (e.g., outside gatherings, parties, and dances).

As hit-and-run attacks by rival gang members, drive-by shootings in the late 1960s and early 1970s were often viewed as an emergent form of gang warfare.[9] They predominate on the West Coast, and especially in Southern California, for several sociodemographic reasons, including lower population concentration or density, the wider separation of neighborhoods, and the subsequent greater usage of automobiles for commuting and personal travel over longer distances. The social ecology of traditional East Coast cities, in contrast, with lower ownership of motor vehicles, narrow and highly congested streets, and high-density populations in high-rise residential units, was more conducive to hit-and-run attacks on foot or bicycles.[10]

Within both geographical regions, drive-bys or "ride-bys" in the last several decades have replaced the large group rumble or melee as the primary mode of serious gang fighting. The old-style rumbles (i.e., where gangs met at appointed places and times to do battle in large groups) were relatively less dangerous encounters because of the types of weapons used (e.g., homemade zip guns that were inaccurate, single shot, and of low muzzle velocity) and rules of fair play were more predominant.[11] After the mid-1960s, however, gang members were more likely to use manufactured guns and semi-automatic weapons, which dramatically increased the lethal risks of face-to-face encounters among rivals. Within this new context, the drive-by shooting proved to be a superior alternative. It provided the means of a quick blitz attack and escape that minimized the immediate risks of retaliation. It also fulfilled many of the intrinsic needs of gang-banging (e.g., impression management as a tough guy, achieving street justice or payback, asserting group loyalty).

Accurate estimates of the extent of drive-by shootings in urban areas are hampered by incomplete information and enormous underreporting of these offenses, especially when they are not associated with serious or lethal injuries.[12] However, we are on better empirical footing when we focus on the common structures and processes underlying drive-by shootings. With this context, notice the similarities in the following descriptions of public shootings derived from police reports:

- The victim, a Syndo Mob member, was working inside his car on the back window. He saw a white van back down the alley. When the van's passenger side door came in front of his car, a Piru/Blood pointed an Uzi machine gun at him and fired eighteen rounds, hitting his car several times but missing him (San Diego. circa 1980s).[13]

- 55-year-old Black female Victim (V) was sitting on the trunk of a parked vehicle in the parting lot of her apartment complex with several others when a vehicle occupied by about five Black males drove past and fired several shots into the crowd, killing the V. Police believed the shooting to be a feud between two groups of Jamaicans (a drug "war" among Rastafarians) and the V got caught in the crossfire (Miami, August 4, 1980).[14]

- 17-year-old Black male victim and a friend were at a fast food chicken restaurant when two unknown Black males pulled up in a vehicle. Driver asked V for a cigarette (which V refused to give him) and the driver pulled a gun and shot the V to death (Miami, September 23, 1980).[15]

- Suspect (S) was riding in an auto with 3 or 4 others. A witness (W), who was a Crips wannabe, called out "What's up Cuzz?" to people in auto. That greeting is used by Crips and is considered an insult by Bloods, who refer to each other as "Blood." S and others in the auto were Bloods. After calling out this greeting, W took off running. V was standing in street visiting with his friends. They had seen W calling everyone "Cuzz" and heard him shout at occupants of this car. As W ran by V's group, he told them there would be trouble. Auto made U-turn and cruised by V's group. Car stopped and S called out "What's up Bloods?" then began shooting. V's group started running. V was shot. Car sped off. S fired 6 shots, but W claimed at least one other fired from auto also. As the car sped away, a neighbor heard someone in the car say that they had shot the "wrong mother fucker" (St. Louis, 1990).[16]

- In an alleged gang feud, the V and his associates were selling drugs at this location as they usually did. S1 drove up, and one yelled to group, asking if they had any fifties to sell. Someone shouted "no," but V walked towards car, asking "huh?" when S2 opened fire, reportedly from a sawed off shotgun. S1 did not speed off in auto but drove slowly from scene. Two groups had been feuding for some time, and had shot at one another the previous summer (St. Louis, 1990).[17]

- At approximately 8:10 PM, numerous shots were fired into a vehicle, which was stopped at a traffic light waiting to turn on another road. The victim vehicle was occupied by three 19- to 20-year-old males. Both passengers were struck by gunfire. The front-seat passenger was mortally wounded. The three male suspects of roughly the same age as the Vs fled north in their vehicle and were apprehended by the police in a high speed pursuit. The shooting was apparently the result of a dispute between the suspects and one of the victims (Las Vegas, Nevada, 1999.)[18]

As suggested by these accounts, drive-by shootings are similar to other assault situations because they often involve some form of mutual confrontation between victims and offenders. Many of these crime events are precipitated by other historical events, serving as a means of retaliation and payback against prior personal affronts and disputes. Their unique signatures, however, derive from the use of firearms and their social ecology (intra-male assaults from automobiles in public places involving multiple offenders).

Many drive-by shootings result in death and serious injuries to the intended targets and "mushrooms" (innocent bystanders who are harmed in the assaults). However, the more common scenario involves the discharge of multiple rounds of ammunition with no serious injuries to anyone. The reasons for the low probability of injuries in drive-by situations are related to practical issues (e.g., the difficulty in hitting a moving target from a distance with a handgun) and the learning of the rules of survival in low-income, urban areas where drive-bys are most likely to occur. These rules include keeping a watchful eye to the street (especially for slow moving vehicles), being aware of ongoing disputes in the neighborhood, and running away quickly when trouble seems imminent.[19] The fact that other methods of dispute resolution and honor defense are available (e.g., verbal abuse, threats, retreat, submission, conciliation) may also contribute to the prevalence of nonlethal forms of agonistic behavior in these violent situations.

Road Rage

Acts of road rage are violent situations involving drivers in traffic. The precipitating event is often some particular action or inaction by a fellow driver that is interpreted by another as offensive or annoying. Slow driving or aggressive driving, tailgating, changing lanes without signaling, momentary delays at stop lights or signs, cutting someone off when a lane ends, and minor "fender benders" are often the specific stimuli that trigger the aggressive attack. Most researchers agree that road rage is often displaced aggression, inflicted upon fellow drivers whose only fault may be that they are in the wrong place at the wrong time. Some road rage situations are cases of mutual combat, whereas other attacks are one-sided affairs in which the victimized party is trying to avoid a confrontation.

As situated transactions among two or more parties, road rage incidents have an underlying structure like other violent events. These incidents are initiated by a triggering act, a sequence of specific actions and counteractions, and termination in a variety of different ways (e.g., by mutual combat, verbal banter, or by one party driving away before further escalation). General rules of reciprocity (e.g., respond-in-kind) and particular subcultural norms (e.g., don't let anyone disrespect you, "real" men don't back down) may also suggest particular paths of appropriate conduct in these situations. However, the fact that these highway confrontations involve strangers who may differ widely in their sociodemographic profiles makes these situations especially difficult to anticipate in terms of normative actions and expectations associated with them. They are, in short, dangerous situations without clear normative rules for guidance.

Based on available survey data and police incident reports, young males are the most likely victims and offenders in road rage situations. For example, an internet poll in 2004 revealed that males were slightly more likely than females to report getting into confrontations with other drivers (40 percent vs. 33 percent). Similar differences were also found between drivers under 25 years old and those older (41 percent vs. 35 percent).[20] When police reports detail incidents involving physical injury, the proportion of road rage incidents among males is even more dramatic.

A closer examination of the situational dynamics in road rage incidents reveal their similarity with other types of confrontational violence. These common elements include the offender's interpretation of the victim's actions as threatening or offensive, face-saving actions by the victim and offender, numerous opportunities to disengage from the anger-provoking situation, and a sort of mutual agreement among the parties in many cases that physical aggression is necessary to resolve the conflict. Notice how these ideas are directly expressed or implied in the following narrative accounts of two road rage incidents provided by the Las Vegas Metropolitan Police Department.

- The victim stated that he got into a traffic altercation with the suspect. The suspect continued to spit on the victim's vehicle and attempted to cut him off. Both subjects pulled into a parking lot. Both got out of their vehicles, and words were exchanged. The suspect hit the victim one time on the left side of the head. The victim fell to the ground. The suspect got into his car and left the area. The victim refused medical assistance and could identify the suspect if seen again (March 2004).

- The two drivers were involved in a traffic altercation. The driver of a Mercedes Benz stated that the driver of a Honda was continually swerving in front of him making numerous unsafe lane changes, cutting him off. The Mercedes driver stopped behind the Honda at a red light, exited his vehicle, and approached the Honda driver's window. He began asking the Honda driver why he was cutting him off when the Honda driver stated "you want to fight!" and began swinging closed fist punches at the Mercedes driver. In an attempt to defend himself, the Mercedes driver stated that he punched the Honda driver under the left eye, leaving a small cut. The drivers were the sole occupants of their vehicles. The Honda driver refused medical response. Due to conflicting stories, no charges were filed (March 2004).

Sexual Violence

Rape and sexual assaults are another context for interpersonal violence in U.S. society. Although it may seem odd to view these crimes as exhibiting particular rules of commission, a closer examination of these violent offenses reveals common behavioral patterns and interaction rituals involved in them. The fact that rapists and other sex offenders are often characterized as emotionally weak and immature men who want to dominate and control women is important because it tells us something about the typical pre-contact behavior, victim-selection factors, and the *modus operandi* underlying these offenses.

The term "sexual predator" is commonly used in the research literature to describe male sex offenders who commit multiple offenses of a sexual nature over an extended period of time. By calling them predators, the assumption is that these offenders engage in a wide variety of stalking and hunting activities to select their prey. Serial killers are often thought to epitomize this image of sexual predation. However, child molesters (pedophiles) who do not kill their victims also develop various strategies and action sequences to stalk and lure young children. Pedophiles who lack the social competence or interpersonal skills to gain the confidence of susceptible children may use voyeurism and child pornography as permanent or temporary alternatives to sexual molestation.

Available police data on incidents of rape and homicide suggest that lethal violence is extremely rare in sexual assaults. For example, there were about 95,000 rapes known to the police in 2004 and 36 homicides with rape as the primary motive or circumstance of the crime.[21] These numbers convert to an extremely low probability of fatal injuries in sexual assaults—a rate of about 1 fatality for every 2,600 known rapes. The low lethality of sexual assaults is explained by evolutionary psychologists as indicative of processes of sexual selection (e.g., low resource males use rape as a reproductive strategy).[22] However, an alternative explanation for this pattern is that strong and unambiguous normative rules are fully entrenched in U.S. society about the maximum thresholds of violence in situations of sexual assaults.[23] The relatively small number of these offenses provides some indirect evidence for both of these explanations.

Sexual assaults that occur in the context of dating relations are often a violation of the normative response sequences associated with consensual sexual behavior. In particular, within the context of normative dating rules and practices in the United States, the typical couple proceeds through successive stages of greater sexual intimacy.[24] This progression is terminated when one member is unwilling to go to the next stage. However, this normative process is violated in "date rape" situations because (1) the offense is motivated by the desire for power and control (rather than sexual intimacy) and/or (2) the offender misinterprets the victim's actions or intentions as consent for sexual intercourse. In either case, it is the violation of the rule of consent that underlies all sexual assault laws.

Street Muggings and Robbery

Interviews and ethnographical studies of armed robberies in action suggest that normative rules of conduct also underlie this type of street violence.[25] These rules or codes of the street involve the selection of crime targets, the *modus operandi*, and the routine action sequences associated with these offenses.

Similar to other offenders, available evidence reveals that street muggers select their particular targets on the basis of accessibility, the expected yield or attractiveness of the target, and the availability of protection or guardianship. Both seasoned and opportunistic street muggers canvas the immediate physical environment for potential targets, but their basis for target selection often differs. For example, opportunistic robbers, by definition, prefer easy and largely unguarded targets, whereas the seasoned mugger calculates more carefully to select targets that offer the maximum yield and lowest risks of resistance. Both types of robbers are qualitatively different from pickpockets, who use charm and stealth to achieve their financial goals.

Street muggers employ a diverse array of methods to make initial contact with their selected targets. Some muggers approach their targets in a face-forward and causal manner, asking them for directions, a cigarette light, or spare change before taking their money or other possessions. Others use a more abrupt and blitz-like attack, grabbing victims while passing by or jumping out of structures and pouncing on them.[26] Methods vary across contexts. Groups of offenders may more easily intimidate victims into submission by the threat of injury. In contrast, lone offenders are far more likely to use or threaten physical injury with lethal instruments (i.e., guns, knives) to control the retaliatory actions of their victims.

Both crime prevention manuals and the norms of street culture provide rules about appropriate conduct during a street mugging. Rules for robbery prevention tell potential victims to avoid particular places (especially at night), limit the carrying of valuables in public, travel with companions, and, if accosted by a criminal, comply by giving them money and valuables without hesitation.

Although far less explicit, the code of the street for robbery offers a complementary set of expectations and normative action patterns on how street muggings should be conducted and resolved. These robbery norms can be identified from offenders' descriptions of their "standard operating procedures" and the action patterns included in police narrative accounts of incidents of street muggings. Specific components of the rules of engagement associated with street mugging include the following:[27]

- Select drug dealers, prostitutes, and others involved in illegal behavior as mugging victims because they are less likely to report their victimization to the police.

- Use only enough physical force against the victim to achieve the prime objective of theft. Some muggers have been known to unload their guns prior to street muggings to insure that they do not kill or seriously injure the victim inadvertently in the heat of the moment.

- Announce the stickup with unarguable clarity and threaten dire consequences if the victim doesn't cooperate. Short, graphic, and stern pronouncements in a form such as, "This is a robbery, give me your money, and don't make any sudden moves or I'll blow your fucking head off!!!"

- Provide some assurance that the victim will not be physically injured if they cooperate. This assurance is abruptly communicated in the initial contact with the victim by statements such as, "This is a robbery, I just want your money, don't make it a murder."

- Keep the victim in check throughout the incident and while leaving the crime scene by creating a convincing illusion of impending death. This is most often accomplished by tough talk and unwavering clarity of the offender's willingness to kill the victim if they offer any resistance.

Although the rules of offending and appropriate behavior of the victim often lead to street robberies with few physical injuries to the victim, it is also true that these rules are breached in many robbery situations. In fact, nearly 1,000 victims were killed in robberies in the U.S. in 2004. Our review of narrative descriptions of street muggings also reveal many acts of largely gratuitous violence directed at the victim when this aggression appeared unnecessary for the commission of the robbery and the successful escape from the crime scene. Thus, normative rules and thresholds are evident in street muggings like other criminal offenses, but there is an assortment of individual and situational factors that may lead to the violation of these rules within particular crime incidents.

Summary

This chapter has tried to demonstrate the presence of implicit and explicit rules of engagement surrounding acts of street violence. Codes of the street provide a level of predictability when standard operating procedures are understood and followed by the participants in public encounters. The rules are different for fistfights, character contests, drive-by shootings, incidents of road rage, sexual assaults, and street muggings. Although the characteristics of the offenders are usually the same (predominantly male), there are diverse thresholds of appropriate behavior for various illegal acts, and the expected codes of conduct can be violated in particular situational contexts.

Notes

[1] Other comprehensive data sources for this quantitative analysis of incidents of physical assault include national crime victimization data (NCVS) and UCR-SHR data. Unfortunately, neither of these alternative data sources have complete coverage of all types of assault incidents (e.g., NCVS do not include homicides, UCR-SHR do not include incident-level data on offenders, victim, and offense attributes for simple assaults and aggravated assaults). The possibility of merging different types of data into the same file (SHR data on national homicides, NCVS for simple and aggravated assaults) raised serious questions about the comparability of the coverage areas and was therefore abandoned. Under these conditions, the best available source for conducting comparative analysis of different types of physical assaults across the same jurisdictions and time frame were the NIBRS data.

[2] NIBRS data for various time periods are available through the Inter-University Consortium for Political and Social Research (ICPSR) at the University of Michigan. The 2001 data were the most recent NIBRS data available through ICPSR at the time of this study. The codebook provides a detailed description of the methodology used to collect these data. We wish to thank Tom Zelenock at the National Archive of Criminal Justice Data at ICPSR for his assistance in constructing the computer code to read the NIBRS data used in this study.

[3] Given their coverage of only 20 states, an obvious question is the representativeness of NIBRS data to national trends. This question can be addressed, in part, by comparing offender, victim, and offense characteristics in national UCR data with NIBRS data. In general, these comparisons reveal similar trends across data sources in the modal profiles for each offender, victim, and offense characteristics. Most departures for particular variables exhibit differences in the range of 5 percent to 15 percent. For example, the proportion of murders involving males as offenders, male victims, strangers, or guns as the lethal weapon are anywhere between 5 and 15 percent lower in NIBRS data than trends reported in the Supplementary Homicide Reports. Given similarity of modal categories and small differences in the absolute magnitudes between categories in NIBRS and UCR data, we contend that NIBRS data in these 20 states can be considered sufficiently representative of national incidents of assaults reported to the police.

The biases associated with the reporting and recording of police data are well known and need not be discussed further here. Accordingly, our conclusions about the possibility of similarities and differences in the structural profiles and situational dynamics of different types of physical assaults are restricted to incidents of violence that are serious enough in terms of their injury and potential injury or public visibility (e.g., occur in public places or take place in the presence of third parties) to warrant the call for police action or direct observations by them. For a discussion of the strengths and limitations of various data sources on crime, see Clayton A. Mosher, Terance D. Miethe, and Dretha Phillips. 2002. *The Mismeasure of Crime.* Thousand Oaks, CA: Sage.

[4] For examples of the research literature on character contests and masculinity, see David F. Luckenbill. 1977. "Criminal Homicide as a Situated Transaction." *Social Problems* 25:177–178; Lonnie Athens. 1985. "Character Contests and Violent Criminal Conduct: A Critique." *Sociological Quarterly* 26:419–431; Gini R. Deibert and Terance D. Miethe. 2003. "Character Contests and Dispute-Related Offenses." *Deviant Behavior* 24:245–267; Kenneth Polk. 1994. *When Men Kill: Scenarios of Masculine Violence.* New York: Cambridge University Press; Elijah Anderson. 1999. *Code of the Street: Decency, Violence, and the Moral Life of the Inner City.* New York: W. W. Norton; Terance D. Miethe and Wendy C. Regoeczi. 2004. *Rethinking Homicide: Exploring the Structure and Process Underlying Deadly Situations.* Cambridge, UK: Cambridge University Press.

[5] For contrasting positions about the necessity of mutual agreements in character contests, see David F. Luckenbill. 1977. "Criminal Homicide as a Situated Transaction." *Social Problems* 25:177–178; Lonnie Athens. 1985. "Character Contests and Violent Criminal Conduct: A Critique." *Sociological Quarterly* 26:419–431.

[6] The phrase "the dozens" is thought to have derived from a slave era custom of selling sick or old slaves in lots of 12 because they were too weak or incapacitated to perform hard labor. Being sold as part of the "dozens" was considered the lowest possible insult. See Geneva Smitherman. 1994. *Black Talk: Words and Phrases from the Hood to the Amen Corner.* New York: Houghton Mifflin.

[7] Wikipedia Encyclopedia. "Playing the Dozens." http://en.wikipedia.org/wiki/Playing_the_dozens.

[8] See Geneva Smitherman. 1994. *Black Talk: Words and Phrases from the Hood to the Amen Corner.* New York: Houghton Mifflin.

[9] See Malcolm Klein. 1971. *Street Gangs and Street Workers.* Englewood Cliffs, NJ: Prentice-Hall; Walter B. Miller. 1975. *Violence by Youth Gangs and Youth Groups as a Crime Problem in Major American Cities.* Washington, DC: U.S. Department of Justice.

[10] William B. Sanders. 1994. *Gangbangs and Drive-Bys: Grounded Culture and Juvenile Gang Violence.* New York: Aldine de Gruyter, p. 66.

[11] For a discussion of these unreliable firearms and gangs, see Walter B. Miller. 1975. *Violence by Youth Gangs and Youth Groups as a Crime Problem in Major American Cities.* Washington, DC: U.S. Department of Justice.

The rules of "fair play" include the squaring off of opponents of equal size and rank, the lack of double-teaming opponents, no "sucker punching," and a mutual understanding of how much force to use in a fight and when the opponent is counted out. The rules of fair play may have been more symbolic than real in their actual use, but they nonetheless appear to have been followed historically in gang fights more than in current practices.

Compared to modern gang warfare, the typical "rumble" appeared to be more verbal than physical, involving extensive jawing and verbal banter with little direct physical contact. Fighting was limited to "square offs" between rival gang leaders or sporadic outbursts by members who were trying to increase their reps as tough guys. Almost inevitably, word of the possible rumble would be leaked to the legal authorities who would gather to prevent the group attack.

[12] One of the few empirical studies on this topic found that drive-by shootings represented about 41 percent of all gang-related assaults in San Diego in the late 1980s. See William B. Sanders. 1994. *Gangbangs and Drive-Bys: Grounded Culture and Juvenile Gang Violence.* New York: Aldine de Gruyter, p. 67. Drive-by shootings in this study were defined as situations in which a member of one gang drives a vehicle into a rival gang's area and shoots at someone. The author also uses the term "hit and run" tactic (p. 65). The number of drive-by shootings would increase dramatically if all incidents of discharge of firearms from within a vehicle or after a quick shot and exit were included in the definition, rather than limiting the definition to attacks against rival gang members or on the "turf" of others. For many residents of low income areas in large West Coast cities, gangbanging (i.e., fights among gang members) and drive-by shootings have become a relatively routine activity of everyday life.

[13] William B. Sanders. 1994. *Gangbangs and Drive-Bys: Grounded Culture and Juvenile Gang Violence.* New York: Aldine de Gruyter, p. 68.

[14] William Wilbanks. 1984. *Murder in Miami: An Analysis of Homicide Patterns and Trends in Dade County (Miami), Florida, 1917–1983.* Lantham, MD: University Press of America, p. 280.

[15] William Wilbanks. 1984. *Murder in Miami: An Analysis of Homicide Patterns and Trends in Dade County (Miami), Florida, 1917–1983.* Lantham, MD: University Press of America, p. 288.

[16] Incident summary from the St. Louis Homicide Project. For a discussion of this project, see Scott Decker, Carol W. Kohfeld, Richard Rosenfeld, and John Sprague. 1991. *St. Louis Homicide Project: Local Responses to a National Problem.* St. Louis: University of Missouri-St. Louis.

[17] Incident summary from the St. Louis Homicide Project.

[18] Las Vegas Police Department (LVPD) "Media Release." July 12, 1999.

[19] Several authors would disagree with this characterization of gang members. William Sanders, for example, alleges that many potential victims of drive-by shootings adopt public postures that are "slow to be mobilized" and a rather relaxed or "kicked-back" perspective when hanging out in public places. Being vigilant about one's personal safety during group leisure activities (e.g., dances, social gatherings) is often thought to put a damper on these situations and may be interpreted as being weak. See William B. Sanders. 1994. *Gangbangs and Drive-Bys: Grounded Culture and Juvenile Gang Violence.* New York: Aldine de Gruyter, p. 70.

[20] These data derive from over 10,000 Internet respondents who completed an online survey on the Web site for *RoadRagers.com.* Survey data are available for 2004 and 2001. This Web site has done other polls on road rage since 2000.

[21] Federal Bureau of Investigation (FBI). 2005. *Crime in the United States, 2004.* Uniform Crime Reports. Washington, DC: Government Printing Office.

[22] See Michael P. Ghiglieri. 1999. *The Dark Side of Man: Tracing the Origins of Male Violence.* Reading, MA: Perseus Books; Martin Daly and Margo Wilson. 1984. *Homicide.* New York: Aldine de Gruyter.

[23] Under all existing state laws, the maximum sentence for nonlethal sex offending is life imprisonment. The death penalty for rape was declared as excessive punishment under the Supreme Court ruling of *Coker v. Georgia* (1978). Given that the maximum penalty is life imprisonment for these offenses, deterrence theory would suggest that the low lethality of sex offending is attributed to the deterrent value of capital punishment for sexual homi-

cides. Based on this explanation, potential sexual homicide offenders are deterred from killing their victims, but not deterred from raping them, by the threat of capital punishment for committing acts of sexual homicide. However, this deterrence argument is contradicted by the fact that it would be in the best interest of the reasoning sex offender to kill their victim because it would decrease their risks of getting caught. It is for these reasons that the deterrent effect of criminal sanctions is not considered a strong explanation for the low lethality of sexual assaults.

[24] Previous research on patterns of sexual behavior provides ample support for this idea of a progression toward greater sexual intimacy. For example, Peter Bentler found that the types of heterosexual experiences formed a Guttman scale in which act A proceeded act B, act B proceeded act C, and continuing this sequence. In terms of actual sexual behaviors, the sequence involved the following behaviors: "continuous lip kissing for one minute," "light petting of the female [above clothing and above the waist] . . . ," "heavy petting [under the clothing] below the waist . . . ," "ventral-to-ventral intercourse," followed by "ventral-dorsal intercourse." For the complete listing of behavioral activities in this heterosexual inventory, see Peter M. Bentler. 1968. "Heterosexual Behavior." *Behavior Research and Therapy* 6(1):21–30.

[25] See Richard T. Wright and Scott H. Decker. 1997. *Armed Robbers in Action: Stickups and Street Culture.* Boston: Northeastern University Press.

[26] See Terance D. Miethe, Richard C. McCorkle, and Shelley J. Listwan. 2006. *Crime Profiles: The Anatomy of Dangerous Persons, Places, and Situations.* Los Angeles: Roxbury Publishing Company, p. 74.

[27] These rules are derived from our analysis of over 1,600 street robberies in Las Vegas over the last 5 years and previous studies of street robbery. See Richard T. Wright and Scott H. Decker. 1997. *Armed Robbers in Action: Stickups and Street Culture.* Boston: Northeastern University Press; David Luckenbill. 1981. "Generating Compliance: The Case of Robbery." *Urban Life* 10:25–46; R. Lejeune. 1977. "The Management of Mugging." *Urban Life* 6:123–148.

Domestic Violence

Violence in the private sphere has experienced enormous changes in legitimacy throughout different periods and cultures. Definitions of the term "domestic violence" vary within scholarly, legal, and popular sources, but most commonly refer to violence between intimate partners. For the purposes of this chapter, domestic violence is more inclusive, referring to all violence that takes place among familial and intimate (sexually involved) parties. Included in this conception of domestic violence are intimate partner abuse, child abuse, elderly abuse, and sibling violence.

PREVALENCE OF DOMESTIC VIOLENCE

There is no doubt that violence among intimates and family members is the most prevalent form of interpersonal aggression. Given the amount of time people spend with primary group members, it should not be surprising to learn that we are most often physically abused by those who presumably love us. From a criminal opportunity perspective, intimates and family members have the highest risks of physical victimization because of their high exposure to motivated offenders (e.g., they live in the same house or in close proximity) and their attractiveness as a victim (e.g., they are visible, accessible, and predictable in terms of their actions/reactions).

The ability to get accurate estimates of the prevalence of domestic violence is hampered by several obvious problems of underreporting and sampling bias. For example, many acts of interpersonal violence among intimates and family members are not reported to the police or in victim surveys because: the offense is considered a private matter; fear of reprisals for reporting; there is reconciliation between the parties; and/or the long historical legacy of social and legal tolerance of acts of domestic abuse.[1] Acts of domestic abuse that involve minor physical injuries, verbal abuse, sibling assaults, or physical neglect of children or elders are especially likely to be underreported. It is also the case that persons who agree to participate in a survey on domestic violence are probably different than those who don't want to be interviewed about this topic. Under these conditions, any estimates of the prevalence of domestic violence are likely to represent only a small fraction of these incidents.

Regardless of the limitations of any particular study or survey, previous research nonetheless paints a rather chilling picture of the prevalence of the various forms of domestic violence. In the case of intimate partner violence, surveys and official reports provide the following estimates of trends in the United States:

- An estimated 8.5 million incidents of intimate partner violence occur each year. The vast majority of these incidents involve female victims. Most of the assaults are relatively minor and consist of pushing, grabbing, shoving, slapping, and hitting. Most injuries involve scratches, bruises, and welts.[2]

- More than 1 million women and 371,000 men are stalked by intimate partners each year.[3]

- Intimate partner violence results in 1,300 deaths nationwide every year. About three-fourths of these victims are women.[4] Between 1976 and 2002, about 11 percent of all homicides were committed by intimates.[5]

- 29 percent of women and 22 percent of men had experienced some form of intimate partner violence (e.g., physical, sexual, or psychological abuse) during their lifetime.[6]

Child abuse involves maltreatment through acts of physical abuse, sexual abuse, emotional abuse, and/or medical neglect. National surveys from service agencies indicate that an estimated 1.5 million children experienced harm-causing abuse or neglect in 1993.[7] This survey also estimated that 2.8 million children were "at risk" of maltreatment. Nearly 3 million children were reported as abused or neglected in 1997.[8] An estimated 3 children die each day from abuse and neglect, resulting in about 1,100 deaths per year.[9] Aside from their direct victimization by child abuse, up to 10 million children witness some form of domestic violence annually.[10]

As a behavior that may easily cross over the line between "acceptable" corporal punishment and physical abuse, spanking remains a dominant form of parental discipline even in contemporary U.S. society. National survey data in 1999 indicates that over 40 percent of parents report that they spank or hit their children for disciplinary purposes.[11]

Elderly abuse is another form of domestic violence that has only recently attracted national attention. In 1975, elderly abuse gained attention from a British medical journal article that used the term "granny battering."[12] Since the mid-1970s and increasingly as the baby-boomer generation ages, elderly abuse has become an important issue in the study of domestic violence.

Estimates of the prevalence of elderly abuse vary widely. A study from 1996 suggests that over 500,000 elderly persons were abused that year.[13] Other studies suggest 2 million older adults are mistreated each year in the United States.[14] On average, figures suggest that the prevalence of elder abuse ranges between 1 and 5 percent.

One of the most underreported and neglected area of domestic violence involves sibling abuse. This type of abuse is not widely recognized by parents or others because it is often expected that siblings fight and engage in other forms of physical aggression. However, it is often the case that the most violent members within a family are the children. In fact, previous research studies have revealed the following trends about sibling violence:

- 42 percent of all children kicked, bit, or punched a sibling at least once in the past year.
- 40 percent of children hit their siblings with an object.
- 16 percent of children reported being "beaten up" by a sibling.
- About 1 percent of children were threatened with a knife or gun by a sibling.[15]

INTIMATE PARTNER VIOLENCE AND ITS RULES OF CONDUCT

The archetypal form of intimate partner abuse is male on female aggression commonly referred to as wife beating.[16] Most theoretical explanations of this behavior focus on aspects of control in marital relations, whereby men are attempting to exert control over their female partners.[17] Recent research has coined a new phrase, "patriarchal terrorism," to emphasize the historical context of husbands controlling and brutalizing their wives.[18] From this perspective, wife beating has been a legitimate means of controlling women throughout history because patriarchy has been the dominant social arrangement that dictates marriage structure in both Western and non-Western societies.[19] Under patriarchy, women are subjugated to the will of men, particularly in marital relationships.

Under the Western laws of antiquity, women were considered the property of their fathers and then their husbands. Several ancient civilizations had rules pertaining to the treatment of women. For instance, women under ancient Roman civil law could be bought or sold, as could children and slaves.[20] Women also had no social or legal standing during this period of time; they were not permitted to appear in court as a complainant. If a woman was victimized in any manner, the offense was considered to be against her husband or her father, who could pursue civil court remedies.[21]

Over the course of the next millennium (approximately 426 CE to 1215 CE), social order in Western civilization was dominated by the Catholic Church. Christian doctrines reinforced patriarchal arrangements whereby a husband was considered dominant over a wife.[22] English common law (dating from the thirteenth century) eliminated the language of wives as property. However, violence against wives was not only legitimate (i.e., socially acceptable form of behavior), but legal as well.

Limits on the magnitude of physical abuse of one's wife have been established through various legal and social norms. For example, the "rule of thumb" gave a husband the right to hit his wife with a stick no wider than his thumb.[23] Although there is no evidence of the codification of this principle in English law, this "rule of thumb" has nonetheless served as part of the folk wisdom surrounding what is "reasonable" in corporal punishment of wives throughout Western history.

By the nineteenth century, the United States had established case law that wife beating was legal as long as the intent was corrective and the punishment inflicted only temporary damage.[24] Only during brief periods between the 1800s and the 1940s was wife abuse addressed with any strong condemnation. It was not until the mid-1970s that domestic violence among intimate partners received widespread attention by the criminal justice system—largely at the insistence of the various women's political and social movements.[25] Under this changing social and legal context, the "rule of thumb" and related principles about legitimate forms of wife beating (e.g., striking the victim with an open hand, hitting less vulnerable body parts) were considered anachronistic and blatantly sexist.

For other regions of the modern world, however, there are both social norms and legal rules that legitimize wife beating and other forms of physical abuse against women. Table 6.1 provides some examples of the wide range of types of domestic violence against women that are permitted in other countries.[26]

The acceptance of wife beating is well established in Islamic law and culture. However, this practice is shrouded in much controversy concerning its use in a modern world. The foundation for wife beating within the *Shari'a* (Islamic law) derives from the *Qur'an* (the Muslim holy book) and its authorization for husbands to beat disobedient wives, the Prophet Muhammad's traditions (i.e., *hadith*), and other biographical material (*Sira*). The legitimacy of wife beating within this cultural context is intrinsically tied to a woman's subservient status in Islam and husbands' custodial control in Muslim society.

As true of other types of violence described in this book, wife beating in Muslim culture is regulated by rules of appropriate conduct. These rules of engagement involve how and when this type of physical aggression is administered.

Under the *Qur'an* (4:34), wife beating is considered a last resort or the final step in dealing with a rebellious or disobedient spouse. There is a specific progression of steps surrounding wife beating: (1) The husband is to verbally admonish her without anger, (2) if that fails, the husband is to sexually desert his wife (i.e., "distance her from the conjugal bed"),

Table 6.1   Rules of Legitimate Violence against Women by Men Around the World

In courts of law, the "honor defense" is legitimate in some Middle Eastern and Latin American countries, allowing fathers or husbands to walk away from murder. For example, husbands are often exonerated from killing an "unfaithful, disobedient or willful wife" on the grounds of "honor."

In 12 Latin American nations, a rapist can be exonerated if he offers to marry the victim and she accepts. In one country, Costa Rica, the rapist can be exonerated even if she refuses his offer. The family of the victim often pressures her to marry the rapist, which they believe restores the family's honor.

In India, more than 5,000 women are killed annually because their in-laws consider their dowries inadequate. Only a minuscule percentage of the murderers are ever criminally prosecuted.

Source: "The Intolerable Status Quo: Violence against Women and Girls." *The Progress of Nations 1997*. The United Nations (http://www.unicef.org/pon97/mainmenu.htm).

and (3) if both measures fail, the husband is exhorted to beat his wife.[27] Beatings that occur without prior warnings are a violation of these rules of engagement.

Muslim clerics and religious foundations have offered various interpretations of the "acceptable" nature and magnitude of wife beating. The permissible rules of conduct in "disciplining" the wife in accordance with the *Qur'an* and *Shari'a* law include the following:[28]

- "Wife beating must never be in exaggerated, blind anger, in order to avoid serious harm [to the woman]."
- "It is forbidden to beat her on the sensitive parts of her body, such as the face, breast, abdomen, and head. Instead, she should be beaten on the arms and legs."
- The rod [for beating] must not be stiff, but slim and lightweight so that no wounds, scars, or bruises are caused.

Despite the variety of relationships and contexts in which intimate violence can occur, there are some typical action patterns and behavioral sequences underlying physical assaults among intimate partners. Similar to other types of violence, arguments become more volatile among intimates when alcohol is present. However, few instances of intimate partner violence spontaneously erupt without any precursors. Most violent encounters begin with (1) verbal arguments that lead to common couple violence or (2) psychological abuse that leads to patriarchal terrorism.[29]

"Common couple violence" is a sporadic reaction to everyday problems.[30] Disagreements about independent friendships and activities, jealousy, infidelity, children, and money can all precipitate mutual violence when the arguments escalate. This violence is often considered legitimate and normative in families. Relatively few injuries are sustained during these arguments, and they are not likely to reach the level of serious violent encounters. Couples usually reconcile quickly without any involvement from legal authorities or social services.

When women are the offenders of lethal attacks against intimate partners, previous research suggests that these homicides have a well-defined behavioral profile. Major aspects of the behavioral sequences underlying these offenses include victim-precipitation (the male victim initiates the deadly encounter by using or threatening physical force) and self-defense (the female offender uses lethal force in response to this threat).[31]

NORMATIVE RULES FOR OTHER TYPES OF DOMESTIC VIOLENCE

Many of the social and legal norms surrounding intimate partner violence are also found within the context of other forms of domestic violence. Both normative proscriptions and prescriptions regulate and control the nature and magnitude of child abuse, elderly abuse, and sibling violence.

For much of recorded history, child abuse was not a meaningful concept. Parents have long been given exclusive power to control and regulate the behavior of their children in any manner they deem appropriate. Up until the last quarter of the twentieth century in the United States, there was widespread social and legal tolerance for various types of nonlethal methods of discipline and control of children. The standard operating rule throughout this history was "the ends (i.e., controlling potentially rebellious or wayward youth) justify the means."

The discovery and clinical recognition of the "battered child syndrome" by Henry Kempe and associates in the early 1960s was a critical event in changing both public perceptions and the legal treatment of child abuse. Mandatory reporting by educators and social service providers of suspected cases of child abuse was legally established to overcome the strong social norm of "minding one's own business." Even within this changing social and legal environment, however, most people are still unwilling to get involved when they witness a case of child abuse.[32]

The rules of permissible behavior concerning corporal punishment of children and its social acceptance have changed in the United States over the last half century. Survey data suggest that the proportion of parents who spank their children has decreased over time. The general rules of appropriate action when parents spank their children have also changed over time. For example, the method and severity of spanking has evolved from a "hickory stick," leather strap/belt, and paddling board that often drew blood or major swelling to an open-handed slap on the buttock, which is far less likely to produce injury. Spankings that involve particular physical instruments (e.g., coat hangers, sticks) directed at more sensitive body parts (e.g., head, chest) have become increasingly prohibited in law and practice. There also appears to be a growing recognition that spanking and other methods of corporal punishment of children should be used as a last resort. The placement of the problem child on "time out" and the denial of privileges for not being responsible are now considered by many to be the preferred types of parental discipline.

General norms and customs in U.S. society have long prescribed that the elderly be treated with dignity and respect. Social inhibitions against abusing the elderly are reinforced by criminal laws that mandate more severe punishment for crimes against these victims. Other than these protective rules, however, there are no normative rules in U.S. society concerning the permissible use of physical violence against the elderly. The only possible exception involves cases of "mercy killings" of a terminally ill spouse. In these situations, both the physical state of the victim (e.g., the victim is suffering from irreversible terminal pain) and the intent of the offender (e.g., the act was done to ease the victim's suffering rather than for personal gain) are fundamental conditions that determine the social and legal tolerance for these spousal killings.[33]

Sibling rivalry burgeoning into sibling violence dates back to the biblical story of Cain killing Abel. Sigmund Freud also explored the issue of sibling rivalry, arguing that competition causes older siblings to resent the birth of a new sibling. However, sibling violence rarely escalates to a homicide; most siblings stop fighting short of major injury.

The low level of injury surrounding sibling violence is attributable to a variety of factors, including immediate parental intervention before the disputes escalate and social conditioning in which children learn that excessive violence among siblings is negatively sanctioned. Within traditional childhood socialization practices, the standard operating norm involving conflict among siblings is the "no hurt" rule. Under this rule of permissible aggression, quarrels and disputes among siblings that involve verbal arguments and even yelling are considered within acceptable limits, but physical threats and injuries are not. The fact that sibling aggression is rarely associated with serious physical injury provides empirical evidence of this "no hurt" rule and the various internal and external control mechanisms used to regulate the nature and magnitude of violence in this context.

SUMMARY

Violence among family members and intimates is a common context for interpersonal violence. The types of domestic violence vary across cultures and historical settings. Similar to other types of violence, acts of intimate partner violence, child abuse, elder abuse, and sibling violence are structured by social and normative rules concerning their nature and gravity. These rules of permissible conduct are most evident in the "rule of thumb" and related principles in wife beating, the movement away from spanking as a primary method of parental discipline for children, and the "no hurt" rule associated with sibling aggression. Violation of the boundaries of violence established by these rules can lead to serious and lethal forms of interpersonal aggression within the context of domestic life.

Notes

[1] For a discussion of the reporting biases in official crime statistics and victimization surveys, see Clayton Mosher, Terance D. Miethe, and Dretha Phillips. 2002. *The Mismeasure of Crime*. Thousand Oaks, CA: Sage.

[2] P. Tjaden, and N. Thoennes. 2000. *Extent, Nature, and Consequences of Intimate Partner Violence: Findings from the National Violence Against Women Survey*. U.S. Department of Justice. Washington, DC: Government Printing Office. NCJ 181867.

[3] P. Tjaden, and N. Thoennes. 2000. *Extent, Nature, and Consequences of Intimate Partner Violence: Findings from the National Violence Against Women Survey*. U.S. Department of Justice. Washington, DC: Government Printing Office. NCJ 181867.

[4] See Centers for Disease Control and Prevention (CDC). 2003. *Costs of Intimate Partner Violence Against Women in the United States*. Atlanta, GA: CDC, National Center for Injury Prevention and Control; Terance D. Miethe and Wendy C. Regoeczi. 2004. *Rethinking Homicide: Exploring the Structure and Process Underlying Deadly Situations*. Cambridge, UK: Cambridge University Press.

[5] See James A. Fox and Marianne W. Zawitz. 2004. *Homicide Trends in the United States*. Washington, DC: Department of Justice. Available online at: http://www.ojp.usdoj.gov/bjs/homicide/homtrnd.htm#contents.

[6] A. L. Coker, K. E. Davis, I. Arias, S. Desai, M. Sanderson, H. M. Brandt, et al. 2002. "Physical and Mental Health Effects of Intimate Partner Violence for Men and Women." *American Journal of Preventive Medicine* 23(4):260–268.

[7] Third National Incident Study of Child Abuse and Neglect (NIS-3). 1993. National Center on Child Abuse and Neglect.

[8] Department of Health and Human Services, National Center on Child Abuse and Neglect. 1999. *Child Maltreatment 1997: Reports from the States to the National Child Abuse and Neglect Data System (NCANDS)*. Washington, DC: U.S. Government Printing Office.

[9] Department of Health and Human Services, Children's Bureau. 2000. *Child Maltreatment 1998: Reports from the States to the National Child Abuse and Neglect Data System (NCANDS)*. Washington, DC: U.S. Government Printing Office.

[10] See Bonnie E. Carlson. 1984. "Children's Observation of Interpersonal Violence." In A. R. Roberts (ed.), *Battered Women and Their Families*. New York: Springer, pp. 147–167; Murray A. Straus. 1992. *Children as Witnesses to Marital Violence: A Risk Factor for Lifelong Problems among a Nationally Representative Sample of American Men and Women*. Report of the Twenty-Third Ross Roundtable. Columbus, OH: Ross Laboratories.

[11] Deborah Daro. 1999. *Public Opinion and Behaviors Regarding Child Abuse Prevention: 1999 Survey*. Chicago: Prevent Child Abuse America Publications.

[12] See Daniel L. Swagerty, Paul Y. Takahashi, and Jonathan M. Evans. 1999. "Elder Mistreatment." *American Family Physician*. Available online at: http://www.aafp.org/afp/990515ap/2804.html.

[13] See The American Public Human Services Association. 1998. *The National Elderly Abuse Incident Study, Final Report*. Available online at: http://www.aoa.gov/eldfam/Elder_Rights/Elder_Abuse/ABuseReport_Full.pdf

[14] Swagerty et al. define mistreatment as "includes physical abuse and neglect, psychological abuse, financial exploitation and violation of rights." See Daniel L. Swagerty, Paul Y. Takahashi, and Jonathan M. Evan. 1999. "Elder Mistreatment." *American Family Physician*. Available online at: http://www.aafp.org/afp/990515ap/2804.html.

[15] These statistics about sibling violence are based on the National Family Violence Survey. See Murray A. Straus and Richard J. Gelles. 1990. *Family Violence in American Families: Risk Factors and Adaptations to Violence in 8,145 Families*. New Brunswick, NY: Transaction Publishers.

[16] See Michael P. Johnson and Kathleen J. Ferraro. 2000. "Research on Domestic Violence in the 1990s: Making Distinctions." *Journal of Marriage and the Family* 62:948–963.

[17] For a review of control based explanations of intimate partner violence, see Richard B. Felson and Steven F. Messner. 2000. "The Control Motive in Intimate Partner Violence." *Social Psychology Quarterly* 63:86–94.

[18] See Michael P. Johnson. 1995. "Patriarchal Terrorism and Common Couple Violence: Two Forms of Violence against Women." *Journal of Marriage and the Family* 57:283–294.

[19] The term "patriarchy" literally means father and is of Greek origin. When used to describe social organization, it labels an assumption of male innate superiority and the correspondent domination of all institutions and women in any given society. See Kristin L. Anderson and Debra Umberson. 2001. "Gendering Violence: Masculinity and Power in Men's Accounts of Domestic Violence." *Gender and Society* 15:358–380.

[20] For a thorough discussion of the historical contexts of violence, see Denise Kindschi Gosselin. 2005. "Intimate Partner Violence Against and By Women." In Alida V. Merlo and Joycelyn M. Pollock (eds.), *Women, Law and Social Control*, 2nd Edition. Boston: Pearson, pp. 170–187.

[21] See Denise Kindschi Gosselin. 2005. "Intimate Partner Violence Against and By Women." In Alida V. Merlo and Joycelyn M. Pollock (eds.), *Women, Law and Social Control*. 2nd Edition. Boston: Pearson, pp. 170–187.

[22] See Ephesians 5:22–24 for a passage regarding the status of wives. "Wives submit yourselves unto your own husbands, as unto the Lord. For the husband is the head of the wife, even as Christ is head of the Church: and he is the saviour of the body. Therefore, as the church is subject unto Christ, so let the wives be to their own husbands in everything" (Holy Bible, 1968, p. 1045), as quoted in Denise Kindschi Gosselin. 2005. "Intimate Partner Violence Against and By Women." In Alida V. Merlo and Joycelyn M. Pollock (eds.), *Women, Law and Social Control*. 2nd Edition. Boston: Pearson, pp. 171–172.

[23] For further discussion on the epistemology of the phrase see Christina Hoff Sommers. 1995. *Who Stole Feminism?: How Women Have Betrayed Women*. New York: Simon & Schuster; Henry A. Kelly. 1994. "Rule of Thumb and the Folklaw of the Husband's Stick." *Journal of Legal Education* 44:341–365. See also the Web sites: http://research.umbc.edu/~korenman/wmst/ruleofthumb.html and http://www.phrases.org.uk/meanings/307000.html.

[24] For a discussion of the two most cited cases regarding the legality of domestic violence in the 1800s, see *Bradley v. State* (1824) and *State v. Rhodes* (1868). Both are discussed at length in Elizabeth Pleck. 2001. "Domestic Tyranny: The Making of Social Policy Against Family Violence from Colonial Times to the Present." In C. Dalton and E. Schneider (eds.), *Battered Women and the Law*. New York: Foundation Press, pp. 10–17; see also Henry A. Kelly. 1994. "Rule of Thumb and the Folklaw of the Husband's Stick." *Journal of Legal Education* 44:341–365.

[25] See Jeffrey Fagan. 1996. "The Criminalization of Domestic Violence: Promises and Limits." Washington, DC: National Institute of Justice.

[26] See Charlotte Bunch. 1997. "The Intolerable Status Quo: Violence against Women and Girls." *The Progress of Nations 1997*. United Nations. Available online at: http://www.unicef.org/pon97/mainmenu.htm.

[27] See "Wife Beating in Islam." http:/answering-islam.org.uk/Silas/wife-beating.htm. Steven Stalinsky and Y. Yehoshua. 2004. "Muslim Clerics on the Religious Rulings Regarding Wife-Beating." Special Report No. 27. The Middle East Media Research Institute. Available online at: http:memri.org.

[28] See Sheikh Mustafa. *The Women of Islam*. Cited in Steven Stalinsky and Y. Yehoshua. 2004. "Muslim Clerics on the Religious Rulings Regarding Wife-Beating." Special Report No. 27. The Middle East Media Research Institute. Available online at: http: memri.org.

[29] See Michael P. Johnson and Kathleen J. Ferraro. 2000. "Research on Domestic Violence in the 1990s: Making Distinctions." *Journal of Marriage and the Family* 62:948–963.

[30] According to Johnson, 94 percent of perpetrators in common couple violence never become severely violent. See Michael P. Johnson. 1995. "Patriarchal Terrorism and Com-

mon Couple Violence: Two Forms of Violence against Women." *Journal of Marriage and the Family* 57:283–294.

[31] See Peter J. Benekos. 2005. "Women as Perpetrators of Murder." In Alida V. Merlo and Joycelyn M. Pollock (eds.), *Women, Law and Social Control.* 2nd Edition. Boston: Pearson, pp. 227–248.

[32] Deborah Daro. 1999. *Public Opinion and Behaviors Regarding Child Abuse Prevention: 1999 Survey.* Chicago: Prevent Child Abuse America Publications.

[33] Although it is difficult to identify normative rules and interaction rituals associated with elder abuse, previous research has recognized several important risk factors that increase the likelihood of an elderly person being abused. Those factors include "excessive physical and psychological demands associated with care-giving; advanced age, poor health, physical frailty and impaired activities of daily living (ADL) on the part of the care recipient; alcohol and other substance abuse by caregivers; the caregiver and care recipient living together; caregiver psychopathology; and a family history of abusive behavior." Depression and dementia also increase the risk of elderly abuse within a care-giving relationship. See Andrew C. Coyne. 2001. "The Relationship between Dementia and Elderly Abuse." *Geriatric Times.* Available online at: http://www.geriatrictimes.com/g010715.html.

Rules and Boundaries of Violence in Sporting Events

All amateur and professional sports are guided by rules that specify how to play the game. These rules define and regulate all aspects of the contest, including the time span, how points are scored and winners determined, and what penalties are assigned for violations of the rules of the game. In most contact sports (e.g., hockey, U.S. football, basketball), physically aggressive play is a crucial aspect of success and a normative expectation for the players.

As a way of controlling the nature and magnitude of sports violence, all sporting events have acceptable thresholds for aggressive play and assign penalties to teams, players, and even fans who violate the rules. For example, hockey players are given time in the penalty box for overly aggressive acts of high sticking, tripping, roughing, and/or boarding the opponent. Basketball uses the language of "fouls" (i.e., technical fouls, personal fouls) to designate illegal physical acts and to award free shots at the basket for those violations. Game misconduct penalties, ejections, and other disqualifications are penalties for some types of rule violations (e.g., throwing punches, bumping or hitting game officials, participation in bench-clearing brawls). Other types of agonistic behavior (e.g., threatening gestures, "trash talking") are common in various sporting events but do not necessarily elicit any official sanctions The penalty for unruly fans is removal from the arena or criminal charges, depending on the gravity of the physical misconduct (e.g., throwing objects at players or officials, fights among rival fans).

This chapter examines the rules of legitimate and illegitimate aggression in sporting events. It explores sports violence in general and within the context of specific types of sports (e.g., boxing, hockey, football, basketball, baseball, roller derby). Classic examples of extreme rule violation within each of these sporting activities are also provided. We begin with a brief discussion of the instrumental value of overt aggression and physical intimidation in contact and noncontact sports.

The Value of Aggression in Sports for Players and Fans

Sports have long provided a legitimate context for acts of interpersonal aggression. The "blood sports" of the early Olympic Games and the Roman circuses, jousting matches in Medieval Europe (and increasingly in jousting clubs in the United States),[1] and current athletic contests offer spoils to the victor and high entertainment value to the spectators. Similar to the early Greek and Roman audiences, fans of modern sporting events often go to these contests in anticipation of some violent encounter (e.g., crashes at auto races, brawls at baseball or basketball games). For many fans of professional hockey, the very definition of a "good game" involves a win by your team and a hearty, gloves-off, multi-participant brawl in the final period. Rick Morrissey, a sports columnist for the *Chicago Tribune*, made the following somewhat tongue-in-cheek comments after the 2006 winter Olympics.

> The reason the snowboard cross, a new event in these Olympics, was so popular was because there was a decent chance of a collision *every single race.* That's what we need to keep in mind when thinking about how to improve the Olympics. There needs to be violence, or at least the chance of mayhem.[2]

Although the rules of the game exert some control over violence in sports, aggression and/or the threat of aggression remain an integral part of these contests. Physical toughness is an instrumental value of team play in all contact sports, and many professional teams have specific players on their rosters whose primary role is that of an "enforcer." These players are usually fearless and intimidating characters whose physical toughness often outshines their athletic abilities. At strategic points in athletic contests (e.g., near the end of the game when the outcome is inevitable), they will enter the game and "send a message" by imposing some physical punishment on a particular opponent.

Violent acts in sports are highly ritualized and scripted events in several additional respects. Rules of violence in sports include definitions of adequate victim provocation, the appropriate behavioral responses to it, the selection of particular targets, and the role of teammates. For most sports, with the exception of using violence for self-defense, acts of aggression by players against fans are strictly prohibited and may result in criminal prosecutions. Similar proscriptions apply to the infliction of serious physical injury against fellow players.

Even in the world of noncontact sporting events (e.g., tennis, bowling, swimming, track and field, golf), acts of physical violence, trash talking, and aggressive gestures have become part of the game. For example, Tiger Woods has perfected the "fist pump" when making a crucial putt, and the stoic and reserved golf fans of the past have been increasingly replaced with a more vocal horde that screams exhortations to "be the man" or "in the hole." The "bad boys" of tennis (i.e., Ilie Nastase, Jimmy Conners, John McEnroe) were notorious for verbal and physical outbursts. Chest bumping, fist pumping, trash talking, and jersey popping are some of the aggressive gestures that have infiltrated many sports, even the previously sedate sport of professional bowling.[3]

Given the highly spirited nature of athletic competition and the availability of lethal weapons (e.g., baseball bats, hockey sticks, race cars), it is somewhat surprising that there are not more serious physical injuries in these contests. Our best explanation for the low rate of serious injuries is the moderating effect of the normative rules of appropriate conduct that are clearly established within each sport's culture. For example, hockey players learn as both spectators and players to immediately drop their sticks before fighting. To send a strong but nonlethal message, they also learn to drop their gloves so they can give their opponent a better punch with a fist! Similarly, a nearly automatic, conditioned response to the "brushback" pitch is for the batter to slam down his bat and make an aggressive step toward the pitcher. These are the rules of proper behavior that athletes learn through years of socialization as fans and players.

RULES OF APPROPRIATE VIOLENCE IN PARTICULAR SPORTS

The specific rules and routines surrounding violence within sports depend on the sporting event. The rules of appropriate violent behavior within the context of boxing, hockey, football, basketball, baseball, and roller derby are described below.

Boxing Rules and Routines

The earliest records of pugilism (i.e., boxing with a clenched fist) are found in the ancient civilizations of Egypt and Greece. Fistfighting was introduced in the twenty-third Olympiad (around 880 BC). Contestants fought entirely naked except for the cestus (heavy leather straps worn on the hands). Strict rules were followed in these contests, including no wrestling, grappling, kicking, or biting. The contest stopped when a fighter lost consciousness or raised his hand in acknowledgement of defeat.[4]

Pugilism in the Roman Empire involved more carnage between participants and was largely a blood sport in the gladiatorial games and circuses. During these events, the cestus was laced with metal to ensure injury to the opponent and an abundant flow of blood. Boxing matches were a staple of local fairs and religious festivals throughout Europe in the Middle Ages.

The various rules of fistfighting in American history derive from the English practice of prizefighting. Jack Broughton in the mid-eighteenth century was especially influential in establishing rules to make boxing matches both safer and fairer. His boxing rules of 1743 specified how the fight would begin (opponents would meet in the middle of a stage), proper conduct during the match ("adversaries could not be hit when down, or seized by the ham, the breeches, or any part below the waist"), and when the opponent was defeated (when he was unable to return to the middle of the square within 30 seconds). In 1867 these boxing codes were revised and published as "The Marquess of Queensberry Rules" (see table 7.1), which became the standard in the modern era of boxing.

The official "weigh in" and prefight media events have often served as a staging area for verbal banter and physical posturing among boxers in the modern era. Muhammad Ali was especially adept at verbal sparring and mocking his opponent in prefight press conferences. Whether used as

---

Table 7.1 Marquess of Queensberry Rules of Boxing

1. To be a fair stand-up boxing match in a 24-foot ring, or as near that size as practicable.

2. No wrestling or hugging allowed.

3. The rounds to be of three minutes' duration, and one minute's time between rounds.

4. If either man falls through weakness or otherwise, he must get up unassisted, 10 seconds to be allowed him to do so, the other man meanwhile to return to his corner, and when the fallen man is on his legs the round is to be resumed and continued until the three minutes have expired. If one man fails to come to the scratch in the 10 seconds allowed, it shall be in the power of the referee to give his award in favour of the other man.

5. A man hanging on the ropes in a helpless state, with his toes off the ground, shall be considered down.

6. No seconds or any other person to be allowed in the ring during the rounds.

7. Should the contest be stopped by any unavoidable interference, the referee to name the time and place as soon as possible for finishing the contest; so that the match must be won and lost, unless the backers of both men agree to draw the stakes.

8. The gloves to be fair-sized boxing gloves of the best quality and new.

9. Should a glove burst, or come off, it must be replaced to the referee's satisfaction.

10. A man on one knee is considered down and if struck is entitled to the stakes.

11. No shoes or boots with springs allowed.

12. The contest in all other respects to be governed by revised rules of the London Prize Ring.

a publicity stunt or indicative of real animosity, prefight events often degenerated into brief physical tussles and minor skirmishes among the fighters. The effects often spilled over to the conduct of the fighters in the actual boxing match.

Although there are both implicit and explicit rules about appropriate fighting behavior in boxing matches, recent history provides several dramatic cases of rule violations within these regulated contests. The most infamous examples of these rule violations in professional boxing include the following:

- Benny Paret died in a brutal professional boxing match with Emile Griffith in 1962. The boxers had fought each other on two other occasions, and this third fight was the grudge match. They did not like each other. Paret's prefight taunting about Griffith's alleged sexual orientation was a festering source of animosities. The fight lasted until the twelfth round when Paret was trapped on the ropes, too exhausted to flee, and was pummeled by Griffith until he collapsed to the canvas. Paret remained in a coma for 10 days before he died.

- Muhammad Ali adopted a fighting style that would later be called the "rope-a-dope" in his title bout with George Foreman in October of 1974. During the early rounds of the fight, Ali backed up against the ropes, cradled his arms in a tight defensive position, and used his gloves and arms to block Foreman's body shots. As Foreman expended his energy by delivering a barrage of body punches, Ali would occasionally go on a brief offensive flurry before reverting back to defensive posturing on the ropes. Ali ultimately knocked out the punched-out and leg weary Foreman in the eighth round. Many fans and sports commentators considered Ali's boxing style in this fight to be an implicit violation of the proper way to fight in a heavyweight boxing match.

- Mike Tyson bit Evander Holyfield on the ear twice during their heavyweight boxing match in 1997. Part of Holyfield's ear was bitten off and had to be surgically re-attached. Tyson was disqualified in the fight, fined $3 million, and his boxing license was revoked by the Nevada Athletic Commission. The brutality of this act added greatly to Tyson's nefarious reputation. Tyson also violated most standard rules of civility when he claimed in a press conference prior to a fight with Lennox Lewis that he would "eat his [Lewis'] children."

- During an April 8, 2006, welterweight title fight in Las Vegas, the boxing match turned into an "all-comers brawl" in the tenth round. Zab Judah hit Floyd Mayweather below the belt; as Mayweather staggered forward in agony, Judah hit him in the back of the head. Mayweather's uncle/trainer jumped into the ring after the two illegal blows. The referee had whistled a time out, so Mayweather was not automatically disqualified because of his trainer's actions and won the title. The Nevada Athletic Commission revoked the trainer's license for one year and fined him $200,000.[5]

There is a newer entry in fighting as a sporting event. In 2001, the Ultimate Fighting Championship (UFC) was launched as a combination martial arts and "no holds barred" form of fighting. It is permissible to hit an opponent who is down, to punch with fists, to kick, wrestle, apply chokeholds, and to hit with elbows. The brutal action "appeals to the video-game generation, especially the coveted 18- to 34-year-old male demographic."[6] Despite permitting actions barred in boxing, UFC claims no competitor has been seriously injured; in comparison, two boxers died from injuries suffered in the ring in 2005. The first UFC event in California was scheduled in a 17,000 seat arena; contestants fight in an eight-sided metal cage. Gate receipts, pay-per-view numbers, and cable telecasts attest to the growing popularity of UFC. Marc Ratner resigned as executive director of the Nevada State Athletic Commission to become a vice president of UFC.

> About 10 years ago I was on a panel with [U.S. Sen.] John McCain and I said we would not think of allowing or sanctioning UFC events in Nevada because it had no rules or regulations. It was like a barroom brawl. Now the UFC has referees, judges, rounds, and rules to make it a regulated, safe sport.

Professional Hockey

Observing several minutes of an ice hockey game reveals that it is a physically aggressive and demanding sport. As with other sports, the nature and level of violence is regulated by implicit and explicit rules of legitimate and illegitimate aggression. Physical acts of hockey aggression that are prohibited within the sport and result in various penalties (e.g., 2-minute minors, 5-minute majors, ejection, and possible suspension) are summarized in table 7.2.

Fights in hockey have components of both spontaneity and design. An especially vicious or cheap shot into the boards or an abrupt and overly forceful cross-check can precipitate a fight; they can also foment lingering resentment and a plan to retaliate at the slightest provocation the next time the two teams meet.

Although any player may instigate a fight, particular players often serve as the enforcers. These players may have marginal hockey skills; they are inserted at particular times for retaliatory and defensive purposes. Circumstances can range from a particularly hard check against a star player to frustration over a blow-out loss in the third period. Goalies and centers are often the team leaders, but as finesse players they usually lack the physical size and strength to defend themselves in scuffles and fights. All NHL teams have at least one player whose physical size and toughness make him the designated guardian and protector of his teammates.

Table 7.2   Examples of Prohibited Physical Acts in the National Hockey League

Boarding:
Any unnecessary contact with a player playing the puck on an obvious "icing" or "off-side" play that results in that player being knocked into the boards. When the opponent suffers face or head injuries, a game misconduct is imposed.

Butt-Ending:
The use of the end of the shaft of the stick in a jabbing motion. A double-minor penalty is assigned for attempts to butt-end an opponent, whereas a major penalty and a game misconduct are given to players who make physical contact in this manner. A match penalty is imposed on a player who injures an opponent as a result of a butt-end.

Cross-Checking:
A check rendered with both hands on the stick and the arms extended when the physical blow is delivered. A minor or major penalty, at the discretion of the referee, is imposed on a player who "cross-checks" an opponent.

Fisticuffs (Instigators):
An instigator is the player in an altercation who by his actions or demeanor demonstrates any/some of the following criteria: distance traveled; gloves off first; first punch thrown; menacing attitude or posture; verbal instigation or threats; conduct in retaliation to a prior game (or season) incident; obvious retribution for a previous incident in the game or season. Instigators are given an instigating minor penalty, a major for fighting, and a 10-minute misconduct.

Fisticuffs (Aggressors):
The aggressor in an altercation shall be the player who continues to throw punches in an attempt to inflict punishment on his opponent who is in a defenseless position or who is an unwilling combatant. A player must be deemed the aggressor when he continues throwing and landing punches in a further attempt to inflict punishment and/or injury on his opponent who is no longer in a position to defend himself. Aggressors of an altercation are given a major penalty for fighting and a game misconduct.

High Sticking:
A "high stick" is one that is carried above the height of the opponent's shoulders. A player is permitted accidental contact on an opponent if the act is committed as a normal windup or follow through of a shooting motion. A minor 2-minute penalty is given for high sticking without injury.

Kicking:
Any player who kicks or attempts to kick another player is given a match penalty (i.e., immediate suspension for the balance of the game, with a substitute player replacing the penalized player after five [5] minutes playing time has elapsed).

Slashing:
Slashing is the act of swinging a stick at an opponent, whether contact is made or not. Nonaggressive stick contact to the pants or front of the shin pads is not penalized as slashing. Slashing results in a 2-minute minor penalty.

Source: NHL Rule Book (2005–06): (http://www.nhl.com/hockeyu/rulebook)

The action sequences in hockey fights are highly ritualized and stereotyped. After the initial provocation, opponents square off, drop the gloves, and proceed to fight. This hockey fighting routine is called "drop the gloves and dance." During the fight, a common strategy is to grab the opponent's jersey and pull it over the back of the neck and arms to hinder the vision of the fighter and his ability to punch back. "Face washing" (running a sweaty glove over the face of an opponent) serves as both the initial provocation and a less physical form of fighting. Referees intervene in fights only when one player has a clear advantage and drives his opponent to the ice.

The "code of the ice" includes a strict prohibition against excessive aggression toward the goalie. As a result, goalies are far less likely than other players to be the victims of malicious attacks. Even in the full-blown melee, the goalie is rarely attacked by another player, unless he skates across the rink to battle the opposing goalie.

Over the last decade, physical injuries from hockey fights have gained national and international attention. Two incidents in the National Hockey League (NHL) clearly violated the normative thresholds of acceptable violence.[7]

- Marty McSorley of the Boston Bruins hit Vancouver Canuck Donald Brashear in the head with his stick during the 2000 season. For this offense, McSorley was criminally convicted of assault and given an 18-month term of probation; he was suspended from the NHL for one year but chose not to appeal for reinstatement after the suspension. As of 2006, McSorley was the third most penalized player in NHL history, with 3,381 minutes. While with the Oilers, he was the enforcer who protected Wayne Gretsky.

- Todd Bertuzzi of the Vancouver Canucks attacked Steve Moore of the Colorado Avalanche with a blind-side punch after trailing him for several seconds toward the end of a 9–2 victory by Colorado in 2004. Many believed Bertuzzi targeted Moore because of his hit (unpenalized) one month earlier on Markus Nasland, a star Canuck player, who was sidelined for three games with a concussion. The blow knocked Moore unconscious; his neck was broken in two places, and he suffered a concussion and facial lacerations. Bertuzzi was charged and pled guilty to assault causing bodily harm. He was suspended from the NHL without pay (losing approximately $500,000) for the remainder of the season and the playoffs. The team was fined $250,000. Bertuzzi was reinstated for the 2005 season.

American Football

Similar to hockey, U.S. football is another contact sport with established normative thresholds of legitimate violence that are reinforced by penalties for misconduct. The term "personal foul" is used to signify breaches of the rules of the game. Examples of personal fouls in football that are due to prohibited physical acts are included in table 7.3.

Football involves a great deal of physical contact. Physical fights are not permitted, but offensive and defensive linemen sometimes square off in brief skirmishes that test the limits of allowable contact, as do defensive backs and wide receivers. Quarterbacks and top running backs are rigorously protected by their offensive linemen against cheap shots and other physical attacks by bigger and stronger opponents. Most acts of physical violence within football are preempted by officials and teammates before they escalate into serious injuries.

The reputations of particular teams and games that involve intense rivalries are common triggering factors for excessive violence in football. In both professional and college football, certain teams are notorious for their aggressiveness, swagger, intimidation, and bravado on the field (e.g., Oakland Raiders, University of Miami Hurricanes, Florida State Seminoles). These reputations grow and intensify in the "big" games involving arch rivals, such as the 'Canes and the Seminoles. During pregame activities, minor skirmishes sometimes occur, particularly if the two teams share the same runway onto the field. Taunts and offensive gestures can precipitate aggressive encounters. Both injuries and ejections are rare in these pregame disturbances. Order is quickly restored, but the animosities flare up again and continue throughout the football game. Intrastate rivals in college football are especially likely to begin with these pregame character contests.

Table 7.3 Some Types of Personal Fouls in Professional Football

Offensive and Defensive Holding:
Restricting the movement of player by grabbing them.

Pass Interference:
Hitting the pass receiver before they have a chance to catch the football or pushing away the defender to catch a pass.

Roughing the Passer:
Hitting the quarterback after the ball has been thrown.

Face Mask:
Grabbing the face mask while tackling an opponent.

Unnecessary Roughness:
Hitting another player after the play is over or when they are out-of-bounds.

Spearing:
Using one's helmet to ram a player who is already on the ground.

Chop Block:
Blocking someone from behind and below the knees.

Taunting:
Throwing the ball at an opponent or other physical actions designed to embarrass or humiliate them.

A major basis for retaliatory aggression involves the payback for demeaning and disrespecting one's opponent. Most retaliation involves minor pushes in the back, a stiff arm to the head, the blind-side block, or the chop-block. Payback is usually exercised during or immediately after the initial taunting or dirty play and typically results in a personal foul on the retaliator for unnecessary roughness. However, for especially egregious acts of disrespect, some level of planning and collusion among teammates occurs to make sure that sufficient payback is imposed. In some cases, this retaliation may also involve displaced aggression against a key player for the opposition (e.g., the place kicker, punter, quarterback).

When compared over time, clear and abrupt acts of retaliatory violence in professional football have decreased in both frequency and gravity. It is exceptionally rare to witness deliberate and calculated instances of "head hunting" within modern football. Formal efforts to minimize retaliatory aggression include the establishment of penalties involving unsportsmanlike conduct for excessive celebrations and taunting. The increased use of fines and suspensions by the NFL is another formal means to preempt or deter excessive violence.

Basketball

Excessive violence in asketball occurs primarily in the context of the "hard foul," retaliatory actions for trash talking and other verbal provocation, and confrontations between players and fans. Fistfights and open brawls are relatively rare within this sport, but the potential for violent encounters is present in all games because of the close proximity of players and fans.

Many acts of excessive aggression in basketball are precipitated by a hard foul by an opponent. These fouls often occur during an unimpeded breakaway to the basket and result from an opponent's frustration due to an errant pass or other type of turnover. When these fouls serve as retaliation for previous actions against another teammate, they happen in a more diverse array of circumstances (e.g., a moving screen that creates hard contact, a well-placed forearm during a rebound). Particular players with reputations for tough play and being "enforcers" are often inserted into the game at strategic points to send a message.

Following the hard foul, the action often follows a defined sequence: the fouled party gets up quickly, begins physical retaliation, and is joined immediately in the fray by teammates. Coaches, referees, and other players intervene to prevent further aggression. Verbal exchanges and minor physical acts like shoving are the most common behavioral responses. The original combatants and players who leave the bench are usually fined and/or suspended.

Trash talking is another common type of agonistic behavior in professional basketball and pick-up games on the street. The mutual verbal banter often escalates into physical fights under conditions of performance differentials (e.g., one team or player is clearly outperforming another) and when the talk becomes excessively loud or offensive and a public affront to one's self-image. The joint combination of trash talking and physical posturing to show one's superiority is particularly likely to trigger a violent response. The ensuing fight is short in duration, often involving only a push or shove. The players are separated quickly, assessed personal fouls or technicals, and play resumes in a somewhat cautious but orderly manner.

Physical confrontations between basketball players and fans often occur while the players are leaving or entering the court. The precipitating event may be some especially caustic heckling or the throwing of an object at the player (e.g., dumping beer on them). Teammates and officials often prevent these acts from escalating to more serious encounters.

There are numerous examples of violent encounters in the National Basketball Association (NBA).

- During an NBA basketball game in 1977, Kermit Washington punched Rudy Tomjanovich with a bone-crushing blow to the face in a blind-side attack. Tomjanovich was running onto the court to assist a fellow teammate when Washington, catching a brief glimpse of a hard-charging opponent, turned around quickly, and then leveled him with one massive punch. Tomjanovich suffered major injuries to his face and skull that ultimately ended his playing career. Washington was fined $10,000 and suspended for 60 days by the NBA.

- During an NBA basketball game in the 1996–97 season, Dennis Rodman of the Chicago Bulls deliberately kicked a cameraman in the groin. Rodman had fallen under the basket and was rising to his feet when the incident occurred. Rodman was suspended by the NBA for 11 games. Other cases of excessive aggression in Rodman's history included the head-butting of the Chicago Bulls' Stacey King in December 1993, resulting in game suspension and $7,500 fine. He was also fined $5,000 for headbutting Utah's John Stockton in March 1994.

- During practice in December 1997, Latrell Sprewell (then with the Golden State Warriors) attacked his coach, P. J. Carlesimo. Carlesimo had presumably yelled at Sprewell to make better passes, and a brief argument ensued. When Carlesimo approached the player, Sprewell threatened to kill him. He then dragged Carlesimo to the ground by his throat and choked him for several seconds before teammates pulled Sprewell off the coach. Sprewell returned about 20 minutes later and punched Carlesimo, again requiring restraint by others present before he stopped. For his actions, Sprewell was suspended for 10 days without pay. The Warriors voided the remainder of his contract, which included $23.7 million over three years. The NBA expelled him from the league, but after arbitration his suspension was reduced to the remainder of the season.

- Near the end of a game between the Indiana Pacers and Detroit Pistons in November 2004, a brawl broke out between Pacer players
and Piston fans. The melee started with a hard foul of the Piston's
Ben Wallace by Ron Artest of the Pacers. Wallace then gave Artest a
hard two-handed shove to the upper chest and chin. Other players
became involved in the dispute, and it de-escalated. While Artest
was lying on the scorer's table, an unidentified fan near midcourt hit
Artest in the face with a cup filled with ice and a beverage. Artest
charged the stands toward the direction of the hurled beverage and
began hitting the fan he thought was the culprit. Videotape captured
other Pacer players entering the fray and hitting fans. Order was
finally restored after the 15-minute fracas. As the Pacer players left
the court for their dressing room, Piston fans continued to yell
obscenities and to pelt the players with cups, drinks, pretzels, pop-
corn, ice, and a folding chair. Ten people, including five Pacers and
five Pistons fans, were charged with misdemeanor assault. The most
serious penalty by the NBA was Artest's suspension for the remainder of the season. Stephen Jackson was suspended for 30 games,
and Jermaine O'Neal was given a 25-game suspension by the league.
- On January 18, 2006, Antonio Davis, then a forward for the New York
Knicks, jumped over the scorer's table and charged into the stands
during a game against the Chicago Bulls. He thought he saw his wife
being threatened by a fan. The NBA suspended him for five games.[8]

Regardless of whether these incidents involved fights among fellow
players or fans, the physical actions of the players were clearly beyond the
limits of legitimate violence within this sport. The brawl involving the Pacers and the Detroit fans has been especially important in sending a clear
message about the need for developing policies and practices for better
control and regulation of sports violence in the United States.

Baseball Violence

Compared to contact sports, baseball is a relatively tranquil and passive sport. The physical structure of baseball stadiums and the game itself
limits the opportunity for contact among rival teams and the fans. Baseball's reputation as the "national pastime" and the romanticized image of
the sport as a family activity further adds to its presumed benevolence.

Contrary to this stereotypical portrayal of professional baseball, the
reality is that this sport is similar to others in the use of aggression for
instrumental and expressive purposes. Especially for pitchers, the projection of the image of an intimidator or aggressive "flame thrower" has enormous instrumental value as a performance-enhancing strategy. For
example, Bob Gibson of the St. Louis Cardinals was one of the most dominant pitchers in the history of Major League Baseball. He was notorious in
the '60s and early '70s for moving batters off the plate by his aggressive

inside pitching. Among modern players, Roger Clemens and Randy Johnson are the most likely candidates for the labels of intimidating, aggressive, and incredibly successful pitchers.

Physical assaults and other types of excessive aggression in baseball are often restricted to the context of the "battery" (the batter, pitcher, and catcher) and aggressive slides. The original dispute is usually between two opposing players, but baseball violence seems to be almost always on the verge of escalating into a collective, bench-clearing event. Regardless of its individual or collective forms, baseball violence is similar to illegitimate aggression in other sports in that its action patterns and behavioral sequences are highly ritualized and routinized.

The most prevalent situational context for violence in baseball involves the "brushback" pitch or the "beanball." The timing of this activity and its recipient are often quite predictable. In fact, the typical precipitating actions for the "high and tight" pitch include (1) a previous history of animosity between the particular batter and pitcher, (2) excessive posing and a slow trot around the bases after hitting a home run, (3) retaliation for a hard slide that injured a teammate, and (4) anger-driven acts of frustration that occur when the game is a blowout and the pitcher is getting "lit up" by the opposing team.

The actions and reactions associated with the brushback pitch follow stereotypically standard sequences. Specifically, after some provocation, the pitcher initiates the interaction ritual by throwing a pitch perilously near a batter, whether a particular opponent or the batter following a home run.

The batter's response to the pitch dictates the subsequent course of action. Previous histories of antagonism and the nature of the brushback pitch (e.g., its speed and particular location) are situational factors that influence the batter's response pattern. Most players know when the brushback is coming and are often prepared to act either with indifference (e.g., by dropping their bats and walking directly to first base if hit) or to seek retaliation immediately.

For off-speed pitches thrown at less vulnerable body parts (e.g., lower back or butt), the normative response sequence often involves the dropping of the bat, a quick stare at the pitcher, followed by a slow jaunt down to first base and little additional conflict. Teammates immediately jump up in the dugout poised for physical combat, but they do not proceed on the field unless the batter takes aggressive action. The primary breach of this action sequence occurs when the pitcher does not remain passive but instead engages in verbal utterances, movement toward the batter, or other antagonistic gestures.

For fastballs at or near the batter's head (i.e., close or actual "beanings"), a violent encounter intensifies quickly. The batter immediately assumes an aggressive posture, shaking the bat at the rival pitcher, taking steps toward him, and releasing a verbal barrage. If intent on physical contact, the batter drops the bat and charges the mound. Coaches, umpires, and other players on the field and in the dugout immediately converge on the scene as dispute mediators and/or fellow combatants in the melee. The primary and secondary battles quickly terminate and order is restored. Whether or not an inside pitch or hit batter results in violent confrontation depends entirely on its context. Brawls and other retaliatory actions rarely follow the hitting of a batter in a close game and when the bases are loaded. Instead, the implicit rules of "aggressive pitching" are that this conduct occurs after sufficient provocation and when it will not materially affect the outcome of the game by the potential ejection of the key participants.

Wayward pitches are also differentially evaluated when they are viewed as deliberate or unintentional. When a pitch simply gets away from the pitcher and strikes a batter unintentionally, the pitcher typically hangs his head and avoids eye contact with the batter. The nonverbal cues signal to the batter, the umpire, and both benches that the hit batter was a mistake and not intentional, immediately de-escalating the situation and pre-empting further retaliation. In contrast, overt acts of staring at the hit batter, taking steps toward the batter, "jawing" at them, and/or hand movements symbolizing "bring it on" suggest some degree of intentionality and provides an unequivocal indication of the pitcher's willingness to fight.

Explicit rules against fighting exist in baseball, and this behavior is controlled to some extent by serious fines and suspensions. For example, in a game between the Washington Nationals and the New York Mets, five batters were hit by pitchers. A relief pitcher for the Nationals and the manager were ejected from the game and both were fined, as was an outfielder.[9] Heated verbal exchanges with umpires are often permitted before coaches are ceremonially "tossed" from the game. Minor altercations between opposing players (e.g., a push or shove, "chest bumping") are also tolerated within limits. However, the use of bats as weapons, attacking umpires, and physical confrontations with fans are clear violations of the normative thresholds for violence in this sport.

The most infamous cases of unacceptable violence in Major League Baseball involved conduct that clearly violated normative standards.

- Juan Marichal attacked catcher John Roseboro with his bat in a game between the Los Angeles Dodgers and San Francisco Giants in 1965. Marichal hit Roseboro at least twice on the top of the head, resulting in a two-inch cut that bled profusely. Roseboro was examined for a possible brain concussion but suffered no permanent injuries. Marichal was suspended for 9 days and fined $1,750. The incident occurred in the context of a late season pennant race between the arch rivals.

- In a successful attempt to score the winning run, Pete Rose barreled over catcher Ray Fosse in the twelfth inning of the 1970 All-Star game. Fosse's shoulder was separated in the collision and he never fully recovered from it. The play symbolized Rose's reputation as

"Charlie Hustle," but it was viewed by many as offensive and unsportsmanlike—particularly because it occurred within the context of a relatively meaningless All-Star game.

- After arguing a third strike call, Roberto Alomar of the Baltimore Orioles spit in the face of Umpire John Hirschbeck in a baseball game in 1996. Alomar was ejected from the game and later received a fine and suspension for his actions.

Rules of Violence in Roller Derby

While most of the sports discussed in this chapter are familiar to many readers, roller derby may not be as well known. A brief summary of the sport follows as well as the rules of violence underlying it.

Roller derby is a sport where two teams of five players roller skate against each other around an oval, sometimes banked, track in sixty-second intervals known as jams. Team positions consist of jammers and blockers. Each team has one jammer and four blockers who skate in a pack. The object of the game is for the jammers to skate around the pack once and then pass the four players of the opposite team in the pack a second time. For every opposing blocker the jammers pass the second time around the track, their team earns one point. However, getting around the pack is a brutal experience marked by tripping, elbowing, and shoving—all of which are tacitly condoned in the sport and celebrated by the fans.

Leo Seltzer invented Roller Derby in 1935. Seltzer's original vision was for it to be a clean sport with stiff fines for fighting. In 1936, a popular skater named Joe Laurney threw an opponent over the railing at a match in Louisville, Kentucky. Laurney was fined $25 and disqualified. The fans, however, heartily approved of this unexpected display of violence. Seltzer adapted the sport to please the audience, and fisticuffs were frequently staged. By 1937, the legacy of roller derby as a rough and violent spectacle on wheels was sealed with additional changes to the rules that added more skaters and more brutality.[10]

While roller derby's popularity waned by the 1980s, it has since been revitalized by all-women leagues in the twenty-first century, even spawning a reality series on cable television.[11] The first of these all-women leagues began in Austin, Texas, in 2001. By 2005, there were over forty all-women leagues nationwide.[12] One player and author described the new phenomenon of roller derby as being "set to a punk-rock sound track, full of fast-paced mayhem, and featuring women behaving very badly."[13]

The spirit of violence is still pervasive in this newest version of roller derby with some modifications. Previously, fights were carefully choreographed. Now, these brawls are practiced among teammates under unwritten fighting rules, such as making an effort to hit helmets and to avoid hitting the face. Teams take fierce names such as the *Putas del Fuego* and the *Hellcats*. Players take intimidating names like *Jenacide, Juana Beat'n, Tara Armov,* and *Venus D'Maulr*.

Perhaps more noteworthy than the rules of violent engagement in these bouts is the culture of violence that allows women a legitimate stage for aggression. By day, these women are lawyers, accountants, teachers, and mothers. By night they are scantily clad skating villains who revel in the opportunity to beat each other up. An Austin, Texas, based Rollergirl notes, "It's funny when new girls start they always ask, 'When is it okay to knock people down?' The answer is pretty much any time you want to."[14]

Other interviews with skaters show a similar interest in participating in violent behavior. In an interview with Alex Cohen, one roller derby girl from Los Angeles said she was raised to be a good girl, but roller derby provides "a great opportunity for sanctioned violence."[15] Veruca Assault of the Holy Rollers in Austin, Texas, explained, "It's a great way to relieve your stress; when you have a bad day you can always just beat the shit out of somebody. That's always nice."[16]

Hair pulling, cussing, and occasionally even spitting are all rewarded by audience and teammate cheers. The official rules vary from league to league, but sanctions for rule violations often match the offense itself. For instance, in the Lonestar Rollergirls League in Austin, Texas, minor penalties include arm wrestling, pillow fights, and a trip down spank alley (customers bring fly swatters to swat at the backsides of offenders as they skate by). A major penalty, which is assessed in rare occasions, calls for a player to sit in a penalty box during a 60-second jam.

Spectator Violence

Another context of violence in athletics that has normative boundaries involves the agonistic behaviors of fans. As spectators of sporting events, we are socialized to behave in particular ways depending on the context. Fans of sporting events involving young kids (e.g., tee-ball, soccer, Pop Warner football, little league baseball) are supposed to offer encouragement for all players on both teams and refrain from disparaging comments. In high school sports, a modicum of verbal banter directed at the opposing team is usually acceptable conduct. Fans of college and professional sports, in contrast, exercise far less civility in their verbal taunts and harassment of the opposition. In fact, some college and professional sports arenas are clearly hostile environments for opponents where local fans take considerable pride in this reputation.[17]

Regardless of the sport, there are strong normative proscriptions against physical contact between fans and the players. Fans are explicitly prohibited from throwing objects at players, running on the field or court during the sporting event, and from any physical battery of the athletes, under penalty of ejection and criminal prosecution. While violations of these normative rules are found throughout history, the low prevalence of physical attacks on athletes in these emotionally charged environments is also a testament to the power of normative regulations.

Situations of mutual assault among rival fans, however, are a more common occurrence in athletic events. While lethal violence has occurred in fights among rival fans, the more typical situation involves the exchange of verbal barrages and posturing with minor physical contact.[18] A brief lucid moment of self-reflection and/or intervention by bystanders often prevents these verbal exchanges from escalating into physical force.

Summary

Violence in sport is similar to violence in other contexts in that there are both legitimate and illegitimate forms of this behavior. When violence in sport exceeds the normative thresholds for the particular type of athletic event, it is often controlled by the penalties and suspensions of players. In contact sports (e.g., boxing, hockey, football), physical aggression is a crucial component required for success. Even the "kinder and gentler" noncontact sports (e.g., golf, tennis, bowling) now include verbal taunts and aggressive gestures.

Regardless of the particular sport, there are both implicit and explicit rules that regulate the nature and severity of violence. Unfortunately, because of a variety of individual and situational factors, there are numerous examples of players who have seriously breached the normative boundaries of violence. The particular inhibiting and facilitating conditions for violation of the rules of violence in sports and other contexts are described in the next chapter.

Notes

[1] Jousting is a growing sport; there are now more than 80 clubs in the United States and several training schools. Clubs hold regional events regularly, the most prominent of which takes place at Long's Peak Scottish/Irish Highland Festival in Estes Park, Colorado. More than 20 "knights" compete before crowds that total 75,000 over the four days of the festival. Jousting was originally a war game for knights preparing for battle. The participants wear more than 50 pounds of armor, and horses also wear armor. While participants enjoy the action, they often say the most fun is the crowd reaction. One participant recounted this story: his opponent's lance struck low on his shield, forcing the top edge up into his jaw, causing his helmet to fly off. Seeing the flying helmet, the crowd at first thought he had been beheaded and shouted in horror. Lisa M. McDivitt. 2006, March 29. "Jousting: A 10-foot Lance, Steel Armor, a Fast Horse." Columbia News Service, *Chicago Tribune*, p. 7.

[2] Rick Morrissey. 2006, February 26. "With Turin Taillights, Some Bright Ideas for Vancouver." *Chicago Tribune*, Sec. 7, p. 1.

[3] Aggressive behavior is also a major part of other sports. For example, stock car racing is not technically a contact sport, but aggressive driving and retaliatory "bumping" to take out other drivers is a basic norm of the sport. One of the major figures in this sport, the late Dale Earnhardt, was nicknamed "the intimidator" because of both his aggressive driving and his personal style. He usually dressed in black with dark sunglasses. Similar to the other sports examined here, there are clear normative rules in stock car racing (a proverbial "code of the road") that shapes how, when, where, and against whom retaliatory aggression should be implemented and directed.

[4] Another Greek fighting contest (pancratium) that combines boxing and wrestling was introduced in subsequent Olympiads. The fight began with a sparring match between the oppo-

nents and continued on the ground. Fighters were permitted to hit with fists, to kick, to break bones, to pull hair, and to strangle their opponents. For a fuller discussion of pugilism and the pancratium, see "Pugilism—Love To Know Article." Available online at: http://50.191encyclopedia,.orga/P/PU/PUGILISM.htm.

[5] Steve Springer. 2006, April 10. "Sorting Out Melee in Ring: Boxing Official Says Referee Right Not to Disqualify Mayweather," *Chicago Tribune*, Sec. 3, p. 3.

[6] Michael Hirsley. 2006, April 11. "New Competitor for Boxing." *Chicago Tribune*, Sec. 3, p. 5.

[7] "History of Criminal Charges on Ice." 2004, June 24. Canadian Press. Available online at: http://www.tsn.ca/nhl/news_story.asp?id=88823.

[8] Brian Hamilton. 2006, January 20. "Courting Trouble: League Suspends Davis for 5 Games." *Chicago Tribune*, Sec. 4, p. 1.

[9] Baseball Bits. 2006, April 11. "Plunkings Net Suspensions." *Chicago Tribune*, Sec. 3, p. 6.

[10] See Keith Coppage. 1999. *Roller Derby to Roller Jam: The Authorized Story of an Unauthorized Sport*. Santa Rosa, CA: Squarebooks.

[11] See A&E's *Rollergirls* Web site: http://www.aetv.com/rollergirls/index.jsp.

[12] See Alex Cohen's broadcast for *All Things Considered* on NPR: "Female Leagues Lead Roller Derby Revival." Available online at:
http://www.npr.org/templates/story/story.php?storyId=4817692.

[13] Tammy Oler. 2005. "Holy Rollers: Is Roller Derby the New Burlesque?" *Bitch* 30:29–34.

[14] See Austin Now's interview with Melissa Joulwan "Melicious" of The Hotrod Honeys. Available online at: http://www.klru.org/austinnow/archives/rollerderby/rollerderby.asp

[15] See Alex Cohen's broadcast for *All Things Considered* on NPR: "Female Leagues Lead Roller Derby Revival." Available online at:
http://www.npr.org/templates/story/story.php?storyId=4817692.

[16] See Michael Lee's interview with Texas Rollergirl Veruca Assault. "Veruca Assault, Roller Derby Queen." Available online at:
http://www.npr.org/templates/story/story.php?storyId=4050950.

[17] Hostile places include entire sport arenas and particular sections within them. Examples include "the dog pound" section of the stadium where the Cleveland Browns play professional football, the Oakland Raiders' end zone section called the "Black Hole," the "pit" (the basketball arena for the University of New Mexico Lobos), the "bleacher bums" on the third base side of the Chicago Cub's Wrigley Field, the student sections at most college campuses, and the location of particular college bands with histories of outrageous behavior (e.g., the Stanford University band, the University of Virginia band).

[18] Incidents of hooliganism (i.e., unruly and destructive behavior usually by groups of young people) are a major exception to this pattern and serve as a special case of mass melees among fans. Hooliganism is most commonly associated with European football clubs (called soccer in the U.S.). The most destructive incident occurred in 1985 at the European Cup game between Juventus (a club from Turin, Italy) and Liverpool F.C. that was held at Heysel Stadium in Brussels, Belgium. A total of 39 people were trampled or crushed to death when a retaining wall collapsed while Juventus fans were fleeing a large group of hooligans supporting Liverpool's team. As a consequence of this incident, Liverpool was banned for 6 years from participating in European football competitions. Another major tragedy associated with fan violence involved 13 people being trampled to death in a riot at the 2002 World Cup qualifying match between South Africa and Zimbabwe. The riot began after South Africa had take a 2–0 lead over the home team (the game was played in Harare, Zimbabwe).

Constraints, Facilitators, and the Ecology of Aggression

Our examination of interpersonal aggression has revealed several patterns about its social ecology (i.e., the offender, victim, and situational elements) and the rules and routines often associated with violent acts. First, most anger-provoking situations do not escalate into acts of physical injuries. Second, interpersonal violence takes place in a relatively small number of situational contexts involving a restricted range of people, places, and circumstances. Third, identifiable fixed-action sequences underlie the nature of interpersonal aggression in different contexts.

This chapter explores how normative rules operate in conjunction with various situational elements to produce the dominant ecological profiles for acts of interpersonal violence. These situational factors are important because they are associated with the two conditions necessary for aggressive behavior: motivation and opportunity. How these factors minimize and enhance the likelihood of serious injury in aggressive encounters and account for the social profile of dangerous persons, places, and situations are discussed below.

Basic Structural Impediments to Aggression

Acts of interpersonal violence require motivated offenders, victims, and opportunity. These basic, necessary conditions place immediate constraints on the likelihood and nature of aggression.

No matter the magnitude of anger or hostility, it is physically impossible for a motivated offender to commit an act of interpersonal violence without an available and accessible victim. It simply cannot be done.[1] Likewise, acts of retaliatory aggression are also not possible if the offended party is not motivated to retaliate. In short, both the likelihood and nature of interpersonal violence are constrained by physical opportunities and the degree of offender motivation.

These basic preemptive conditions explain much of the social ecology of interpersonal violence. To illustrate this point, consider the social profiles of the victims and offenders of physical assault and the situational context in which these acts occur.

Serious physical assaults in the United States are extremely patterned in the structural profiles of offender, victim, and situational attributes. Most homicides known to the police are represented by a relatively small number of distinct combinations of individual and offense characteristics.[2] These dominant profiles include characteristics associated with domestic violence (i.e., situations involving male adult offenders assaulting adult female acquaintances or spouses in the home) and disputes among male acquaintances of the same age and race.

Although numerous theories have been developed to account for the nature and distribution of interpersonal violence, the dominant contexts for these offenses is easily explained by the basic conditions of motivation and opportunity. Specifically, people spend far more time with family members and others who have similar demographic characteristics (e.g., persons of the same age and same race) because U.S. society remains highly segregated. Coupled with the greater interaction among primary group members is the increased exposure to various anger-provoking circumstances that derive from these intimate relationships and personal histories. Under these conditions of multiple sources of offender motivation and opportunity, it should not be surprising that attacks among primary group members within or near the home are the primary contexts for serious physical assaults that require police intervention.

The joint impact of motivation and opportunity also explains why some particular combinations of individual and offense attributes are rarely observed in serious physical assaults. For example, assaults among strangers rarely occur in the victim's home, and these particular incidents are exceptionally uncommon in interracial attacks and/or those involving female offenders. These violent situations are uncommon because (1) strangers are not often invited to spend time in or near someone else's home, (2) other family members provide protection in the home from attacks by strangers, and (3) racial segregation and gender stratification diminishes further the opportunity for home-specific violent encounters.

As discussed in chapter 7, the basic physical structure of human interaction in many athletic contests also affects the motivating stimuli and opportunity for violence in sports. For example, most fights in baseball begin with the battery—the pitcher, catcher, and opposing batter. This is the primary context for baseball fights because it (1) provides a direct forum for anger-provoking actions and (2) offers the immediate physical opportunity to retaliate. Opposing outfielders rarely initiate baseball brawls because these players have little opportunity for personal contact throughout the game. Physical distance and limited opportunity for personal contact also diminish the chances of fights among hockey goalies.

Opportunity and motivation are the basic prerequisites for interpersonal aggression. However, even when a person has sufficient motivation for physical violence and the opportunity to engage in such behavior, other regulatory factors control the magnitude of the aggression and the specific target. Checks and balances on physical aggression are addressed below.

WHY ARE PHYSICAL INJURIES RARE IN AGGRESSIVE ACTS?

Physical aggression and its consequences are a bit of an enigma in U.S. society. As described in previous chapters, values that embrace violence are widely espoused in various media sources (e.g., television, film, music). Within some low-income areas of large cities and particular social groups (e.g., young males), physical violence is an expected and demanded response to threatening situations.[3] Yet, if physical violence is a cultural expectation, then why do most anger-provoking situations end without serious or lethal injuries?

It is our contention that acts of serious physical violence are relatively rare even within the most violent segments of U.S. society because there are various normative rules and other social constraints that limit the amount of physical injuries in aggressive situations. These constraints derive from socialization experiences, internal mechanisms of avoidance and self-control, and the external threat of legal sanction.

Socialization Experiences

Socialization involves the joint processes of the internalization and institutionalization of patterns of behavior. Members of a society are properly socialized when they have learned the normative rules of appropriate conduct, internalize them as personal preferences, and apply them to their behavior in everyday life.

The typical American is inundated with images of violence and its appropriate uses. Most of us have also had direct experiences with aggressive behavior, usually in the context of fights with siblings or classmates in school. Early childhood and adolescent experiences provide both positive and negative information about the cognitive and physical elements of aggressive behavior. These socialization experiences form the basis for learning how to act aggressively and how to control its use across different contexts.

Based on these direct and vicarious experiences with violence, humans internalize various scripts on aggressive situations that are subsequently triggered by external cues. For learning and social cognition theorists, these scripts offer cognitive road maps for anticipating how particular violent situations will play out. It is these shared scripts of anticipated action that are really the normative rules of engagement and disengagement in violent situations. These rules tell us how to fight, when to fight, when to retreat, and how to anticipate the reactions of others to situational cues.

From this basic theoretical perspective, one obvious explanation for the low level of injury in most aggressive situations is that people are socialized in various ways to preempt their violent actions and reactions. These preemptive actions derive from basic normative rules in interaction rituals and other social proscriptions.

The folk wisdoms and informal principles that represent nonviolent messages include advice and encouragement for "picking your battles wisely," "discretion is the better part of valor," and numerous dicta about being tolerant and non-retaliatory (e.g., "taking the higher road [by walking away]," developing a "tough skin," "taking it like a man," "turning the other cheek," and "rolling with the punches"). Principles of fair play, norms of reciprocity, and street jargon about "watching the back" of friends and family members also minimize the likelihood of grievances escalating into incidents with serious physical consequences. However, these basic principles are only effective in de-escalating potentially violent situations when both parties subscribe to the same normative standards.

Another important component of one's socialization experiences is learning the "right" and "wrong" way to initiate an argument or disputes. A sure-fired way of escalating a grievance is by "getting in one's face," "getting loud," "talking shit," and taking these aggressive actions in a public place. In contrast, the "right" way to initiate grievance proceedings to minimize its misinterpretation as a personal affront or "fighting words" is to use a dispassionate tone and to remove the subsequent verbal discussion from the immediate stage of public scrutiny. Taking a nonconfrontational approach, while possibly escalating the level of anger in some cases, is often an effective means of diffusing even the most volatile situations.

Avoidance and Internal Self-Controls

Mammals avoid many aggressive situations by flight, and the same type of reactions can prevent the escalation of violence when confronted with human aggression. Humans also have the capacity for self-reflection and to monitor their own behavior. This ability for internal self-control allows humans to decide when "fighting words" deserve a retaliatory response and when anger-provoking situations are best ignored or treated through nonphysical means.

Most incidents of potentially violent encounters are immediately circumvented by avoidance behaviors and the unwillingness of one party to agree to participate physically in the conflict situation.[4] This is especially true in potential road rage situations that are preempted by one driver's refusal to engage in mutual combat. The same preemptive reactions regulate situations involving verbal taunting in sports or other contexts from developing into violent encounters. Similar to other animals, humans avoid emerging violent situations out of fear of physical injury, previous conditioning, and the recognition that physical confrontation in many contexts is simply not worth the risks.

The avoidance of conflict situations often reflects higher levels of self-control. Persons with these traits are, by definition, more likely to reflect on their behavior, exercise greater rationality in their decision making, and exhibit low levels of impulsivity. Persons with high self-control may have greater ability to simply ignore minor verbal or physical threats to one's social status or reputation. Enhanced self-control may also enable reasoning offenders to use their cognitive skills to interpret anger-provoking stimuli and to design an appropriate, measured response.

Through the dual processes of cognitive rehearsal and internal self-control, many potentially violent situations are quickly diffused before they escalate. Both the initial aggressor and his/her target may thwart physical confrontations through the use of nonviolent methods of dispute resolution (e.g., avoidance behavior, verbal exchanges, defensive posturing). These alternative methods are less likely to produce injury. Self-control is a major inhibiting factor that may minimize injuries in all types of aggressive situations, including acts of gratuitous and displaced aggression.[5]

External Controls from Legal Sanctions

The threat of legal sanction for willfully injuring another person is a primary source of external control that may impede the escalation of violent situations. The threat of legal punishment is assumed to reduce violent inclinations when societal reaction (i.e., punishment) is swift, severe, and certain.

When used to explain the nonviolent conclusion of most dangerous situations, deterrence theory argues that personal desires to inflict serious injuries on antagonists and other particular targets are held in check and curtailed by the threat of severe punishment. The deterrence doctrine predicts that most violent encounters will be resolved through nonphysical force because the risks of legal sanction for inflicting physical injuries exceed the subjective benefits from these actions.

Previous research on the deterrent effect of punishments, however, questions the crime-inhibiting influence of legal sanctions for violent offenses because of the nature of these offenses.[6] Specifically, these offenses are often viewed as impulsive, spontaneous acts done in the heat of passion (i.e., noninstrumental crimes of rage and anger). Given that people in these particular situations are unable to think about the consequences of their actions, it is often assumed that acts of physical violence are the least likely offenses to be deterred by the threat of legal sanctions.

Critics of the applicability of the deterrence effect for violent offenses, however, often fail to recognize the level of planning, calculation, and/or rationality that underlies even spontaneous outbursts of violence. In fact, there is ample evidence that some level of rational reflection of consequences is found among nearly all offenders, violent or otherwise.[7] This alternative view supports our contention that external sources of social control like criminal penalties may be a major contributory factor in the nonphysical resolution of most anger-provoking situations.

FACILITATING FACTORS IN SERIOUS AND LETHAL AGGRESSION

Our examination of the social ecology of physical assaults indicated that criminal offenses involving the threat of serious injury or lethal violence are extremely patterned in terms of their offender, victim, and offense attributes. Most of these serious offenses occur in the context of domestic violence and public disputes among males. The key task for criminologists is to explain these patterns of dangerous persons, places, and situations.

Our explanation for the causes and social distribution of serious physical assaults involves elements of both norm violation (when violence exceeds its socially acceptable limits in particular contexts) and normative compliance (when serious violence is the expected and demanded cultural response). Various facilitating conditions for serious aggressive acts that represent norm violations and compliance are described below.

Normative Violations vs. Normative Compliance

Depending on its context, physical violence resulting in serious injury to its victims may be a viewed as either an act of normative compliance or deviant behavior. Under most macro-cultural theories of criminal behavior, acts of serious physical injuries are considered a violation of normative rules of fair play or a deviant adaptation to achieve goals through illegitimate institutional means.[8] For most subcultural theories, however, serious acts of interpersonal violence may be viewed as normative compliance to a "code of the street" or another subcultural value system in which violence is the expected, tolerated, or demanded response to threatening situations.[9]

The distinction between normative and deviant violence is important because it helps identify how and to what extent various facilitating factors influence the expression of serious aggression. These facilitating factors include individual predispositions toward violence, dangerous places, enabling hardware or instruments, and the role of third parties and bystanders.

Individual Propensities toward Violence

Regardless of its origins (e.g., harsh and inconsistent parental discipline, low impulse control, chemical imbalances), previous research on the arrest trajectories of juvenile and adult offenders suggest clear individual differences in the propensity toward violence. Some juveniles persist and others desist in their criminal behavior over the life course.[10] Low self-control is often identified as a major causal factor in explaining the age-crime curve (i.e., the increased rates of criminal behavior during adolescence, peaking in the mid 20s, and decreasing thereafter) and the persistence of criminal behavior among particular people over the life course.

Individuals with a high propensity toward violence represent only a minority of offenders within all segments of society. The collective tolerance for serial acts of aggression varies across geographical context. In middle-class America, acts of persistent violent offending are considered deviant conduct that is often treated with harsh criminal sanctions (e.g., juvenile certification as adults, long prison sentences). Within large, urban, low-income neighborhoods, the habitually violent offender may be equally feared but often operates with greater immunity against legal prosecution.

Gender is a powerful correlate of violent propensity, both in isolation and in combination with social class, age, and race. Regardless of whether serious aggression represents normatively appropriate or deviant conduct, males predominate as both offenders and victims in acts of physical violence. The crime-producing effect of gender is usually attributed to attempts to maintain, defend, or assert one's masculine identity. Threats to masculinity are especially salient risk factors for physical violence among young, low-income, and minority males who lack access to conventional means of demonstrating one's social status (e.g., having a high paying job, educational advancement). Character contests and other ritualized violent confrontations serve as a public forum to assert one's masculinity and to build a "bad ass" reputation so others will not mess with you. It is within this context that physical violence is both normative and functional behavior.

Some authors claim girls are growing more physically aggressive as traditional expectations about feminine behavior change and girls become attracted to the power of assertive physicality. Social and cultural factors have glamorized violence, and physical aggression is more frequently seen as an acceptable way for girls to work out their anger and frustrations.[11] Powerpuff girls fight on television, and movies have gun-wielding heroines (*Lara Croft, Tomb Raider; Charlie's Angels*), lethal female protagonists (*Kill Bill*), and women prize fighters (*Million Dollar Baby*). Movies like *Mean Girls* and *Thirteen* chronicle the heartless and mean-spirited treatment teenage girls can dish out.

The provisions of Title IX in 1975 mandated that education systems provide girls an equal opportunity to participate in sports. In 1970, one in twenty-seven high school girls played a varsity sport; by 2002 it was one in three. In 1970 the ratio of boys to girls playing a varsity sport was 35 to 1. In 2002, four million boys and three million girls played varsity sports: a ratio of 1.33 to 1.[12]

> Girls are getting physical and learning the very positive message that
> their bodies can be physically powerful in ways that are not sexual.
> These very positive changes in girls result from unleashing them from

the traditional bonds of femininity and are evident in assertiveness, participation in sports, and active rather than passive psychological coping strategies.[13]

Some believe these changes have caused an increase in violent interactions involving girls. Mike Males uses government statistics to refute that contention.[14] In terms of the focus of this book, these cultural developments affect the socialization process of girls, changing the structural obstacles that previously might have barred access to the same normative rules of violence for boys.

Deborah Prothrow-Stith and Howard Spivak find that media violence is the major contributing factor in violence becoming more acceptable for girls.

> The changes in girls' behavior have followed the last decade and a half of media portrayals of female superheroes beating people up and getting beaten up just as male superheroes do—the feminization of the superhero. The other risk factors for violence—poverty, witnessing and victimization, alcohol and other drug use, and availability of guns—have not changed differentially for boys and girls. No other changes in a risk factor are as dramatic as the shift toward violence in the images of women and girls in the media that has occurred over the last two decades.[15]

In their book, *Sugar and Spice and No Longer Nice: How We Can Stop Girls' Violence*, Prothrow-Stith and Spivak talk about one of the authors attending a church service where the minister referred to the "love of violence as a religion, with rituals, celebrations, tools of the trade, mythology, and a significant following."[16] They thought the analogy was very useful to explain why people enjoy watching portrayals of characters on television or in the movies exacting violent revenge. "The problem is that in this society violence equals power; violence is admired and glamorized. It is the superheroes' successful solution for a problem—the ultimate strategy."[17] They find that the risk factors and reasons for violence are now the same for boys and girls.

> The cycle of violence (exposing children to violence increases their risk for involvement in violence later in life) applies to girls as well as boys. And for girls, just as is the case for boys, fighting is a frightening indication that social and cultural norms (this society's apparent love of violence) and media portrayals of these norms (the glamorization of violence) are the problem. Equating power with violence sets the stage for everyone, *including girls*, to use violence to gain power and control over a situation.[18]

Dangerous Places

Just as individuals vary in their histories of violence, so do neighborhoods and other physical locations. The tempo, pace, rhythm, physical ambience, and the characteristics of inhabitants contribute to the relative dangerousness of different places. The language of "hot spots" is often used to describe these dangerous physical locations.[19] Other terms used to describe both the social and physical elements of these dangerous places include "micro environments" and "domains."[20]

The social and physical properties of particular settings both enable and constrain the nature and magnitude of violent offenses. In fact, criminal opportunity theory suggests that the relative dangerousness of particular physical locations (e.g., the home, the street, bars, schools, work settings) is a product of their proximity and exposure to motivated offenders, the attractiveness of the crime target (i.e., visibility, accessibility, subjective utility, expected yield), and the level of protection or guardianship of the potential victim. Specific examples of how some places facilitate and impede the escalation of physical violence are described below.

The Home.   The home of the victim or offender has structural features that contribute to its attractiveness as a location for serious and lethal violence. Homes are facilitative places for interpersonal violence because they are bounded physical structures where legal rules and social norms of privacy limit public scrutiny and outside intrusion.[21] Familiarity with the victim's behavior in a variety of different contexts, histories of previous conflict with primary group members in the offender's household, the greater amount of time spent with family members and intimate partners within the home, and the knowledge of the location of various weapons in the dwelling further contribute to the home as a premier location for violent behavior. When the victim is an intruder in one's home, there are both legal and social norms that justify, and thereby also facilitate, the use of serious and lethal physical force for purposes of self-defense.

There are some constraints on the use of physical force in disputes within the home of the victim or offender. In particular, other household members are likely to intervene in physical disputes among family members and intimate partners that occur within the home. Presumably, feelings of affection toward other family members and intimate partners should also constrain and minimize the likelihood of serious injuries in disputes among loved ones. However, one-fourth of all homicides involve family members and intimate partners, and the vast majority of domestic violence homicides occur within the home. The facilitative effect of the home environment is greater than its constraining influence on the severity of interpersonal violence.[22]

Streets and Bars.   Streets and drinking establishments, especially at night, are a common physical context for physical assaults. These places facilitate violence through the characteristics of their inhabitants (e.g., primarily young males), the presence of alcohol that may impede judgment or provide "liquid courage," and the presentation of a public forum for the demonstration of masculinity. Character contests that derive from threats to masculinity, perceived sexual entitlements, and jealousy are far more likely in these types of physical settings, which involve both a relevant peer group and a social audience. Specific street corners and particular bars may also attract certain customers because of their reputations as being tough or rowdy places.

Constraints on the dangerousness of particular street locations and drinking establishments are imposed through environmental design and various types of target-hardening strategies. Most nightclubs in urban areas, for example, have bouncers who remove unruly customers and maintain some semblance of order. Electronic surveillance equipment is also installed in strategic locations to serve as a visual deterrent for serious misconduct. Police patrol practices, in particular "hot spots," provide further constraints on physical violence. However, in many cases, these social control efforts provide minimal reductions in the dangerousness of particular areas and, when they are effective, often just displace aggression to other nearby locations (e.g., fights occur in parking lots outside the nightclub rather than inside it).

Schools and Work Settings. Both schools and work settings are physically bounded environments that involve extensive interactions with similarly situated others (e.g., classmates, coworkers). Competition among rivals and the prevalence of these mutual interactions increase the risks of conflict in these environments.

Highly publicized incidents of school shootings (e.g., Columbine High School) and workplace violence have increased policy efforts to minimize the risks of physical assaults in these social environments. Increased private security and added technology (e.g., the use of metal detectors) have been the common response to violence in these settings. Peer counseling and mediation have also been instituted in both environments as a preemptive strategy. Similar to other public settings (e.g., bars and streets), social control efforts have constrained the opportunity for physical violence. Nonetheless, these places remain highly facilitative contexts for violent encounters because of their basic structural features (i.e., the concentration of similarly situated people makes them primary staging areas for physical displays of masculine competitiveness).

Facilitating Hardware

There are nearly an infinite number of ways to inflict serious and lethal injuries in assault situations. Wooden clubs and rocks were the weapon of choice in prehistoric times, whereas swords, knives, and metal-laced clubs became the fashionable weaponry in the Dark and Middle Ages. Firearms are now the primary weapon of lethal assaults in contemporary American society.[23]

Facilitative hardware for the commission of physical assaults involves any object that is visible, accessible, and readily usable. Many ordinary household objects (e.g., kitchen knives, ice picks, bottles, hammers, bricks, baseball bats) are widely accessible and available weapons that require little skill to inflict serious injuries. However, by requiring direct physical contact with the other person, injuries from these weapons may be easily circumvented by evasive movements or strength differentials between the antagonists.

Compared to other weaponry, firearms are especially facilitative hardware for serious assaults because they are widely available, require no direct physical contact between the parties, cause severe and lethal injuries to their victims, and neutralize any strength differentials. However, firearms may also impede the escalation of physical aggression in several ways. For example, the mere brandishing of a firearm at the beginning of a volatile situation may provide an immediate cue for the opponent to withdraw and to desist from aggressive actions.[24] Some previous research has also concluded that greater civilian firearm ownership serves as a general deterrent for various predatory crimes (i.e., potential criminals are inhibited or constrained from physical attacks when they believe that citizens are armed with firearms).[25] Under these conditions, firearms both facilitate and constrain the escalation of interpersonal disputes.

The Role of Third Parties and Bystanders

Many violent situations in public places occur in the presence of bystanders and third parties (e.g., friends, relatives). Depending on the interpersonal relationships among these people, the presence of others may either facilitate or impede the escalation of physical violence. The defense of a third party is often a triggering event in violent encounters. Even when third parties are not present in the particular situation, the offender's perceptions of the anticipated reactions of "significant others" affects their likely response to various anger-provoking stimuli.

The primary means by which third parties and bystanders facilitate physical aggression is through their actions and their inactions. For many street fights involving young males, other people in the vicinity often serve as "cheerleaders" who encourage the escalation of the violent encounter through verbal taunts and various physical behaviors (e.g., pushing the parties toward each other, blocking retreat routes, supplying a weapon). Inactivity from bystanders may also be interpreted as tacit approval for physical aggression in this setting. In order to "save face" among their peers and friends, many young males may feel compelled to escalate the level of violence in public disputes—even when they are not necessarily predisposed to acting aggressively. In hindsight, many violent offenders claim that they basically "had to do it" because of the social pressure to maintain one's reputation or status.

As a constraining factor in aggressive situations, third parties and bystanders reduce the likelihood of escalation through direct intervention. After a brief verbal or minor physical scuffle, significant others often will become directly involved in the fracas and restrain their friends from further activity. Immediate calls for help by other friends or summons for police assistance are other ways in which third parties are sources of de-escalation. Normative rules (like "minding your own business") often discourage the direct involvement of bystanders in these public disputes, but there are numerous examples of good Samaritans who intervene to prevent further injuries.

Drug and Alcohol Abuse

Similar to other situational factors, drug and alcohol abuse by the victim, offender, or both parties may both facilitate and constrain the escalation of violent encounters. As an inhibiting factor, substance abuse may impede one's cognitive ability to process anger-provoking stimuli (e.g., being too drunk to recognize that others are threatening or insulting you). It may also impair one's physical ability to retaliate even if the cues are perceived.

Drug and alcohol abuse, however, are more typically viewed as facilitators of aggression for several reasons. In particular, alcohol is often dubbed "liquid courage" because it impedes rational judgment and enables its abuser to resort to verbal and physical actions that may depart from normative rules of proper conduct. Both the drunken brawl among persons similarly situated and the individual drunkard who provokes another into physical attacks through verbally abusive and caustic behavior are the stereotypical image of how substance abuse facilitates acts of interpersonal violence. The fact that the majority of homicides involve alcohol abuse by one or both parties provides strong evidence of the relative power of substance abuse as a facilitator rather than inhibitor of interpersonal violence.[26]

Cultural Conflict and Normative Ambiguity

The final set of situational factors that facilitate acts of interpersonal violence involves the variety of mixed and conflicting messages that humans receive and interpret on a daily basis about the normative appropriateness of violence. The cultural conflict that derives from mixed messages and normative ambiguity is most clearly represented in Elijah Anderson's discussion of the context-specific differences in attitudes and behavior when being "decent folk" versus "street." This normative ambiguity is a central feature of contemporary U.S. life across various social groups and contexts.

Major "gray areas" concerning what are the appropriate interaction rituals and normative routines facilitate various types of aggressive behavior. In situations of cultural conflict, the distinction between violence due to normative compliance and violence as deviant behavior is largely meaningless. We hope several examples will illustrate this point.

Consider whether interpersonal violence is an appropriate or inappropriate response by adolescent males for purposes of self-defense. When a young male is under imminent and immediate threat of serious injury or loss of life, both the legal and normative codes of modern U.S. society would clearly justify self-defense responses up to and including lethal force. However, do the proper normative rules about how much violence is acceptable change if the initial threat is less imminent, involves nonlethal actions, or the victim is operating under an entirely preemptive strategy? Under these alternative conditions, lethal violence would not be legally justified in any current jurisdiction, but its social acceptability would vary substantially. Juveniles and young adults in such a normatively ambiguous context could easily draw on some particular rule and principle to justify their use of physical force in any situational context.

Another situation marked by normative ambiguity is drug trafficking. During the 1980s, many urban areas experienced alarming levels of lethal violence in the context of drug trafficking (especially crack cocaine). Killings involved dealers, rival dealers, and buyers. However, once the normative rules of drug dealing had been established (e.g., territories established, recognition that all parties will be armed with guns), the level of lethal violence associated with illegal drug transactions declined.[27] Under this interpretation, the establishment of clear operating rules about street-level drug transactions provided a normative constraint on the escalation of violence in this context.

Normative ambiguity also provides an explanation for the continuation of domestic violence in modern society. Although legal protection for abused spouses and children has improved considerably in the last three decades, patriarchal normative beliefs about male sovereignty still provide a facilitating context for violent situations. Similarly, "talk" about the value of nonviolent solutions to problems often fails to stand up to the reality of anger, frustration, and alternative messages provided by peers, family members, and mass media that endorse violence as a legitimate normative response to threatening situations. Our mixed cultural messages about physical aggression are more likely to facilitate and encourage the use of interpersonal violence.

SUMMARY

Interpersonal violence is guided by normative rules of appropriate conduct and is enabled and constrained by a variety of individual and situational factors. We have argued that acts of serious physical violence are relatively rare even within the most violent segments of U.S. society because of the operation of various normative rules and other social constraints that limit the amount of physical injuries in aggressive situations. These constraints derive from socialization experiences, internal mechanisms of avoidance and self-control, and the external threat of legal sanction. In contrast, serious physical assaults are facilitated by differences in an individual's propensity toward violence, the structural properties of particular places, the availability of weapons, the presence of a social audience, and the presence of normative ambiguity.

The joint contribution of these constraining and facilitating factors helps explain the low level of physical injury in assault situations and the social ecology of interpersonal violence. Depending on its social context, physical aggression may represent either normative compliance to expected behavioral patterns or a deviant adaptation to the frustration and strains of everyday life.

Notes

[1] This is also true when other people are not available as targets for displaced aggression. For some types of anger-provoking cues (e.g., frustration, jealousy, revenge, infidelity, "mad dogging," or "grilling"), offenders may resort to alternative forms of aggression (e.g., self-inflicted aggression, "irritability" aggression directed at inanimate objects) as an immediate response to the provocation. These particular aggressive reactions are especially likely when the original source of the frustration and other human targets are not readily accessible and available. Without a target for its expression, the likelihood of anger-elicited aggression will dissipate over time.

[2] For empirical evidence of the level of situational clustering in homicide, see Terance D. Miethe and Wendy C. Regoeczi. 2004. *Rethinking Homicide: Exploring the Structure and Process Underlying Deadly Situations*. Cambridge, UK: Cambridge University Press. These authors show that the majority of homicides in the U.S. over the last thirty years occur in a relatively small number of situational contexts.

[3] Elijah Anderson. 1999. *Code of the Street: Decency, Violence, and the Moral Life of the Inner City*. New York: W. W. Norton.

[4] Research on the sequential dynamics of character contests suggests that these violent situations occur when there is a mutual agreement among the parties that violence is the appropriate way of "saving face." However, serious injuries may still result from situations in which one of the parties refuses to participate and is injured in an attempt to escape or disengage. Our major point here is that when one party is able to withdraw quickly from the violent situation, the possibility of physical injury will be diminished considerably.

[5] The concept of self-control is the major causal factor in various theories of criminality. For the most comprehensive treatment of self-control in this context, see Michael R. Gottfredson and Travis Hirschi. 1990. *A General Theory of Crime*. Stanford, CA: Stanford University Press.

[6] See William J. Chambliss. 1967. "Types of Deviance and the Effectiveness of Legal Sanctions." *Wisconsin Law Review* Summer:703–719; Jack P. Gibbs. 1975. *Crime, Punishment, and Deterrence*. New York: Elsevier; William C. Bailey and Ruth D. Peterson. 1999. "Capital Punishment, Homicide, and Deterrence." In M. Dwayne Smith and Margaret A. Zahn (eds.), *Homicide: A Sourcebook of Social Research*. Thousand Oaks, CA: Sage, pp. 257–276.

[7] The best illustration of the rationality of presumably impulsive acts involves the theft behavior of kleptomaniacs. By definition, kleptomaniacs have an uncontrollable desire to steal. However, if their behavior is resistant to external threats of legal sanction, why is it that most kleptomaniacs only steal at particular times and, especially, when security officers are not within plain view? Previous theories and research using a symbolic interactionist's framework contend that humans engage in reflective appraisals before they act in particular situations. The idea that humans think before they act provides further support for the possible deterrent effect of legal sanctions for minimizing the severity of victim injury in all anger-provoking situations.

[8] This perspective is best represented by Robert Merton's anomie theory and the micro-level extensions of this theory associated with Robert Agnew's general strain theory. Under the original formulation, violent behavior is a deviant adaptation that emanates from the frustration of being unable to achieve the cultural goals of material success through legitimate, institutionalized means. At the individual level of analysis, the inability to achieve posi-

tively valued goals, the loss of positive stimuli, and the exposure to negative stimuli from the outside environment are different sources of strain. According to this theory, strain that results from negative treatment by others leads to increased anger and frustration which, in turn, may lead to physical aggression or other criminal activity. For a complete description of these theories, see Robert Agnew. 1992. "Foundation for a General Strain Theory of Crime and Delinquency." *Criminology* 30(1):47–87; Robert Agnew. 1997. "The Nature and Determinants of Strain: Another Look at Durkheim and Merton." In Robert Agnew and Nikos Passas (eds.), *The Future of Anomie Theory*. Boston: Northeastern University Press, pp. 27–51; George B. Vold, Thomas J. Bernard, and Jeffrey B. Snipes. 1998. *Theoretical Criminology*. 4th Edition. New York: Oxford University Press.

[9] Subcultural theories that fall within this perspective include the work of Wolfgang and Ferracuti on "the subculture of violence," Harvey's notion of "a subculture of exasperation," and Anderson's "code of the street" (see chapter 2). Each of these formulations suggests that violence reflects normative compliance to prevailing conditions of daily life within particular groups and socially disadvantaged neighborhoods in large urban areas. See Marvin Wolfgang and Franco Ferracuti. 1967. *The Subculture of Violence: Toward an Integrated Theory in Criminology*. London: Tavistock; William B. Harvey. 1986. "Homicide among Young Black Adults: Life in the Subculture of Exasperation." In Darnell F. Hawkins (ed.), *Homicide among Black Americans*. Lanham, MD: University Press of America, pp. 153–171; Elijah Anderson. 1999. *Code of the Street: Decency, Violence, and the Moral Life of the Inner City*. New York: W. W. Norton.

[10] See Terri Moffitt. 1993. "Life-Course-Persistent and Adolescent-Limited Antisocial Behavior: A Developmental Taxonomy." *Psychological Review* 100:674–701; Terri Moffitt, Avshalom Caspi, Honalee Harrington, and Barry J. Milne. 2002. "Males on the Life-Course-Persistent and Adolescence-Limited Antisocial Pathways: Follow-up at Age 26 Years." *Development and Psychopathology* 14:139–157; Robert J. Sampson and John H. Laub. 2003. "Life-Course Desisters? Trajectories of Crime among Delinquent Boys Followed to Age 70." *Criminology* 41(3):301–340.

[11] Laura Ciolkowski. 2005, February 19. "An Expert Looks at Aggression in Girls." *Chicago Tribune*, Sec. 14, p. 5

[12] James Garbarino. 2006. *See Jane Hit: Why Girls Are Growing More Violent and What We Can Do about It*. New York: Penguin, p. 79.

[13] Ibid., p. 17.

[14] Laura Ciolkowski. 2005, February 19. "An Expert Looks at Aggression in Girls." *Chicago Tribune*, Sec. 14, p. 5

[15] Deborah Prothrow-Stith and Howard R. Spivak. 2006. *Sugar and Spice and No Longer Nice: How We Can Stop Girls' Violence*. San Francisco: Jossey-Bass, pp. 80–81.

[16] Ibid., p. 82.

[17] Ibid., p. 81.

[18] Ibid., p. 32.

[19] See Lawrence W. Sherman, Patrick R. Gartin, and Michael E. Buerger. 1989. "Hot Spots of Predatory Crime: Routine Activities and the Criminology of Place." *Criminology* 27:27–55.

[20] See R. N. Davidson. 1989. "Micro-Environments of Violence." In D. Evans and D. Herbert (eds.), *The Geography of Crime*. London: Routledge, pp. 59–85; James P. Lynch. 1987. "Routine Activity and Victimization at Work." *Journal of Quantitative Criminology* 3:283–300; Terance D. Miethe and Robert F. Meier. 1994. *Crime and Its Social Context: Toward an Integrated Theory of Offenders, Victims, and Situations*. Albany: State University of New York Press.

[21] The "discovery" of child abuse and domestic violence in the last half century has increased public awareness of these problems and increased legal policies for possible deterrence (e.g., mandatory arrest policies for domestic violence). Unfortunately, physical abuse within the home by family members continues with wide immunity in the United States and other countries. Among several countries of the world (e.g., Muslim countries of the Middle East and Southwestern Asia), husbands are still permitted to use lethal punishment

against their wives in cases of infidelity because of the failure of courts to prosecute these cases and the offering of monetary compensation to the victims' families.

[22] Analysis of the FBI's Supplemental Homicide Reports for the 1990s indicates that about one-fourth of homicides without missing data on the victim-offender relationship involved the killing of family members or intimate partners. See Terance D. Miethe and Wendy C. Regoeczi. 2004. *Rethinking Homicide: Exploring the Structure and Process Underlying Deadly Situations.* Cambridge, UK: Cambridge University Press.

[23] See Terance D. Miethe and Wendy C. Regoeczi. 2004. *Rethinking Homicide: Exploring the Structure and Process Underlying Deadly Situations.* Cambridge, UK: Cambridge University Press.

[24] An alternative view is that the presence of a weapon serves as a situational cue that elicits aggressive responses. See Leonard Berkowitz and A. LePage. 1967. "Weapons as Aggression-Eliciting Stimuli." *Journal of Personality and Social Psychology* 7:202–207.

[25] See Gary Kleck. 1991. *Point Blank: Guns and Violence in America.* Hawthorne, NY: Aldine de Gruyter.

[26] For a review of the empirical research on substance abuse and violent offending, see Robert Nash Parker and Linda Rebhun. 1995. *Alcohol and Homicide: A Deadly Combination of Two American Traditions.* Albany: State University of New York Press; Kathleen Auerhahn and Robert Nash Parker. 1999. "Drugs, Alcohol, and Homicide." In M. Dwayne Smith and Margaret A. Zahn (eds.), *Studying and Preventing Homicide: Issues and Challenges.* Thousand Oaks, CA: Sage, pp. 97–114.

[27] Alternative explanations for this pattern of decreased lethal violence in the context of drug trafficking include (1) the effectiveness of law enforcement in eliminating the most dangerous and violent dealers or (2) the death through homicide of the most dangerous and violent drug dealers. However, given market mechanisms of supply-demand and the readily available supply of other dealers to take the place of a rival dealer, we think that the change in the rules of engagement in drug dealing is an equally plausible and, in some ways, a better explanation for the decreased violence of illegal drug transactions.

The Control of
Physical Aggression

We have explored many examples to demonstrate that the onset and commission of acts of interpersonal violence are highly regulated by normative rules of appropriate conduct. If situations of interpersonal violence are so rule-bound and patterned, knowledge of their basic structural features and the fixed-action sequences underlying them should be especially important in the development of realistic strategies for the reduction of physical violence.

A wide range of antiviolence programs and policies have been implemented to control interpersonal violence. These programs have involved various neurophysiological approaches, social opportunity restructuring, deterrence, and anger-management therapies. After reviewing current approaches to the prevention of interpersonal violence, this final chapter explores what is lacking in all of these policies and programs.

We argue that existing violence preventatives do not acknowledge that violence and aggression is normative and rule-bound behavior. However, just because violence is normative does not mean that the norms that regulate violent encounters cannot be changed. In fact, these norms already are changing, and nonviolent encounters continue to evolve as the dominant means for dispute resolution. By addressing the sources of both offender motivation and criminal opportunity, our alternative intervention strategy focuses on changing the normative rules of violence and the situational facilitators and constraints that help regulate these behavioral patterns.

CURRENT INTERVENTION AND PREVENTION PRACTICES

Crime control policies have been directed at both aspects of criminality and at crime itself. Deterrence, incapacitation, and rehabilitation are crime control strategies that focus on the sources of criminal motivation and the differential propensity for particular social groups and individuals to engage in criminal behavior. Policies associated with the reduction of the physical opportunity for criminal acts include efforts at environmental redesign and situational crime prevention programs.

Traditional Methods of Controlling Individual Propensities

A wide variety of social control and social betterment measures have been proposed and used to reduce risks of interpersonal violence for individuals. Biologically-based theories and research have increased our understanding of the nature of the physiological response to anger-provoking stimuli. Various social psychological theories describe the learning of violent behavior through behavioral modeling and vicarious learning. Subcultural theories provide explanations for the social distribution of interpersonal violence and its disproportionate distribution among males, youth, ethnic and racial minorities, the urban, and the poor. The doctrines of deterrence and incapacitation offer swift, certain, and severe punishment as the primary means of controlling risks of interpersonal violence.

Neurophysiological Responses. Many of the behavioral reactions to anger-eliciting stimuli are direct physiological and automatic responses. For persons who suffer from low impulse control and hyperactivity, various drugs are available to help regulate thought processes and behavioral responses. Different types of psychotropic drugs are also widely available to control one's mood and other mental states. By assisting internal mechanisms of the brain that regulate social behavior, the use of these drugs provides an available means of maintaining self-control.

Given the wide variety of motives and motivations for interpersonal violence, it seems unlikely that emphases on neurophysiological reactions will substantially limit and control the expression of interpersonal violence. The fact that much violence is a planned and calculated response to particular external or internal threats diminishes the ability of neurophysiological mechanisms, in and of themselves, to decrease propensities toward interpersonal aggression.

Eliminating Social Conditions of Frustration-Aggression. Under strain theories of criminality, frustration caused by the inability to achieve positively valued goals (e.g., money, status) through institutionalized means is a fundamental source of anger that underlies interpersonal violence. A wide array of educational and economic programs have been proposed and implemented throughout the last quarter century to improve the socioeconomic plight of the poor and disadvantaged in our society. These various social betterment programs (e.g., Head Start, magnet schools, busing, affirmative action, youth employment) are designed to address structural sources of inequality and the frustrations that emanate from blocked opportunities.

Although laudable as attempts to improve the social conditions of particular persons and groups, the ability of these social betterment measures to substantially improve the life chance of the disadvantaged is limited by the very structure of class-based societies. As noted by several authors, there will always be relative deprivation in U.S. society and thus strain and frustration caused by the inability for all groups to be successful in the pursuit of the American dream.[1] Whether the source of frustration and anger derives from material success, masculine competitiveness, relatively low status among one's peers, or the loss of other positively valued goals, interpersonal violence remains a likely response even when social conditions are improving for the groups and people most affected by them.

Changing Pro-Violent Values and Anger Management. The use of interpersonal aggression has been widely endorsed in American culture as a method of dispute resolution. Violence is a clear cultural message in film and television. Within particular subgroups (e.g., young, urban, minority males) physical violence is expected and even demanded as a public response to anger-provoking situations. Under these conditions, the only way to control violence is by changing this historical and cultural legacy of aggression in our society and developing realistic strategies for more constructive means for the diffusion of anger and hostility.

The primary means by which antiviolence values have been promoted is through various types of anger-management programs. School counselors, clinicians, probation officers, peer associations (e.g., peer mediation groups), and human relations officials in work organizations have all devised curriculum, workshops, and other support programs to offer training and counseling in nonviolent methods of conflict resolution. Most of these programs focus on enhancing recognition of personal anger issues and the development of more cathartic ways to release and resolve anger and conflict. Despite clinical uses of anger-management therapies, mass media portrayals of these types of programming remain dismissive and sarcastic.[2]

The promotion of nonviolence as a cultural theme and the establishment of various types of anger-management programs is a long-term solution to interpersonal violence. Unfortunately, these remedies do not address the fundamental conditions in a society that promote aggression in this first place (e.g., social differentiation, sexual rivalry, resource deprivation, loss of valued goals). It is also unrealistic to think that simply promoting antiviolence messages through the mass media, family, and/or work organizations is going to substantially alter the continued prevalence and use of interpersonal violence as a method of conflict resolution and resource for goal attainment.

Severe and Certain Punishment. The primary mechanism for the social control of interpersonal violence through the criminal justice system involves the threat and imposition of swift, certain, and severe punishment. For potential violent offenders who think about the consequences of their actions, criminal punishments may serve as a deterrent to serious physical injury of victims. For those who have committed violent offenses and been sanctioned for them, long imprisonment or other serious sanctions (e.g., death penalty) may function as a specific deterrent to prevent future criminal violence by this particular offender.

The utility of criminal sanctions as a deterrent to interpersonal violence is often questioned because of the spontaneous and impulsive nature of many of these acts. If the typical violent offender does not take the step of reasoning about potential consequences of behavior, the threat of legal sanction will have no bearing on actions taken. However, there is some evidence that even "impulsive" violent offenders exercise some degree of planning and calculation in their offending behavior (e.g., the selection of their target, its location and timing). Under these conditions, the threat of legal sanction may provide some control over interpersonal violence, but it is only likely to deter the violent behavior of potential offenders who have an assortment of other means and resources to diffuse aggression and resolve conflict situations. While deterrence theory does not address the informal sanctions associated with normative violations, some researchers have also argued that deterrence theory will not work without addressing the informal sanctions associated with using aggression and violence.[3]

Opportunity Reduction Strategies. Rather than focusing on the motivations for offending, a number of crime prevention strategies are directed at decreasing the physical opportunity for predatory violence. These opportunity-reduction programs in the mid-twentieth century were called crime prevention through environmental design. The language of target-hardening and situational crime prevention is now used to describe crime-reduction programs that focus on restricting the opportunity for the commission of criminal acts.[4]

Based on the research on hot spots and dangerous places, basic changes in the nature of work and leisure activities have taken place to decrease the opportunity for predatory violence. Convenience stores have redesigned their counters and check-out stations to make it more difficult to enter and exit the premises without full surveillance; multiple employees work during nighttime hours to provide greater security; the sale of alcohol is limited during late evening hours; private security officers are employed to monitor large public activities; building complexes have been redesigned to provide high surveillability of public spaces; and increased exterior lighting has decreased the physical opportunity for a blitz assault from a secluded and dark area. All of these efforts are designed to make it more difficult for motivated offenders to engage in predatory attacks.

Two of the most controversial efforts at target-hardening involve the debate about gun control and self-defense training. Critics of gun-control policies contend that an armed citizenry sends a strong deterrent message to potential offenders, thereby decreasing the likelihood of predatory crimes. Self-defense training in the martial arts is thought to provide a similar preemptive function. In contrast, proponents of gun control argue that the guns are facilitative hardware for crime commission, and the mere presence of a weapon is a situational cue that is likely to elicit, rather than suppress, aggressive responses. Self-defense training and the subsequent taking of a defensive posture during a conflict situation may be viewed as an open invitation for future aggressive actions.

Although these efforts at environmental redesign and target-hardening have the potential to reduce the physical opportunities for aggressive encounters, the old adage "where there is a will, there is a way" remains true. Persons who are sufficiently motivated to engage in violence for various instrumental purposes will make their own opportunities and circumvent many of the self-defense actions of potential victims. Under these conditions, opportunity-reduction programs are similar to other violence-prevention initiatives in that they offer at best a limited potential to reduce interpersonal aggression.[5]

THE LEGACY AND CHANGES OF NORMATIVE VIOLENCE

Previous efforts at reducing interpersonal aggression have focused on changing offender motivation or eliminating the physical opportunities for particular offenses. None of the violence prevention policies or initiatives discussed above take into account the normative nature of violence. Without considering the patterns and normalcy of violence, the effectiveness of all of these antiviolence measures will be limited. In order to curb violence and aggression, we maintain that society must critically assess the social norms that condone violence. So what are those norms?

As discussed throughout this book, violence has historically been a legitimate means to resolve disputes and most of these actions stop before serious bodily injury occurs. While most research on cultural norms and violence has focused on subcultural theories, it is our contention that violence is tacitly and sometimes overtly condoned in mainstream culture.[6]

> In our society the idea of retribution through violence is a basic article of faith. . . . It is normal for us, a fact of value in our culture. It isn't surprising that those of us who feel unjustly treated . . . resort to violence to redress that sense of injustice.[7]

This normative violence, however, may be changing. In the mid-1990s, violence in the United States fell.[8] What are possible explanations for this decline? If changes in norms are the answer, where did the change originate? Where do we learn norms about violence? Previous research has established family, peers, media, and schools as primary socializing agents. Our contention is that particular attention should be focused on how schools and masculinity have contributed to changes in the normalcy of violence.

Changes in Normative Violence through the Education System

Violence within schools is an enduring phenomenon and may be one arena in which norms about violence can be reconstructed.[9] Contemporary disciplinary policies in schools have been explicitly refocused on curbing behavioral problems, including aggression. During the 1990s and continuing today, violence in schools began receiving considerably more attention than in previous eras. Three new antiviolence policies in schools may have contributed to de-normalizing violence. These policies are zero tolerance, the medicalization of school discipline, and the conflict resolution movement.

Congress in 1994 established several "get tough" on school crime and violence policies that fostered an era of school discipline known as "zero tolerance."[10] Expulsion was mandated for a variety of student offenses, including fighting. Some researchers and the National Center for Education Statistics contend that these policies deterred crime and contributed to lower delinquency rates in schools.[11]

Behavioral and social psychology research suggests that people become conditioned to rules and learn to accept new expectations placed on them.[12] Educators and parents may now be less willing to tacitly condone violence among students because of the severity of potential consequences. Students may be learning the new normative roles expected of them in regard to violence.

The increased punitiveness toward school violence in the 1990s is one context for changing the normative rules of human aggression. Two additional social changes that may affect these rules and patterns of violence include (1) the rise in medical treatment for disruptive behavior and (2) the growth of conflict resolution and peer mediation in schools.

Beginning in the 1990s, both medical and educational personnel increasingly characterized disruptive children as having a medical condition. For example, Attention Deficit Disorder (ADD) is one of the most commonly diagnosed behavioral disorders in children. The criteria for ADD diagnosis are very broad and many practitioners suspect that it is over-diagnosed, particularly in boys.[13] Increasingly, parents are reluctant to have their children treated with psychotropic medications to manage minor behavioral problems, and parents reinforce behaviors that are less disruptive and less violent to avoid these diagnoses.

Conflict resolution skills and peer mediation training also spread dramatically in the 1990s. These violence prevention programs are focused on teaching young people to handle their feelings and aggression in productive manners instead of violent (destructive) ways. Because of the nature of resocializing and teaching students how to handle their conflicts without aggression, these programs are contributing to de-normalizing violence in U.S. schools and perhaps the wider American culture as well.

The combined effects of increased punitiveness, medicalization of discipline, and innovations in problem solving have changed how youngsters handle problems that were previously resolved through aggression. While the potential for these programs is great, we suggest that all educational policies and programs be mindful of the normalcy of violence that has pervaded human and animal behavior throughout history. Another key element of the normative structure of violence in both schools and other contexts is its intrinsic link to masculinity.

Changes in Normative Violence Associated with Gender

In the late 1990s, researchers began focusing on the problems of school age boys.[14] A series of pop culture books and articles proposed that boys were getting short-changed in the modern educational system, which led to more scholarly research on the subject. More and more boys receive mixed messages about what it means to be masculine, but hegemonic masculinity that espouses norms of male dominance still exists. According to this perspective, idealized masculinity endorses male physical strength, an adventurous spirit, emotional neutrality, control, assertiveness, competitiveness, and rationality.[15]

These norms are prominent and contribute to the increasing number of college athletes who participate in the more violent sports such as football and lacrosse being charged with sexual assault. The football programs at Colorado, Nebraska, Brigham Young, and Navy all faced such allegations, as did the Duke lacrosse team. Kathy Redmond, the founder of the National Coalition Against Violent Athletes, states, "People are so concerned with being part of the team, with the so-called masculine roles, that the line between right and wrong gets blurred." The promotion of hyper-masculinity is also highly visible in locker rooms, and coaches have widely chastised their male athletes for being "soft" and "playing like women." For example, Bobby Knight, now at Texas Tech and formerly at Indiana, was famous for leaving tampons in the lockers of players he felt weren't performing up to snuff.[16]

Elementary and secondary schools have a number of female educators and administrators who do not necessarily condone the behaviors associated with dominant masculinity. Boys today are more likely to be disciplined severely and often medicated when they behave in stereotypically boyish fashion.[17] Thus, boys are now in a state of confusion about what it is to be a male and what it is to be masculine. The problem of gender identity can affect the amount of violence in which boys engage.

Some research has described the state of affairs for boys today as anomic, confusing, and filled with mixed messages. As boys navigate the transition from grade school to middle school, their masculinity is called into question. Boys negotiate the dichotomous social labels of being "babies" and being "cool." When their self-identities and masculinities are threatened (usually by other boys), boys aggress against the person who makes them feel badly. Boys attack their peers when they feel challenged as a way of self-protection and because it is often the only means of expressing that aggression in a normative manner.[18] Thus, researchers advocate a position of sympathy for boys focused on eliminating labels like "sissy" or "momma's boy" and downplaying traditional patriarchal male values such as aggression.[19]

Deborah Prothrow-Stith encountered an interesting illustration of the conflicting messages boys receive. She had been invited to speak about violence at a luncheon. One of the hostesses mentioned that her son had been beaten by a girl and that everyone in the small town seemed incredulous that he would have allowed that to happen. The family of his girlfriend made her break up with him because they believed something must be wrong with him. Even school personnel did not acknowledge that his choice of nonviolence was positive. Although the mother was proud of her son's choice, she was very disturbed by the lack of support throughout the community for his actions; in fact, there seemed to be an outright celebration of the girl's violent behavior toward her son.[20]

In their book *Sugar and Spice and No Longer Nice,* Prothrow-Stith and Howard Spivak discuss changes that have occurred in socialization patterns.

> Well over a decade ago, psychologist and researcher Leonard Eron stated that if America is to truly reduce youth violence, boys must be socialized more like girls have traditionally been socialized. Instead, over the ensuing years, we as a society have done the opposite, socializing our girls like boys. Now our girls are demonstrating the violent behavior of boys. If parents ever had any doubt about the impact of cultural values and the media on their children, then the past decade of increased fighting among girls answers that—and pretty clearly too! Girls are not genetically protected from the violent junk in the media and toxic cultural influences. Girls may be resilient to violence, but they are obviously not immune to it.[21]

Prothrow-Stith and Spivak found that there is evidence girls may turn to violence for some of the same reasons boys do—"to prove she is not a wimp, to build a reputation and avoid future victimization, to mark her property (her man), to defend her mother against insults, and for the fun of it."[22] Their conclusion is that this is not progress.

> They say maybe it's a good thing that girls are finally defending themselves and outwardly expressing their anger rather than being passive-aggressive or internalizing. We say no. That kind of outward expression of anger, more typical of boys and men, is a problem. Boys and men should not be the model for handling anger. The skills of self-defense include prevention, negotiation, empathy, and conflict resolution, not just fighting back; this is a lesson for boys and girls, men and women. Handling anger in productive ways requires nonviolent con-

flict resolution skills. These are skills that must be taught, practiced, and admired and made popular.[23]

Cheryl Dellasega founded Club Ophelia in 2002 to help girls learn to handle their aggression. "One of the principles behind the groups is that girls tend to be tenacious about their anger, with resentments continuing to simmer long after the fisticuffs have ended."[24] Other classroom-based programs teach anger management and impulse control, including Seattle's Second Step program, which started in 1986. The program targets boys and girls from ages 4 to 14 and has been tested in 25,000 schools. Images of Me is a self-awareness program for girls that teaches mediation and communication skills in Maryland.[25]

Gender identities and norms are culturally and historically specific. The legacy of violence among men and boys has been documented throughout history and in most societies. Family and school environments need to socialize boys and girls to problem solve without violence. Widespread and significant shifts in childhood socialization regarding normative aggression may indeed prove to be the best violence preventative in the years to come.

Conclusions and a Short-Term Remedy

As a type of situational crime prevention, we contend that the most basic way to reduce the gravity of interpersonal violence is by increasing public awareness of the normative rules and routines that govern its use in contemporary U.S. society. By increasing knowledge of the situational contexts that foster, encourage, and promote interpersonal violence, the immediate short-term solution for much of this problem is the simple ability of potential offenders and victims to recognize the "danger signs" and to "walk away" rather than fight. Moreover, the process of walking away, particularly for young males, must be de-stigmatized.

Most acts of interpersonal violence can be easily preempted by acts of omission and commission by the offending parties. The road rager and the offender who uses violence as a status-enhancing resource will get little satisfaction or reward if the targeted victim simply acquiesces to the demands. Similarly, many potential violent encounters dissipate quickly into nonviolent situations when an offended party fails to "talk loud," "get in someone's face," or otherwise challenge another in verbal banter. The basic recognition of the rules of engagement in violent encounters, the fixed-action patterns that often underlie their situational dynamics, and the awareness of how third parties, available hardware, and particular physical locations may facilitate interpersonal violence is the most basic advice that can be given to reduce the nature and magnitude of interpersonal violence.

Similar to the image of a caged animal with no options but to attack, it is common to view violent situations as inevitable—in many cases because one or both parties felt like they "had to do it." Although we recognize such possibilities in the case of self-defense actions, many of these situations could have been preempted by various types of actions prior to the escalation of violence. At various points preceding and during violent encounters, the combatants have numerous opportunities to desist from physical assaults. By promoting ideas about preemptive disengagement, the likelihood of escalation into lethal encounters is greatly minimized.

The optimal benefit of the reduction of interpersonal aggression will arise when the recognition of the rules of engagement and disengagement are supplemented with cultural changes and greater economic opportunities. The message has more resonance when people have more means for seeking nonviolent solutions to the struggles and strains of everyday life and more rewards for pursuing that path. Until fundamental changes in the structure of U.S. society take place, the only feasible solution to interpersonal violence is the avoidance of it through greater recognition of the normative rules and routines that characterize the commission of violent acts at particular times, at particular places, and among particular groups of people.

Notes

[1] See, for example, Steven Messner and Richard Rosenfeld. 2005. *Crime and the America Dream.* Belmont, CA: Wadsworth.

[2] In 2003, Jack Nicholson and Adam Sandler starred in a feature film titled *Anger Management* in which the therapist was portrayed as erratic and patients with anger control problems were portrayed as seriously disturbed, volatile, and totally uncontrolled animals.

[3] See Mark Stafford and Mark Warr. 1993. "A Reconceptualization of General and Specific Deterrence." *Journal of Research in Crime & Delinquency* 30:123–135.

[4] For a review of these crime prevention programs, see Ronald V. Clarke. 1997. *Situational Crime Prevention: Successful Case Studies.* New York: Harrow and Heston.

[5] It is important to note that even if opportunity-reduction strategies did reduce the risks of violent victimization for some groups, there would likely be some displacement of violence to those who are less protected. Within this context, previous research has examined the effectiveness of neighborhood watch programs and other citizen-based crime prevention programs from the perspective of "spatial injustice." From this perspective, gains in crime reduction may be offset by the displacement of crime to more vulnerable targets. When applied to the study of interpersonal aggression, it is possible that efforts to redesign public spaces to increase their surveillability and guardianship may simply move acts of physical violence to more secluded private spaces (e.g., within homes). The extent to which such displacement of crime occurs has not been fully investigated in previous research on crime prevention programs. For a review and discussion of these ideas, see Ronald V. Clarke. 1997. *Situational Crime Prevention: Successful Case Studies.* New York: Harrow and Heston; Terance D. Miethe. 1991. "Citizen-Based Crime Control Activity and Victimization Risks: An Examination of Displacement and Free-Rider Effects." *Criminology* 29(3):419–439.

[6] Don Merten suggests that violence is not part of mainstream culture, meaning the "core cultural elements found primarily, but not exclusively, among the suburban middle class." However, it is tacitly condoned by parental action and more often, inaction. See Don E. Merten. 1994. "The Cultural Context of Aggression: The Transition to Junior High School." *Anthropology and Education Quarterly* 25:29–43. Merten also contends that violence is not truly subcultural but rather included in mainstream culture in hidden ways.

For a discussion of the subculture of violence theories see Felson et al., 1994. "The Subculture of Violence and Delinquency: Individual vs. School Context Effects." *Social Forces* 73:155–173.

[7] James Garbarino. 2000. *Lost Boys: Why Our Sons Turn Violent and How We Can Save Them*, New York: Anchor, p. 133.

[8] For example, the homicide offense rate decreased from 9.4 per 100,000 residents in 1990, to 8.2 in 1995, and decreased further to 5.5 per 100,000 by the year 2000, where it remained in 2004. See Federal Bureau of Investigation (FBI). 2005. *Crime in the United States: Uniform Crime Reports*. Washington, DC: Government Printing Office.

[9] See A. Troy Adams. 2000. "The Status of School Discipline and Violence." *Annals of the American Academy of Political and Social Science* 567:140–156.

[10] The zero tolerance policy was generated by a larger package of federal school violence prevention initiatives. This legislation and its amendments required schools to expel students for at least one year if a hearing officer determined that the student brought a weapon or drug paraphernalia to school and engaged in violence. Schools were threatened that their federal funding would be withheld if they did not comply. Amendments have increased the punitiveness of school discipline across several types of offenses, including fighting, spitting, or threats. See Ronnie Cassella. 2003. "Zero Tolerance Policy in Schools: Rationale, Consequences, and Alternatives." *Teachers College Record* 105:872–892.

[11] The conclusion that school crime fell as a result of zero tolerance policies is based on the research of Sheley and Wright. See Joseph Sheley and James Wright. 1998. *High School Youths*. Washington, DC: National Institute of Justice; J. F. DeVoe, K. Peter, M. Noonan, T. D. Snyder, and K. Baum. 2005. *Indicators of School Crime and Safety: 2005* (NCES 2006–001/NCJ 210697). U.S. Departments of Education and Justice. Washington, DC: U.S. Government Printing Office. However, according to Skiba and Leone (2001), there are no decreases in school violence resulting from zero tolerance policies. See Russell Skiba and Peter Leone. 2001. "Zero Tolerance and School Security Measures: A Failed Experiment." In Tammy Johnson, Jennifer Boyden, and William Pitts (eds.), *Racial Profiling and Punishment in U.S. Schools*. Oakland, CA: Applied Research Center, pp. 34–38.

[12] See Ronnie Cassella. 2003. "Zero Tolerance Policy in Schools: Rationale, Consequences, and Alternatives." *Teachers College Record* 105:872–892.

[13] See, for example, A. Troy Adams. 2000. "The Status of School Discipline and Violence." *Annals of the American Academy of Political and Social Science* 567:140–156.

[14] See Christine Skelton. 2001. *Schooling the Boys: Masculinities and Primary Education*. Buckingham: Open University Press. See also, Cathy Young. 2001. "Where the Boys Are: Is America Shortchanging Male Children?" *Reason Magazine* Feb.:24–31.

[15] See Christine Skelton's discussion in Christine Skeleton. 1997. "Primary Boys and Hegomonic Masculinities." *British Journal of Sociology of Education* 18:349–369.

[16] Jessica Reaves. 2006, April 9. "Winning Streak Can Cover Violent One." *Chicago Tribune*, Sec. 2, pp. 1, 4.

[17] Young (2001:25) states, "Traditional schoolmarmish distastes for unruly young males may be amplified by modern gender politics. Some educators clearly see boys as budding sexists and predators in need of re-education." See Cathy Young. 2001. "Where the Boys Are: Is America Shortchanging Male Children?" *Reason Magazine* Feb.:24–31.

[18] See Merten's qualitative study of boys and aggression in Don E. Merten. 1994. "The Cultural Context of Aggression: The Transition to Junior High School." *Anthropology and Education Quarterly* 25:29–43.

[19] William Pollack suggests that boys are caught in a cultural trap that leaves them scared and confused about what their roles are. He suggests that violence in males begins in childhood when a boy is introduced to adult male norms that suggest anger and violence are the only socially acceptable means of self expression for boys. See William Pollack. 1999. *Real Boys: Rescuing Our Sons from the Myths of Boyhood*. New York: Henry Holt and Company. Pollack's (1999) theory is further supported by a host of other research that sug-

gests boys began using violence in the middle school years as a means of negotiating the changes in their statuses from child to adolescent. See also, Dan Kindlon and Michael Thompson. 1999. *Raising Cain: Protecting the Emotional Life of Boys*. New York: Ballantine Books; Shawn C. McGuffey and B. Lindsay Rich. 1999. "Playing in the Gender Transgression Zone: Race, Class and Hegemonic Masculinity in Middle Childhood." *Gender and Society* 13:608–627; Don E. Merten. 1994. "The Cultural Context of Aggression: The Transition to Junior High School." *Anthropology and Education Quarterly* 25:29–43.

[20] Deborah Prothrow-Stith and Howard R. Spivak. 2006. *Sugar and Spice and No Longer Nice: How We Can Stop Girls' Violence*, San Francisco: Jossey-Bass.

[21] Ibid., pp. 29–30.

[22] Prothrow-Stith and Spivak, p. 31.

[23] Ibid., pp. 29–30.

[24] Jeffrey Kluger. 2006, May 1. "Taming Wild Girls." *Time* (167)18:55.

[25] Ibid.

References

Adams, A. Troy. 2000. "The Status of School Discipline and Violence." *Annals of the American Academy of Political and Social Science* 567:140–156.

Agnew, Robert. 1992. "Foundation for a General Strain Theory of Crime and Delinquency." Criminology 30(1):47–87.

Agnew, Robert. 1997. "The Nature and Determinants of Strain: Another Look at Durkheim and Merton." In Robert Agnew and Nikos Passas (eds.), *The Future of Anomie Theory*. Boston: Northeastern University Press, pp. 27–51.

Altmann, S. A. 1967. "The Structure of Primate Communication." In S. A. Altmann (ed.), *Social Communication Among Primates*. Chicago: University of Chicago Press, pp. 235–262.

American Public Human Services Association. 1998. *The National Elderly Abuse Incident Study, Final Report*. Available online at: http://www.aoa.gov/eldfam/Elder_Rights/Elder_Abuse/ABuseReport_Full.pdf

Anderson, Elijah. 1998. "The Social Ecology of Youth Violence." *Crime and Justice: A Review of Research* 24:64–103.

Anderson, Elijah. 1999. *Code of the Street: Decency, Violence, and the Moral Life of the Inner City*. New York: W. W. Norton.

Anderson, Craig A. and Karen E. Dill. 2000. "Video Games and Aggressive Thoughts, Feelings, and Behavior in the Laboratory and in Life." *Journal of Personality and Social Psychology* 78(4):772–790.

Anderson, Kristin L. and Debra Umberson. 2001. "Gendering Violence: Masculinity and Power in Men's Accounts of Domestic Violence." *Gender and Society* 15:358–380.

Athens, Lonnie. 1985. "Character Contests and Violent Criminal Conduct: A Critique." *Sociological Quarterly* 26:419–431.

Auerhahn, Kathleen and Robert Nash Parker. 1999. "Drugs, Alcohol, and Homicide." In M. Dwayne Smith and Margaret A. Zahn (eds.), *Studying and Preventing Homicide: Issues and Challenges*. Thousand Oaks, CA: Sage, pp. 97–114.

Bailey, William C. and Ruth D. Peterson. 1999. "Capital Punishment, Homicide, and Deterrence." In M. Dwayne Smith and Margaret A. Zahn (eds.), *Homicide: A Sourcebook of Social Research*. Thousand Oaks, CA: Sage, pp. 257–276.

Bandura, Albert. 1973. *Aggression: A Social Learning Analysis*. Englewood Cliffs, NJ: Prentice Hall.

Bandura, Albert. 1983. "Psychological Mechanisms of Aggression." In Russell G. Geen and Edward I. Donnerstein (eds.), *Aggression: Theoretical and Empirical Reviews*, Vol. 1. New York: Academic Press, pp. 1–40.

Bandura, Albert. 1999. "Social Cognitive Theory of Personality." In Lawrence A. Pervin and Oliver P. John (eds.), *Handbook of Personality: Theory and Research*. 2nd Edition. New York: The Guilford Press, pp. 154–218.

Barclay, Gordon C. and Cynthia Tavares. 2000. *International Comparisons of Criminal Justice Statistics, 1998*. London: British Home Office.

Baron, Robert A. and Donn Byrne. 1994. *Social Psychology: Understanding Human Interaction*. 7th Edition. Boston: Allyn & Bacon.

Benekos, Peter J. 2006. "Women as Perpetrators of Murder." In A. Merlo and J. Pollock (eds.), *Women, Law and Social Control*. 2nd Edition. Boston: Allyn & Bacon, pp. 227–248.

Bentler, Peter M. 1968. "Heterosexual Behavior." *Behavior Research and Therapy* 6(1):21–30.

Berkowitz, Leonard and A. LePage. 1967. "Weapons as Aggression-Eliciting Stimuli." *Journal of Personality and Social Psychology* 7:202–207.

Brearley, Harold C. 1932. *Homicide in the United States*. Chapel Hill: University of North Carolina Press.

Bunch, Charlotte. 1997. "The Intolerable Status Quo: Violence against Women and Girls." *The Progress of Nations 1997*. New York: The United Nations. Available online at: http://www.unicef.org/pon97/mainmenu.htm.

Calhoun, J. B. 1962. "The Ecology and Sociology of the Norway Rat." U.S. Department of Health, Education, and Welfare, Public Health Service Publication No. 1008. Washington, DC: U.S. Government Printing Office.

Carlson, Bonnie E. 1984. "Children's Observation of Interpersonal Violence." In A. R. Roberts (ed.), *Battered Women and Their Families*. New York: Springer, pp. 147–167.

Cases, O., I. Seif, J. Grimsby, P. Gaspar, K. Chen, S. Pournin, U. Muller, M. Aguet, C. Babinnet, J. C. Shih, and E. De Maeyer. 1995. "Aggressive Behavior and Altered Amounts of Brain Serotonin and Norepinephrine in Mice Lacking MAOA." *Science* 268:1763–1766.

Cassella, Ronnie. 2003. "Zero Tolerance Policy in Schools: Rationale, Consequences, and Alternatives." *Teachers College Record* 105:872–892.

Catalano, Shannan M. 2005. *Criminal Victimization, 2004*. Department of Justice, Bureau of Justice Statistics (Report No. NCJ 210674). Washington, DC: U.S. Government Printing Office.

Centers for Disease Control and Prevention (CDC). 2003. *Costs of Intimate Partner Violence against Women in the United States*. Atlanta, GA: CDC, National Center for Injury Prevention and Control.

Centers for Disease Control and Prevention. 2006. *Youth Risk Behavior Surveillance—United States, 2005*. Surveillance Summaries, June 9, 2006. MMWR 2006; 55 (No. SS-5).

Chambliss, William J. 1967. "Types of Deviance and the Effectiveness of Legal Sanctions." *Wisconsin Law Review* Summer:703–719.

Clarke, Ronald V. 1997. *Situational Crime Prevention: Successful Case Studies*. New York: Harrow and Heston.

Cochran, Hamilton. 1963. *Noted American Duels and Hostile Encounters*. Philadelphia: Chilton Books.

Cohen, Albert. 1955. *Delinquent Boys*. New York: Free Press.

Cohen, Lawrence E. and Marcus Felson. 1979. "Social Change and Crime Rate Trends: A Routine Activity Approach." *American Sociological Review* 44:588–608.

Collins, Randall. 2005. *Interaction Ritual Chains*. Princeton, NJ: Princeton University Press.

Cook, Philip J. and John H. Laub. 1998. "The Unprecedented Epidemic in Youth Violence." *Crime and Justice: A Review of Research* 24:27–64.

Cornish, Derek B. and Ronald V. Clarke. 1986. *The Reasoning Criminal: Rational Choice Perspectives on Offending*. New York: Springer-Verlag.

Coyne, Andrew C. 2001. "The Relationship between Dementia and Elderly Abuse." *Geriatric Times*. Available online at: http://www.geriatrictimes.com/g010715.html.

Daly, Martin and Margo Wilson. 1988. *Homicide*. New York: Aldine de Gruyter.

Daly, Martin and Margo Wilson. 1999. "An Evolutionary Psychological Perspective on Homicide." In M. Dwayne Smith and Margaret A. Zahn (eds.), *Studying and Preventing Homicide: Issues and Challengers*. Thousand Oaks, CA: Sage.

Daro, Deborah. 1999. *Public Opinion and Behaviors Regarding Child Abuse Prevention: 1999 Survey*. Chicago: Prevent Child Abuse America Publications.

Darwin, Charles. 1896. *The Expression of Emotions in Man and Animals*. New York: D. Appleton.

Davidson, R. N. 1989. "Micro-Environments of Violence." In D. Evans and D. Herbert (eds.), *The Geography of Crime*. London: Routledge, pp. 59–85.

Decker, Scott, Carol W. Kohfeld, Richard Rosenfeld, and John Sprague. 1991. *St. Louis Homicide Project: Local Responses to a National Problem*. St. Louis: University of Missouri-St. Louis.

Deibert, Gini R. and Terance D. Miethe. 2003. "Character Contests and Dispute-Related Offenses." *Deviant Behavior* 24:245–267.

Department of Health and Human Services, Children's Bureau. 2000. *Child Maltreatment 1998: Reports from the States to the National Child Abuse and Neglect Data System (NCANDS)*. Washington, DC: U.S. Government Printing Office.

Department of Health and Human Services, National Center on Child Abuse and Neglect. 1999. *Child Maltreatment 1997: Reports from the States to the National Child Abuse and Neglect Data System (NCANDS)*. Washington, DC: U.S. Government Printing Office.

Dollard, J., N. Doob, N. E. Miller, O. H. Mowrer, and R. R. Sears. 1939. *Frustration and Aggression*. New Haven, CT: Yale University Press.

Eibl-Eiebesfeldt, I. 1961. "The Fighting Behavior of Animals." *Scientific American* 205:112–122.

Eisenberg, J. F. and P. Leyhausen. 1972. "The Phylogenesis of Predatory Behavior in Mammals." *Zeitschrift fur Tierpsychologie* 30:59–93.

Elias, Norbert. 1982. *The Civilizing Process II: Power and Civility*. New York: Pantheon.

Ellis, Lee and Anthony Walsh. 2000. *Criminology: A Global Perspective*. Boston: Allyn & Bacon.

Eron, L. 1995. Testimony before the Senate Committee on Commerce, Science, and Transportation, Subcommittee on Communications. June 12, 1995. Cited in Media Use in America. 2003. *Issue Briefs*. Universal City, CA: Mediascope Press.

Fagan, Jeffrey. 1996. *The Criminalization of Domestic Violence: Promises and Limits*. Washington, DC: National Institute of Justice.

Fagan, Jeffrey and Deanna L. Wilkinson. 1998. "Guns, Youth Violence, and Social Identity in Inner Cities." In Mark Moore and Michael Tonry (eds.), *Crime and Justice: An Annual Review of Research*, Vol. 24. Chicago: University of Chicago Press, pp. 105–188.

Federal Bureau of Investigation (FBI). 1960–2004. *Crime in the United States: Uniform Crime Reports. Select Years.* Washington, DC: U.S. Government Printing Office.

Felson, Richard B. 1983. "Aggression and Violence between Siblings." *Social Psychology Quarterly* 46:271–285.

Felson, Richard B., Allen E. Liska, Scott J. South, and Thomas L. McNulty. 1994. "The Subculture of Violence and Delinquency: Individual vs. School Context Effects." *Social Forces* 73:155–173.

Felson, Richard B. and Steven F. Messner. 2000. "The Control Motive in Intimate Partner Violence." *Social Psychology Quarterly* 63:86–94.

Fishbein, Diana. 2001. *Biobehavioral Perspectives in Criminology.* Belmont, CA: Wadsworth.

Fox, James A. and Marianne W. Zawitz. 2004. *Homicide Trends in the United States.* Washington, DC: Department of Justice. Available online at: http://www.ojp.usdoj.gov/bjs/homicide/homtrnd.htm#contents.

Foucault, Michel. 1977. *Discipline and Punish.* New York: Pantheon.

Freedman, Jonathan. 2002. *Media Violence and Its Effect on Aggression: Assessing the Scientific Evidence.* Toronto: University of Toronto Press.

Freud, Sigmund. 1950. *Beyond the Pleasure Principle* (J. Strachey, translation). New York: Liveright.

Gabel, S., J. Stadler, J. Bjorn, R. Shindledecker, and C. J. Bowen. 1995. "Homovanillic Acid and Monamine Oxidase in Sons of Substance-Abusing Fathers: Relationship to Conduct Disorders." *Journal of Studies on Alcohol* 56:135–139.

Garfinkel, Harold. 1956. "Conditions of Successful Degradation Ceremonies." *American Journal of Sociology* 61:420–424.

Gartner, Rosemary, K. Baker, and Fred Pampel. 1990. "Gender Stratification and the Gender Gap in Homicide Victimization." *Social Problems* 37:593–612.

Geen, Russell G. 1998. "Aggression and Antisocial Behavior." In Daniel T. Gilbert, Susan T. Fiske, and Gardner Lindzey (eds.), *The Handbook of Social Psychology*, Vol. 2. 4th Edition. Boston: McGraw-Hill.

Gelles, Richard J. 2000. "Estimating the Incidence and Prevalence of Violence against Women: National Data Systems and Sources." *Violence Against Women* 6(7):784–804.

Gerbner, George. 1998. "Cultivation Analysis: An Overview." *Mass Communication and Society* 1(3/4):177–184.

Ghuglieri, Michael P. 1999. *The Dark Side of Man: Tracing the Origins of Male Violence.* Reading, MA: Perseus Books.

Gibbs, Jack P. 1975. *Crime, Punishment, and Deterrence.* New York: Elsevier.

Goffman, Erving. 1959. *The Presentation of Self in Everyday Life.* Garden City, NY: Doubleday Anchor Books.

Goffman, Erving. 1963. *Behavior in Public Places: Notes on the Social Organization of Gatherings.* Glencoe, IL: Free Press.

Goffman, Erving. 1967. *Interaction Rituals: Essays on Face-to-Face Behavior.* Garden City, NY: Doubleday.

Gosselin, Denise Kindschi. 2006. "Intimate Partner Violence against and by Women." In A. Merlo and J. Pollock (eds.), *Women, Law and Social Control.* 2nd Edition. Boston: Allyn & Bacon, pp. 170–187.

Gottfredson, Michael R. and Travis Hirsch. 1990. *A General Theory of Crime*. Stanford, CA: Stanford University Press

Gove, Walter R. 1975. *The Labeling of Deviance: Evaluating a Perspective*. New York: Halsted.

Grabianowski, Ed."How Duels Work." Available online at: http://people.howstuffworks.com/duel.htm.

Grant, E. C. 1963. "An Analysis of the Social Behaviour of the Male Laboratory Rat." *Behaviour* 21:260–281.

Gross, N. 1998, Feb. 16. "The Entertainment Glut." *Business Week*.

Gurr, Ted Robert. 1979. "On the History of Violent Crime in Europe and America." In H.D. Graham and T. R. Gurr (eds.), *Violence in America: Historical and Comparative Perspectives*. Beverly Hills, CA: Sage.

Gurr, Ted Robert. 1981. "Historical Trends in Violent Crime: A Critical Review of the Evidence." In M. Tonry and N. Morris (eds.), *Crime and Justice: An Annual Review of Research*. Chicago: University of Chicago Press, pp. 295–353.

Hartnagel, Timothy. 1982. "Modernization, Female Social Roles, and Female Crime: A Cross-National Comparison." *The Sociological Quarterly* 23(4):477–490.

Harvey, William B. 1986. "Homicide among Young Black Adults: Life in the Subculture of Exasperation." In D. F. Hawkins (ed.), *Homicide among Black Americans*. Lanham, MD: University Press of America, pp. 153–171.

Hediger, H. 1950. *Wild Animals in Captivity: An Outline of the Biology of Zoological Gardens*. London: Butterworth's Scientific.

Hewitt, John P. 1997. *Self and Society: A Symbolic Interactionist Social Psychology*. 7th Edition. Boston: Allyn & Bacon.

Hickey, Eric W. 1997. *Serial Murderers and their Victims*. 2nd Edition. Belmont, CA: Wadsworth.

Hindelang, Michael S., Michael Gottfredson, and James Garofalo. 1978. *Victims of Personal Crime*. Cambridge, MA: Ballinger.

Hirschi, Travis. 1969. *Causes of Delinquency*. Berkeley: University of California Press.

Hoff Sommers, Christina. 1995. *Who Stole Feminism?: How Women Have Betrayed Women*. New York: Simon & Schuster.

Holland, Barbara. 2003. *Gentlemen's Blood: A History of Dueling from Swords at Dawn to Pistols at Dusk*. London: Bloomsbury Publishing.

Horowitz, I. 2002. *Taking Life: Genocide and State Power*. 5th Edition. New Brunswick, NJ: Transaction Publishers.

Hotaling, Gerald T., Murray A. Straus, and Alan J. Lincoln. 1989. "Intrafamily Violence, and Crime and Violence Outside the Family." *Crime and Justice* 11:315–375.

Human Rights Watch. 2000, April 24. "Human Rights in Saudi Arabia: A Deafening Silence." AP.

Johnson, Herbert A. and Nancy Travis Wolfe. 2003. *History of Criminal Justice*. 3rd Edition. Cincinnati, OH: Anderson Publishing.

Johnson, Michael P. 1995. "Patriarchal Terrorism and Common Couple Violence: Two Forms of Violence against Women." *Journal of Marriage and the Family* 57:283–294.

Johnson, Michael P. and Kathleen J. Ferraro. 2000. "Research on Domestic Violence in the 1990s: Making Distinctions." *Journal of Marriage and the Family* 62:948–963.

Klein, Malcolm. 1971. *Street Gangs and Street Workers*. Englewood Cliffs, NJ: Prentice Hall.

Kummer, H. 1968. *Social Organization of Hamadryads Baboons: A Field Study.* Chicago: University of Chicago Press.

Kelly, Henry A. 1994. "Rule of Thumb and the Folklaw of the Husband's Stick." *Journal of Legal Education* 44:341–365.

Kennedy, Leslie W. and Vincent F. Sacco. 1996. *Crime Counts: A Criminal Event Analysis.* Scarborough, Ontario: Nelson Canada.

Kindlon, Dan and Michael Thompson. 1999. *Raising Cain: Protecting the Emotional Life of Boys.* New York: Ballantine Books.

Kleck, Gary. 1991. *Point Blank: Guns and Violence in America.* Hawthorne, NY: Aldine de Gruyter.

Lane, Roger. 1997. *Murder in America: A History.* Columbus: Ohio State University.

Lejeune, R. 1977. "The Management of Mugging." *Urban Life* 6:123–148.

Lemert, Edwin M. 1951. *Social Pathology: A Systematic Approach to the Theory of Sociopathic Behavior.* New York: McGraw-Hill.

Lippman, Matthew, Sean McConville, and Mordechai Yerushalmi. 1988. *Islamic Criminal Law and Procedure: An Introduction.* New York: Praeger.

Lofland, John. 1969. *Deviance and Identity.* Englewood Cliffs, NJ: Prentice Hall.

Lorenz, Konrad. 1966. *On Aggression.* New York: Harcourt, Brace, and World.

Luckenbill, David F. 1977. "Criminal Homicide as a Situated Transaction." *Social Problems* 25:176–186.

Luckenbill, David F. 1981. "Generating Compliance: The Case of Robbery." *Urban Life* 10:25–46.

Lynch, James P. 1987. "Routine Activity and Victimization at Work." *Journal of Quantitative Criminology* 3:283–300.

Matz, David. 1964. *Delinquency and Drift.* New York: John Wiley.

Mazur, Alan. 1985. "A Biosocial Model of Status in Face-to-Face Primate Groups." *Social Forces* 64:377–403.

Mazur, Alan and Allen Booth. 1998. "Testosterone and Dominance in Men." *Behavior and Brain Sciences* 21:353–363.

McGuffey, C. Shawn and B. Lindsay Rich. 1999. "Playing in the Gender Transgression Zone: Race, Class and Hegemonic Masculinity in Middle Childhood." *Gender and Society* 13:608–627.

McHale, Susan M., Kimberley A. Updegraff, Corinna J. Tucker, and Ann C. Crouter. 2000. "Step in or Stay out? Parents' Roles in Adolescent Siblings' Relationships." *Journal of Marriage and the Family* 62:746–760.

Mead, George Herbert. 1934. *Mind, Self, and Society.* Chicago: University of Chicago Press.

Media Use in America. 2003. *Issue Briefs.* Universal City, CA: Mediascope Press.

Meier, Robert F., Leslie W. Kennedy, and Vincent F. Sacco. 2001. *The Process and Structure of Crime: Crime Events and Crime Analysis. Advances in Criminological Theory,* Vol. 9. New Brunswick, NJ: Transaction.

Merten, Don E. 1994. "The Cultural Context of Aggression: The Transition to Junior High School." *Anthropology and Education Quarterly* 25:29–43.

Messner, Steven and Richard Rosenfeld. 2005. *Crime and the America Dream.* Belmont, CA: Wadsworth.

Miethe, Terance D. 1991. "Citizen-Based Crime Control Activity and Victimization Risks: An Examination of Displacement and Free-Rider Effects." *Criminology* 29(3):419–439.

Miethe, Terance D. and Hong Lu. 2005. *Punishment: A Comparative Historical Perspective.* Cambridge, UK: Cambridge University Press.

Miethe, Terance D., Richard C. McCorkle, and Shelley J. Listwan. 2006. *Crime Profiles: The Anatomy of Dangerous Persons, Places, and Situations*. 3rd Edition. Los Angeles: Roxbury Publishing Company.

Miethe, Terance D. and Robert F. Meier. 1990. "Criminal Opportunity and Victimization Rates: A Structural-Choice Theory of Criminal Victimization." *Journal of Research in Crime and Delinquency* 27:243–266.

Miethe, Terance D. and Robert F. Meier. 1994. *Crime and Its Social Context: Toward an Integrated Theory of Offenders, Victims, and Situations*. Albany: State University of New York Press.

Miethe, Terance D. and Wendy C. Regoeczi. 2004. *Rethinking Homicide: Exploring the Structure and Process Underlying Deadly Situations*. Cambridge, UK: Cambridge University Press.

Miller, Walter B. 1958. "Lower Class Culture as a Generating Milieu of Gang Delinquency." *Journal of Social Issues* 14:5–19.

Miller, Walter B. 1975. *Violence by Youth Gangs and Youth Groups as a Crime Problem in Major American Cities*. Washington, DC: U.S. Department of Justice.

Moffitt, Terri E. 1993. "Life-Course-Persistent and Adolescent-Limited Antisocial Behavior: A Developmental Taxonomy." *Psychological Review* 100:674–701.

Moffitt, Terri E., G. L. Brammer, A. Caspi, J. P. Fawcett, M. Raleigh, A. Yuwiler, and P. Silva. 1998. "Whole Blood Serotonin Relates to Violence in an Epidemiological Study." *Biological Psychiatry* 43:446–457.

Moffitt, Terri E., Avshalom Caspi, Honalee Harrington, and Barry J. Milne. 2002. "Males on the Life-Course-Persistent and Adolescence-Limited Antisocial Pathways: Follow-up at Age 26 Years." *Development and Psychopathology* 14:139–157.

Monkkonen, Eric H. (ed.). 1991. *Crime and Justice in American History. The Colonies and Early Republic*, Vol 1. and 2. Westport, CT: Meckler Publishing.

Moore, Mark H. and Michael Tonry. 1998. "Youth Violence in America." In M. Moore and M. Tonry (eds.), *Crime and Justice: An Annual Review of Research*, Vol. 24. Chicago: University of Chicago Press, pp. 1–24.

Morgan, M. and J. Shanahan. 1996. "Two Decades of Cultivation Analysis: An Appraisal and a Meta-Analysis." In B. Burleson (ed.), *Communication Yearbook 2020*. Thousand Oaks, CA: Safe, pp. 1–45.

Mosher, Clayton A., Terance D. Miethe, and Dretha Phillips. 2002. *The Mismeasure of Crime*. Thousand Oaks, CA: Sage.

Moyer, Kenneth E. 1976. *The Psychobiology of Aggression*. New York: Harper and Row.

Moyer, Kenneth E. 1987. *Violence and Aggression: A Physiological Perspective*. New York: Paragon House.

Myers, David G. 1999. *Social Psychology*. 6th Edition. Boston: McGraw-Hill.

National Center for Education Statistics. 1998. *Indicators of School Crime and Safety*. Washington, DC: U.S. Department of Education.

National Crime Victimization Survey. 2001. *School Crime Supplement*. U.S. Department of Justice, Bureau of Justice Statistics. Washington, DC: U.S. Government Printing Office.

National Crime Victimization Survey. 2002. *Criminal Victimization in the United States*. U.S. Department of Justice, Bureau of Justice Statistics. Washington, DC: U.S. Government Printing Office.

National Crime Victimization Survey. 2002. *Criminal Victimization in the United States, 2002. Download Spreadsheet Version (Table 2)*. U.S. Department of Justice, Bureau of Justice Statistics. Washington, DC.

National Crime Victimization Survey. 2004. *Criminal Victimization in the United States*. U.S. Department of Justice, Bureau of Justice Statistics. Washington, DC: U.S. Government Printing Office.

Newman, Graeme. 1978. *The Punishment Response*. Philadelphia: J.P. Lippincott.

Oliver, William. 1994. *The Violent Social World of Black Men*. New York: Lexington.

Pagelow, Mildred Daley. 1989. "The Incidence and Prevalence of Criminal Abuse of Other Family Members." *Crime and Justice* 11:263–313.

Parker, Robert Nash. 1995. "Bringing 'Booze' Back in: The Relationship between Alcohol and Homicide." *Journal of Research in Crime and Delinquency* 32:3–38.

Parker, Robert Nash and Linda Rebhun. 1995. *Alcohol and Homicide: A Deadly Combination of Two American Traditions*. Albany: State University of New York Press.

Perlman, Michal and Hildy Ross. 1997. "The Benefits of Parent Intervention in Children's Disputes: An Examination of the Concurrent Changes in Children's Fighting Styles." *Child Development* 64:690–700.

Pillemer, Karl and David Finkelhor. 1988. "The Prevalence of Elder Abuse: A Random Sample Survey." *Gerontologist* 28:51–57.

Pleck, Elizabeth. 2001. "Domestic Tyranny: The Making of Social Policy against Family Violence from Colonial Times to the Present." In C. Dalton & E. Schneider (eds.), *Battered Women and the Law*. New York: Foundation Press, pp. 10–17.

Polk, Kenneth. 1994. *When Men Kill: Scenarios of Masculine Violence*. Cambridge, UK: Cambridge University Press.

Pollack, William. 1999. *Real Boys: Rescuing Our Sons from the Myths of Boyhood*. New York: Henry Holt and Company.

Raffaelli, Marcela. 1992. "Sibling Conflict in Early Adolescence." *Journal of Marriage and the Family* 54:652–663.

Reiss, Albert J. Jr. and Jeffrey A. Roth. 1993. *Understanding and Preventing Violence*. Washington, DC: National Academy Press.

Rennison, Callie M. 2005. *Intimate Partner Violence, 1993–2001*. Department of Justice, Bureau of Justice Statistics (Report No. NCJ 197838). Washington, DC: U.S. Government Printing Office.

Renzetti, Claire M. 1992. *Violent Betrayal: Partner Abuse in Lesbian Relationships*. Thousand Oaks, CA: Sage.

Renzetti, Claire and Charles H. Miley. 1996. *Violence in Gay and Lesbian Domestic Partnerships*. New York: Hawthorne Press.

Rodman, Hyman. 1963. "The Lower Class Value Stretch." *Social Forces* 42:205–215.

Rowe, David C. 2002. *Biology and Crime*. Los Angeles: Roxbury Publishing Company.

Sacco, Vincent F. and Leslie W. Kennedy. 2002. *The Criminal Event: Perspectives in Space and Time*. 2nd Edition. Belmont, CA: Wadsworth.

Sampson, Robert J. and W. Bryon Groves. 1989. "Community Structure and Crime: Testing Social-Disorganization Theory." *American Journal of Sociology* 94:774–802.

Sampson, Robert J. and John H. Laub. 2003. "Life-Course Desisters? Trajectories of Crime among Delinquent Boys Followed to Age 70." *Criminology* 41(3):301–340.

Sampson, Robert J., Stephen W. Raudenbush, and Felton Earls. 1997. "Neighborhoods and Violent Crime: A Multilevel Study of Collective Efficacy." *Science* 277:918–920.

Sampson, Robert J. and William Julius Wilson. 1995. "Toward a Theory of Race, Crime, and Urban Inequality." In John Hagan and Ruth D. Peterson (eds.), *Crime and Inequality*. Stanford, CA: Stanford University Press.

Sanders, William B. 1994. *Gangbangs and Drive-Bys: Grounded Culture and Juvenile Gang Violence.* New York: Aldine de Gruyter.

Schoenberger, Dale T. 1971. *The Gunfighters.* Caldwell, ID: The Caxton Printers.

Shaw, Clifford and Henry McKay. 1942. *Juvenile Delinquency and Urban Areas.* Chicago: University of Chicago Press.

Sheley, Joseph and James Wright. 1998. *High School Youths.* Washington, DC: National Institute of Justice.

Sherman, Lawrence W., Patrick R. Gartin, and Michael E. Buerger. 1989. "Hot Spots of Predatory Crime: Routine Activities and the Criminology of Place." *Criminology* 27:27–55.

Short, James F. Jr. and Fred L. Strodtbeck. 1965. *Group Process and Gang Delinquency.* Chicago: University of Chicago Press.

Signorielli. N. 1990. "Television's Mean and Dangerous World: A Continuation of the Cultural Indicators Perspective." In N. Signorielli and M. Morgan (eds.), *Cultivation Analysis: New Directions in Media Effects Research.* Newbury Park, CA: Sage, pp. 85–106.

Signorielli, N. and M. Morgan. 1990. *Cultivation Analysis: New Directions in Media Effects Research.* Newbury Park, CA: Sage.

Sivard, R. L. 1991. *World Military and Social Expenditures.* Washington, DC: World Priorities.

Skelton, Christine. 1997. "Primary Boys and Hegemonic Masculinities." *British Journal of Sociology of Education* 18:349–369.

Skelton, Christine. 2001. *Schooling the Boys: Masculinities and Primary Education.* Buckingham: Open University Press.

Skiba, Russell and Peter Leone. 2001. "Zero Tolerance and School Security Measures: A Failed Experiment." In Tammy Johnson, Jennifer Boyden, and William Pittz (eds.), *Racial Profiling and Punishment in U.S. Schools.* Oakland, CA: Applied Research Center, pp. 34–38.

Smitherman, Geneva. 1994. *Black Talk: Words and Phrases from the Hood to the Amen Corner.* New York: Houghton Mifflin.

Sommers, Christina Hoff. 1995. *Who Stole Feminism?: How Women Have Betrayed Women.* New York: Simon & Schuster.

Spierenburg, Pieter. 1998. *Men and Violence: Gender, Honor and Rituals in Modern Europe and America.* Columbus: Ohio State University Press.

Stafford, Mark and Mark Warr. 1993. "A Reconceptualization of General and Specific Deterrence." *Journal of Research in Crime & Delinquency* 30:123–135.

Stalinsky, Steven and Y. Yehoshua. 2004. "Muslim Clerics on the Religious Rulings Regarding Wife-Beating." Special Report No. 27. The Middle East Media Research Institute. Available online at: http: memri.org.

Steckmesser, Kent Ladd. 1965. *The Western Hero in History and Legend.* Norman: University of Oklahoma Press.

Straus, Murray A. 1992. *Children as Witnesses to Marital Violence: A Risk Factor for Lifelong Problems among a Nationally Representative Sample of American Men and Women.* Report of the Twenty-Third Ross Roundtable. Columbus, OH: Ross Laboratories.

Straus, Murray A. and Richard Gelles. 1990. *Family Violence in American Families: Risk Factors and Adaptations to Violence in 8,145 Families.* New Brunswick, NY: Transaction Publishers.

Straus, Murrray A., Richard Gelles, and Susan Steinmetz. 1980. *Behind Closed Doors—Violence in the American Family.* New York: Anchor Press/Doubleday.

Sutherland, Edwin H. 1947. *Principles of Criminology*. 4th Edition. Philadelphia: J.B. Lippincott.

Sutherland, Edwin H. and Donald R. Cressey. 1966. *Principles of Criminology*. 7th Edition. Philadelphia: J.B. Lippincott.

Swagerty, Daniel L., Paul Y. Takahashi, and Jonathan M. Evans. 1999. "Elder Mistreatment." *American Family Physician*. Available online at: http://www.aafp.org/afp/990515ap/2804.html.

Sykes, Gresham and David Matza. 1957. "Techniques of Neutralization: A Theory of Delinquency." *American Journal of Sociology* 22:664–670.

Tedeschi, James T. and Richard B. Felson. 1994. *Violence, Aggression, and Coercive Actions*. Washington, DC: American Psychological Association.

Tinbergen, N. 1990. *Social Behaviour in Animals*. London: Chapman and Hall.

Tjaden, P., and N. Thoennes. 2000. *Extent, Nature, and Consequences of Intimate Partner Violence: Findings from the National Violence against Women Survey*. U.S. Department of Justice (Report No. NCJ 181867). Washington, DC: Government Printing Office.

Volavka, Jan. 1995. *Neurobiology of Violence*. Washington, DC: American Psychiatric Press.

Vold, George B., Thomas J. Bernard, and Jeffrey B. Snipes. 1998. *Theoretical Criminology*. 4th Edition. New York: Oxford University Press.

Warr, Mark. 2002. *Companions in Crime: The Social Aspects of Criminal Conduct*. Cambridge, UK: Cambridge University Press.

Wilbanks, William. 1984. *Murder in Miami: An Analysis of Homicide Patterns and Trends in Dade County (Miami), Florida, 1917–1983*. Lanham, MD: University Press of America.

Wilcox, Pamela, Kenneth Land, and Scott Hunt. 2003. *Criminal Circumstances: A Dynamic Multicontextual Criminal Opportunity Theory*. New York: Aldine de Gruyter.

Wilson, Edward O. 2000. *Sociobiology: The New Synthesis*. 25th Anniversary Edition. Cambridge, MA: The Belknap Press of Harvard University.

Wilson, John Lyde. 1838. *The American Code: Code of Honor; or, Rules for the Government of Principals and Seconds in Dueling*. Available online at: www.cbc2.org/faculty/dabbott/duAmericanCode.html.

Wilson, William Julius. 1991. "Studying Inner-City Social Dislocations: The Challenge of Public Agenda Research." *American Sociological Review* 56:1–14.

Wilson, William Julius. 1996. *When Work Disappears: The World of the New Urban Poor*. New York: Knopf.

Wolfgang, Marvin. 1958. *Patterns of Criminal Homicide*. Philadelphia: University of Pennsylvania Press.

Wolfgang, Marvin and Franco Ferracuti. 1967. *The Subculture of Violence: Toward an Integrated Theory in Criminology*. London: Tavistock.

Wright, Richard T. and Scott H. Decker. 1997. *Armed Robbers in Action: Stickups and Street Culture*. Boston: Northeastern University Press.

Young, Cathy. 2001. "Where the Boys Are: Is America Shortchanging Male Children?" *Reason Magazine* Feb.:24–31.

Index